The Ragas of Northern Indian Music

The first part of the book traces the history of Indian music and the continuity of its theory and practice for more than two thousand years. It is based on many years' research into the vast ancient Sanskrit literature of music. These valuable technical treatises, which lie in the form of scarcely catalogued manuscripts throughout the public and private libraries of India, had hitherto remained unemplored. Part Two transcribes and studies in detail fifty typical Raga-s. Each is preceded by a Sanskrit poem in translation which depicts the atmosphere; then follows an analysis of the scale, covering its intervals and expression, a study of the theme with its characteristic motives and finally a typical development.

The present work is based on the author's two-volume *Northern Indian Music* published in London (but not America) some ten years ago, but long out of print and much sought after by students. It was described by Colin Mason in the *Manchester Guardian* as "of immense value to any practical musician" and "an invaluable addition to the very scanty literature of a fascinating and neglected subject." This new version contains a number of additional Raga-s; the earlier text has been extensively revised and many music examples redrawn for greater clarity and accuracy. Some abridgement has taken place, but only of material which appeared originally for the benefit of Indian readers unfamiliar with Western staff notation, those able to read Sanskrit, and specialists in Sanskrit literature. The book provides modern composers outside India with a source of new inspiration and enables practising musicians to play and study some of the endlessly variegated modes for which Indian music is unique.

Alain Danielou was Director of the International Institute for Comparative Music Studies and Documentation, Berlin, and adviser for Oriental Music to the International Music Council (UNESCO). Born in Paris, he pursued scientific and artistic studies before specialising in musicology. He travelled extensively in North Africa, the Middle East, China and Japan and then settled in India, where he studied Indian music and philosophy, Hindi and Sanskrit, and made a unique collection (over 800) of Sanskrit manuscripts on music. In 1949 he was appointed Research Professor of Music at Banaras Hindu University and in 1954 became Director of the Adyar Library and Research Centre in Madras. In 1959 he returned to Europe, joining the Ecole Francaise d'Extréme Orient in Paris, and subsequently became Director of Studies of the Centre d'Etudes de Musique Orientale of Paris. He has written extensively in both French and English on Oriental Music and on many aspects of Indian history and culture, and has also published two novels. He was the general editor of the three UNESCO collections of records: "Anthology of the Orient" (Barenreiter Musicaphon), "Musical Sources" (Philips, Holland) and "Musical Altas" (EMI, Italy).

ALSO BY ALAIN DANIELOU

BOOKS

Introduction to the study of Musical scales

Northern Indian Music
  2 vols, Halcyon Press and Christopher Johnson, London 1949–1953.
Traité de Musicologie Comparée
  Editions Hermann, Paris 1959.
La musique du Cambodge et du Laos
  Institut Français d'Indologie, Pondicherry 1957
Tableau Comparatif des Intervalles Musicaux
  Institut Français d'Indologie, Pondicherry 1958.
La Musique des Puranas
  Texte Sanskrit, traduction Française, Institut Français d'Indologie,
  Pondicherry 1959.
Le Gitâlamkara
  l'ouvrage original de Bharata sur la musique, Texte Sanskrit, traduction
  Institut Français d'Indologie, Pondicherry 1960
Le Roman de l'anneau
  translated from the Tamil, NRF, Paris 1961.
The Ankle Bracelet
  New Directions, New York 1965
Yoga, Méthode de Réintégration
  l'Arche, Paris 1952.
Yoga, Method of Reintegration
  Christopher Johnson, London 1950.
Le Polythéisme Hindou
  Buchet-Chastel, Paris 1960
Hindu Polytheism
  Bollingen Series, New York 1964
Le Bétail des Dieux
  roman, Buchet-Chastel, Paris 1962.
L'Erotisme Divinisé
  Buchet-Chastel, Paris 1963.
Les Quatre Sens de la Vie
  Librairie Académique Perrin, Paris 1963.
India
  in the series "Traditions Musicales", Buchet-Chastel, Paris 1966.
Semantique Musicale
  Editions Hermann, Paris 1967.
Trois Chansons de Rabindranath Tagore
  (Chant et Piano), Ricordi, Paris 1962.

RECORD ALBUMS WITH EXTENSIVE NOTES:

Anthologie de la Musique de l'Inde
  Ducretet-Thomson, Paris
Religious Music of India
  Folkways, New York
Folk Music of India
  Columbia, New York
Unesco Anthology of the Orient
  Bärenreiter, Kassel

THE
RĀGA-S OF NORTHERN INDIAN MUSIC

ALAIN DANIÉLOU

DIRECTOR OF
THE INTERNATIONAL INSTITUTE
FOR COMPARATIVE MUSIC STUDIES
AND DOCUMENTATION,
BERLIN

Munshiram Manoharlal
Publishers Pvt. Ltd.

ISBN 978-81-215-0225-2
Reprinted 1991, 1997, 2003, 2007, 2010, **2014**
First Indian edition 1980

PRINTED IN INDIA
Published by Vikram Jain *for*
Munshiram Manoharlal Publishers Pvt. Ltd.
PO Box 5715, 54 Rani Jhansi Road, New Delhi 110 055, INDIA

www.mrmlbooks.com

CONTENTS

PART II
NOTATION AND ANALYSIS OF THE RĀGA-S

FOREWORD

THE *rāga*-s of which notations appear in this book conform to the Benares Musical Tradition. They have been noted as played on the North Indian *Vīnā* by the late Shivendranāth Basu of Benares and with his kind help and advice. They often differ slightly from those noted by Bhātkhande and other modern compilers who belong to other schools (gharana-s).

A. D.

PART I

INDIAN MUSICAL THEORY

"Extracting the essence of the Scriptures, I shall explain the origin of Intelligible Sound which is the only means of achieving the four aims of life—virtue, success, pleasure and liberation." (*Sangīta-darpana*, 1–29.)

"The Man who understands the inner meaning of the sound of the harp, who knows intervals, modal scales and rhythms, shall travel without effort on the way to liberation." (*Yājna-valkya Smriti*, III, 115.)

CHAPTER I

THE HISTORY OF INDIAN MUSIC

"Animals tamed or wild, and children even, delight in musical sounds. Who can depict their beauty?" (*Sangīta-darpana,* 1-31.)

THERE are three main layers of civilization in India, an aboriginal culture speaking Munda languages, a Dravidian culture speaking Dravidian languages and probably representing the high culture the Aryans met with when they conquered North-Western India, and an Aryan culture speaking Sanskritic languages.

The history of music in India has remained linked with these different cultural backgrounds which have never achieved a real unity. We meet today aboriginal music among the Munda-speaking tribes, a Dravidian music in Southern India and a Northern Sanskritic musical tradition. Obviously there has been much exchange of theoretical data and considerable mutual as well as external influences. Yet the fact remains today that we find in India very distinct musical systems which correspond in the main to the linguistic and ethnic divisions of the country.

The fact that the theory of music came, even in Dravidian areas, to be in the hands of a Sanskritic Brahmanical class that looked to the Aryan *Veda*-s as the source of all knowledge led to considerable misconceptions as regards the origin and theory of non-Aryan music.

Yet this affected more the theory than the practice, and the music itself, whether it be art music or folklore, has maintained very definite characteristics.

There is evidence of early musical contacts between India and the Middle and Far East.

The ancient *Kinnari Vīnā* (Vīnā of the Kin-nara-s) or Kin seems to have been known in China as the Ch'in. It is a stringed instrument said to have been played by the first Emperor, Fu-Hsi (c. 3000 B.C.). The mythical Kin-nara-s, a word which may mean "men of Kin", may have been originally the Chinese. The Ch'in is further mentioned in ancient Chinese chronicles, such as the *Chi Ki* (second century B.C.), in connection with events of the sixth or seventh century. According to the *Li Chi*, Confucius (551–578 B.C.) always had his Ch'in at his side when at home, and carried it with him when he went for a walk or on a journey.

In *Genesis* (iv, 21 and xxxi, 27) a stringed instrument of a similar kind is called Kinnor. David used to play the Kinnor as well as the Nebel (harp or lyre).

The antiquity of Indian theatrical art and musical theory was well known to the ancient world. According to Strabo (*Geography* x, 11, 17) the Greeks considered that music "from the triple point of view of melody, rhythm and instruments" came to them originally from Thrace and Asia. Further, "the poets, who make the whole of Asia, including India, the land or sacred territory of Dionysos, claim that the origin of music is almost entirely Asiatic. Thus, one of them, speaking of the lyre, will say: the strings of the cithara of Asia resound."

Megasthenes (quoted by Arrian in his *Indika*, VII, 8, written in 150 B.C.) tells us that Dionysos "taught the Indians to worship the other Gods and himself by playing cymbals and drums; he also taught them the satyr dance which the Greeks call kordax".

"This is because they are, of all peoples, the greatest lovers of music and have practised dancing with great love since the days when Bacchus and his companions led their bacchanalia in the land of India." (Arrian: *Anabasis of Alexander* VI, 3, 10.)

Megasthenes had come to India in 302 B.C. He reported that the Indians counted 153 kings and 6042 years between Dionysos and Alexander (who entered the Punjab in 329 B.C.). Similar information is also given by Pliny the Elder who, however, gives the number of years as 6451. By comparing these Greek dates with those of the dynasties given in the various *Purāna*-s, several attempts have been made to identify Dionysos with some early figure of Indian history (particularly Manu or Krishna). However, from the similarity of the legends and the symbols, there can be no doubt that Dionysos is Shiva and that the dates refer to his chief incarnation, as described in the

Shaiva Purāna-s, which give approximately the same dates.

Dionysos is the Greek name of a prehistoric divinity whom the Indians call Shiva (the auspicious). Shiva, represented as a nude and lustful god wandering through the primeval forest, is said to have been the first teacher of the oldest system of music and dancing in India. Up to a comparatively recent period this system seems to have remained distinct from that which traces its origin to the Vedic Aryans. A number of treatises on music, some of which are still extant, refer to the Shiva school of music which seems to be derived from a pre-Aryan civilization.

A fundamental characteristic of the Shiva school of music is the conception that basic modes must, for symbolic reasons, be pentatonic,[1] hence the classification of all heptatonic forms as variants of fundamental pentatonic modes.

The Vedic Aryans brought to India another conception of music, to which were added later important Iranian and Greek elements. This led to the development of a musical theory distinct from the Shivaite. The contrast in the basis of their parallel systems is still felt in the music of Northern India.

A general Sanskritic theory of music, termed *Gāndharva Veda*, was elaborated at a very early date. From such summaries as have survived, it seems that the *Gāndharva Veda* studied every use of musical sound, not only in different musical forms and systems but also in physics, medicine and magic.

The rise of Buddhism brought about a sharp deviation in the ancient approach to the arts and sciences. During this time the *Gāndharva Veda*, together with several of the other sacred sciences, disappeared. Fragments of some of its texts may still survive in unpublished manuscripts. A short account of the contents of the *Gāndharva Veda*, said to have been collected from such sources, has been published in an encyclopedic work in Hindi, *Hindutva*, by Motilal Gaud (Benares, 1928).

Musical theory and the theory of language in India were considered by the Sanskrit theorists as two parallel branches of one general science of sound. Both have often been codified

---

[1] Shivaite philosophy attaches great importance to the number 5 as a symbol of life.

by the same writers. The names of Vashishtha, Yajnavalkya, Nārada, Kashyapa, Pānini, are mentioned among the early musicologist-grammarians. Nandikeshvara is famous as the author of a work on the structure and content of language in its broader sense as well as of a treatise on music. His work on linguistics is believed to be anterior to the *Mahābhāshya* of Patanjali (attributed to the second century B.C.) into which it is usually incorporated, though it is thought to be probably posterior to the grammarian Pānini, who seems to have lived not later than the sixth century B.C.

The Four Schools (Mata-s)

In A.D. 1550, the late medieval author Rāmāmātya wrote: "The science of music has both in theory and in practice degenerated into conflicting views." (*Svaramela-kalānidhi*, I, 24.) This was not an accurate statement. The various forms of music found on the Indian continent did not come from a common source and the efforts made by theorists after the tenth century to explain all the musical facts in terms of a theory which was considered to be unique and of divine origin required a great deal of intricate musical exegesis. The earlier writers trace the origin of the musical system, which they describe, to one of four different teachers each representing a different musical tradition. Hence there are four distinct systems or *mata*-s known as expounded by Shiva (or Someshvara), Bharata, Hanumanta, and Kallinātha. These systems undoubtedly had a distinct origin and belong very probably to the different cultures that came together on the Indian continent and which have retained to our day distinct characteristics in spite of century-old attempts to relate them to one another.

The basic (shuddha) scale of Southern or Karnātaka music is and has always been fundamentally different from the basic scale of Northern or Hindusthani music. It cannot be said that these scales are formed from one another any more than the Dravidian languages are connected to the Indo-European ones.

There is also evidence in Bengal and Orissa of independent musical systems. In Assam, Nepal, and most Himalayan countries musical forms are found which belong to the Sino-

Tibetan family.

Many of the "low castes" and primitive tribes in India, often descendants of independent peoples with a civilization of their own, have kept to our day original musical forms that bear no relation to those defined in the *Nātya Shāstra* or the *Sangīta-ratnākara*. The case is particularly striking for the *Ahīr*-s (ancient Abhira-s) of Northern India. In many regions, particularly in a few valleys of the Himalayas, there remain archaic forms of music with an upper tonic and a descending scale, the study of which would be of great interest towards the understanding of some of the ancient texts.

Although the various schools of music in present-day India lay claim to the same ancient treatises, there remain such important differences in musical practice that the meaning of the texts has to be forced to a sometimes incredible extent, so that they may appear to refer to musical systems completely different from those they describe. Hardly any of the modes of Southern Indian music is identical with a Northern Indian mode, yet each one claims the same origin. Even in the North, *rāga*-s and styles differ from one province to the other.

It is a common belief in Southern India that Southern music represents the more ancient school while Northern music has evolved under external influences. Except in minor points, this opinion, however, does not appear to correspond with the facts. Both systems are extremely ancient. Southern Indian music was subjected to systematic reforms, one of the main reformers being Venkata Makhin in the seventeenth century. Northern Indian classical music, on the other hand, though it lent itself easily to temporary fashions, did not attempt to systematize *rāga*-s or styles. In many instances it seems to have remained the same in spite of temporary changes. It still conforms with the definitions in some of the most ancient books.

The stories that relate how the various styles of Northern Indian music were developed by musicians of the Mohammedan period seem usually unfounded. Under Moslem rule, age-old stories were retold as if they had happened at the court of Akbar, so as to make them acceptable to new rulers and win the praise and honours bestowed on the creative artists of the day. Such transfer of legends is frequent everywhere. We should therefore not be surprised to find ancient musical forms and musical instruments being given Persian-sounding names and starting a new career as the innovations of the Moghul court.

The assumption that the scales and styles now used by the "Ustads" of Northern India pertain to, or have been influenced by Turkish, Arab or Persian melody-types is unlikely. The structure of Arab and Persian music is quite different from that of Indian music. It is difficult to see how the one could have seriously influenced the other without losing its distinct character—unless one is referring merely to the setting of certain types of poetry, or to certain mannerisms or ways of sitting or of placing the voice.

The Turkish system was also known to late medieval Hindu scholars who occasionally mention Persian and Turkish music (the latter under the name of Turushka).

Amir Khusrau (A.D. 1253–1319), a Turkish musician and scholar at the Persian court of Delhi, wrote that Indian music was so difficult and so refined that no foreigner could totally master it, even after twenty years of practice.

The Sanskrit Writers on Music

The main Sanskrit treatises on music present, at first sight, a mass of conflicting definitions. However, a careful study of the divergences and similarities between various groups of texts shows that these belong to different schools and have been mixed without discrimination. The original works, based upon a coherent theory, are easy to classify. The rest represent more or less adapted compilations of which each element has to be dealt with separately. Unfortunately, only fragments of the earlier works are now available.

The Sanskrit writers on musical theory belong to four main periods. The first concerns authors mentioned in the *Purāna-s* (the "ancient scriptures") and in the Epics (*Mahābhārata* and *Rāmāyana*); the second, those mentioned in early medieval works. The third period concerns the authors who wrote between the medieval Hindu revival and the Moslem invasion. The last or modern period is that of Sanskrit writers under Moslem and European rule. Exact dates can usually be ascertained only for the authors of the two last periods.

Among the important landmarks of musical literature must be regarded the chapters on music of some of the *Purāna*-s, particularly the *Vishnu-dharmottara, Mārkandeya Purāna* and *Vāyu Purāna*. The Hindus regard these texts as extremely ancient. This seems to be confirmed by the technical terms used in reference to music. Purāṇic texts are, however, often difficult to interpret because of the lack of critical editions and of the abundance of copyists' errors in technical passages.[1]

Many of the available works of the early period have been re-written over and over again. This is quite natural for they were teachers' text-books and not library records. Thus, to accept the date of their latest re-editing as the earliest date of compilation, as some over-cautious scholars have a tendency to do, may give an erroneous picture of musical history.

The available early works refer either to the *Gāndharva Veda* or to the Shaiva tradition as their authority. In these we find theories easier to understand. Taking into account the changes that have occurred in the scale, in the tonic, etc., the interpretation of the early works should present no difficult problem except that of restoring the corrupt portions of the text.

First Period (Puranic-Vedic-Epic)

An approximate chronology of the most important writers belonging to the early period may be established with the help of a few works that have partly survived, although any attempt to fix definite dates or periods can only be conjectural. References in Vedic, Puranic and Epic literature permit us to place most of the legendary authors of the early period in the pre-Buddhist age.

A chronological chart can be drawn showing the relative antiquity of authors mentioned or quoted in the works available in full or in fragments. Although far from being exhaustive, this chart shows the relationship between the most important Sanskrit writers on music of the early period, which must have extended over many centuries. Most of these early works are archaic in their language.

The main works of Nandikeshvara, the main Shivaite

---

[1] See Alain Daniélou, *Textes des Purāna-s sur la Théorie Musicale*, Institut Francais d'Indologie, 1959.

author, on the philosophy of music are now believed to be lost, but fragments of them are incorporated in later works.

A small surviving part of an anonymous manuscript in the Bikaner Library, called the *Rudra-damarudbhava-sūtra-viva-rana* (published by Mādhava Krishna Sarma in the *New Indian Antiquary*, June, 1943),[1] explains the formation of musical sounds on the basis of the *Maheshvara Sūtra*-s, an esoteric arrangement of syllabic sounds, which Nandikeshvara also accepts as the philosophical basis of the Sanskrit language and, in fact, of all language. This text seems to be either a fragment of Nandikeshvara's work or a study directly based upon it. The first part of the manuscript is a fragment of another work, in no way connected with the second part. This first part deals with the qualities and defects of singers in verses also found in the *Sangīta-ratnākara* of Shārngadeva.

A part of Nandikeshvara's work on dancing, the *Abhinaya-darpana*, has been published (Calcutta, 1934, with English translation by Manomohan Ghosh). An earlier translation by Ananda K. Coomaraswamy appeared under the title *The Mirror of Gesture* (Harvard University Press, 1917).

Further fragments of Nandikeshvara's technical writings on dancing and music, the *Bharata-arnava* in particular, remain unpublished. Manuscripts are to be found in the Tanjore and Madras libraries.

The Different Nārada-s

There are three separate authors known by the name of Nārada. One, the author of the *Nāradīya Shikshā*, is probably the earliest writer on profane music, some of whose writings have survived. He is quoted by all subsequent writers of the early period, who in turn are quoted by later Nārada-s, the authors of the *Sangīta-makaranda* and the *Chatvārimshach'-hata-rāga-nirūpanam*.

According to tradition, the *Nāradīya Shikshā* forms part of the later Vedic literature. Although some attempts have been made to date this work rather late, there is no concrete evidence to disprove the tradition. The fact that the *Nāradīya Shikshā* mentions the names of only a few of the earliest

[1] Translated by A. Daniélou, in the *Journal of the Madras Music Academy*, 1951.

authorities on music who are also mentioned in the *Vashishtha* and *Yājnavalkya Shikshā*-s, seems to confirm it as an early work. If we were to consider the *Nāradīya Shikshā* as a late work, we should have to account for some other very early work of the same description forming the link between Vedic chant and profane music as mentioned by Yāshtika, Nārada II, Kohala, Matanga and practically all subsequent authors. There seems to be no sufficient reason to doubt the authenticity of the available *Nāradīya Shikshā*.

The *Panchama Samhitā* and *Nārada Samhitā* are probably the work of the second Nārada, the author of the *Sangīta-makaranda*.

The *Chatvārimshach'hata-rāga-nirūpanam* is a much later work.

The Bharata Problem

The main available work attributed to Bharata, the *Nātya Shāstra*, is a compilation which has been variously dated between the second century B.C. and the fourth century A.D. It mentions Kohala and Dattila but not Matanga, and probably contains fragments of the work of Nandikeshvara, Kohala etc., and the earlier Bharata. It may in fact be doubted whether a sage named Bharata ever wrote the *Nātya Shāstra*. The Bharata Vriddha (Bharata the Elder) mentioned by Shāradātanaya, as distinct from the author of the *Nātya Shāstra*, is probably the author of the *Gītālamkāra*, a much older treatise belonging to the Shaiva school and quoted in the Panchatantra, the book of fables, dated about 300 B.C. The word "bharata" designates a dance-actor.[1] It was a common name in the title of all the treatises on stage technique. Thus we hear of Ādi Bharata, Nandikeshvara Bharata, Arjuna Bharata, Matanga Bharata, Kohala Bharata, etc. *Bharata Nātya Shāstra* would then simply mean "the text-book of the dance-actor". It is, in fact, a practical compilation of authoritative works on the subject periodically brought up to date.

The *Nātya Shāstra*, therefore, cannot be taken as a sure basis to determine the chronology. We should not be surprised to find Bharata himself mentioning several later authors as his sons. They all, however, belong to an earlier period and

[1] Some Celtic scholars link the Celtic word "bard" to the Sanskrit Bharata.

must obviously precede the last revision of the *Nātya Shāstra*.
According to tradition Bharata had four sons—Shāndilya,
Vātsya, Kohala and Dattila.

"I taught the perfect practice (of music) to my sons,
Shāndilya, Vātsya, Kohala and Dattila." (*Nātya Shāstra*,
1–26.)

"The family of Bharata-s will be made famous in the future
by the Bharata-s—Kohala, and, after him, Vātsya, Shāndilya,
Dattila." (*Nātya Shāstra*, 36, 70–71.)

These obviously later additions only mean that these four
authors are considered the direct heirs to the tradition of the
earlier Bharata. Their work, therefore, has great authority.

Matanga

It appears at first difficult to ascribe Matanga, the author
of the *Brihaddeshī*, to a definite period. The text mentions a
number of early authors, including Yāshtika and Bharata. It
has also an extensive commentary which mentions further
writers, including Nandikeshvara, Kohala and Dattila. Some
medieval and later authors have considered this commentary
as the work of Matanga himself. But this is unlikely since it
mentions Kohala, who, in a passage reproduced by Kallinātha,
quotes Matanga. The name and the story of the sage Matanga
are mentioned in the *Rāmāyana* and the *Mahābhārata* and in
several *Purāna*-s. This places him definitely in the early
period.

The Three Chatura-s

A quotation by Tumburu is found in Kallinātha's commentary on the *Sangīta-ratnākara* (1, 3, 10–16). In the commentary on the 27th verse of Matanga's *Brihaddeshī*, however,
the same quotation is attributed to Chatura. Chatura is a
name given to Kallinātha himself and the *Brihaddeshī* commentary might be considered late enough to quote him.
Simhabhūpāla—more than a century before Kallinātha—
repeatedly quotes from the *Brihaddeshī* commentary which he
seems to consider the work of Matanga himself. It would
therefore appear that the title of Chatura (clever) was also
given to the early writer Tumburu, the same name having
been used later for Kallinātha and also for Dāmodara Mishra,
the author of the *Sangīta-darpana*.

Mātrigupta and Rudrata

The Mātrigupta mentioned by Nārada (in the *Chatvārim-shach'hata-rāga-nirūpanam*, and as Mātragupta, in the *Sangīta makaranda*) has sometimes been identified with the celebrated poet Mātrigupta of the seventh century. This is not absolutely impossible, although it is unlikely.

Similarly, the Rudrata mentioned by the author of the commentary on the *Brihaddeshī* and also by Abhinava Gupta (tenth century) has been said to be either the ninth-century author of the *Kāvyālankāra*, or Rudra Bhatta, the author of the *Shringāratilaka*.

Such attributions should not be attempted without concrete evidence. Sanskrit literature on music extends over so vast a period that similarities of name are bound to occur. The difficulty is to distinguish between numerous authors of the same name. We know of at least ten Bhatta-s, authors of different works, six Soma-s or Someshvara-s, five Nārāyana-s, four Dāmodara-s, etc. Among the existent works we have two *Sangīta-ratnākara*-s, three *Sangīta-nārāyana*-s, four *Bharata Shāstra*-s, four *Rāga-mālā*-s, and so on. Hasty identifications are sure to lead to mistakes such as have already been made in the case of the different Dāmodara-s.

If the commentary on the *Brihaddeshī* is really the work of Matanga, the boundary of the Epic-Puranic period in the list given below must be placed before Gāndharva Rājā. The relative chronology is not otherwise altered.

An attempt at relative chronology based on the mention of earlier authors in existing texts begins on the next page.

THE FIRST PERIOD

The first period extends from prehistoric ages to the *Purāna-Mahābhārata* period.[1]

I

The teachers of the Sāma Veda

SAMA VEDA
Gāndharva Veda

The main teachers are in probable succession:

BRAHMĀ, *Prajāpati*,
Kashyapa+,[2] Brihaspati, Vishvakarman, Angirasa+, Gautama+, Bharadvāja, Soma Sharman, Vashishtha+, Yajñavalkya+, Tumburu+, Vishvāvasu,

NARADA I+, (*Shikshā*)
Agastya, Āyu, Aruvān, Ushanā, Ekadhanvi, Kanva, Kusha, Kritavrana, Kratuh, Gālava, Chyavana, Durvāsā, Dhruva, Dhaumya, Nishthyūti, Parvata, Pulastya, Pulaha, Pratimardani, Bhavana, Manu, Medhātithi, Rāmajāmadagni, Raibhya, Vatsa, Vāmanajāmadagni, Vālmiki, Vishvāmitra, Shankulāksha, Shatānanda, Sanvartta, Sthūlashirā, Sthūlāksha, Susharmā, Bhārgava.
Then come: Yāshtika+, Anjaneya+, Ashvattara, Kambala, Mārkandeya+ (Purāna?), Vāyu+ (Purāna?).

BHARATA+
All the above names are mentioned in the *Nātya Shāstra+*. Later come Tandu and

MATANGA+

*   *   *   *

II

Parallel to the *Gāndharva Veda* runs the Shiva tradition of which the main teachers are:

[1] By the *Purāna-Mahābharata* period we mean the general historical period envisaged in these books and not the particular date of their final recension.

[2] Authors by whom some writings on music are available and still existing works are marked with +.

SHIVA

Shankara, Shambhu, Parameshthī, Vighnesha, Shashānka, Shashimaulī, Indra.

Then: Chandī, Shanmukha, Bhringi, Kuvera, Vikrama, Gaurī, Pārvatī, Mahādeva, Vallabha, Shārdūla I, Sadā Shiva+, Svati, Rāvana,

NANDIKESHVARA+

These names are mainly mentioned by Nandikeshvara and in the *Brihaddeshī's*+ commentary.

* * * *

To the third tradition, that of *Hanumāna*, appear to belong: Atri, Kapila, Bhrigu,

HANUMĀNA

Angada, Kinnaresha, Kushika, Guna, Sarasvatī, Bali, Yaksha, Daksha, Vyāla, Samudra, Shashi, Bhāskara, Shauri, Gopipati, Shrīnātha, Shrīvatsa, Hari I, Hari II, Harishchandra.

Later come: Chitraratha, Gāndharva Rāja I, Arjuna, Rambhā, Kshetrapāla, Ugrasena.

These names are mainly mentioned in the *Sangīta Makaranda*+, the commentary on the *Brihaddeshī*+ and the work of Gāndharva Rāja II+.

* * * *

All the names so far mentioned are anterior to the *Purāna*-s and the Epics (*Mahābhārata, Rāmāyana*).

* * * *

Then come a series of authors who seem to have lived between the Epic-Puranic age and the first century of the Christian era, such as:

Kirtidhāra Āchārya, Mātragupta, Kshemarāja, Lohita Bhattaka, Sumantu, Kshetrapāla, Ugrasena, Bhatta Tandu, Shārdūla II,

KOHALA+

Devendra, Durgā Shakti+, Ganeshvara, Pārvatīpati, Sharva. Vātsya, Vāsuki, Shāndilya, Vishākhila+,

DATTILA+,
NĀRADA II+, (*Sangīta Makaranda*)+,

Rudrata, Chatura+

Brihaddeshī's commentary+

Māghesha, Girisutā, Gāndharva Rāja II+,

NĀRADA III (*Chatvārimshach'hata Rāganirūpanam*)+

Several names mentioned in later works may be variants of the names of earlier authors, chosen for the sake of the metre, as all the treatises are in verse form. Pārvatī-pati (the husband of Pārvatī) and Sharva (the refuge), for example, are names of Shiva; they may stand for Shiva, the first expounder of music, or for some of his later followers; Māghesha (Lord of riches) may be Indra, Kamalāsyaka may be Brahma. Yet it would be incautious to make such assertions without evidence since these are names that occur frequently.

The Kshemarāja mentioned by Kohala cannot be the celebrated disciple of Abhinava Gupta, since Kohala's latest possible time is the fourth century A.D., six centuries before Abhinava Gupta.

The Second (Buddhist) Period

This period extends from the Epic-Puranic period to the early medieval Hindu revival. We may generally term it Buddhist because, according to Hindu tradition, Buddhism rose and declined in India within the limits of this millenium.

A few importants works that probably belong to the beginning of this period are extant (see previous chart). These include extensive fragments of Kohala.

The lower limit of the early first period works is set by the fact that Kohala and Dattila are mentioned in the *Nātya Shāstra* of which the last re-editing, as we have already seen, is variously dated between the second century B.C. and the fourth century A.D., the first of these dates being the more likely.

Very few of the numerous musical works of this second period have so far been found, neither have they been edited nor studied. In most cases we have to content ourselves with authors' names without attempting to establish their chronological relationship. The authors who can safely be attributed to this period are those not mentioned by any writer of the pre-Puranic-Epic period but mentioned as ancient authorities by authors of the tenth, eleventh and twelfth centuries (chiefly Abhinava Gupta, Shāradātanaya, Nānya Bhūpāla, Pārshvadeva and Shārngadeva).

This gives us a list of names, some of which may, however,

belong to the first period or to the earlier part of the third period.

The main writers of this second (Buddhist) period are:
Āstika, Apisali (author of a *Shikshā*), Uttara, Uvata, Umāpati, Kātyāyana, Kāmadeva, Kumbhodbhava, Ghantaka, Chhatraka, Datta, Devarāja (who may be Devendra), Drauhini, Dhenuka, Priyātithi, Bindu Rāja, Brihat Kashyapa, Bhatta, Bhatta Yantra, Bhatta Sumanas, Bhatta Vriddhi, Bhatta Gopāla, Bhatta Shubhākara (commentator on *Nāradīya Shikshā*), Rahula, Vena, Vyāsa, Vāchaspati, Shrī Harsha (different from the patron of the seventh-century poet Bāna), Sakali garbha, Sūrya (may be Bhāskara), Sureshvara, Someshvara I (different from the two later Someshvara-s, authors respectively of *Mānasollāsa* and *Sangīta Ratnāvalī*).

The Third (Medieval) Period

The main authors of this period can be divided into two groups:

I.   Udbhata (late eighth century): comm. on *Nātya Shāstra*.
Lollata (between Udbhata and Abhinava Gupta, c. 825): comm. on *Nātya Shāstra*.
Shankuka (id., c. 850): comm. on *Nātya Shāstra*.
Utpala Deva (early tenth century; the teacher of Abhinava's teacher).
Nrisimha Gupta (Abhinava's teacher and father).
Abhinava Gupta (end of tenth century): *Abhinava-bhārati*, comm. on *Nātya Shāstra*.
Bhoja (King) (1010–1055).
Simhana (eleventh century or early thirteenth, before Hammira).
Abhaya Deva (a Jain) (1063–   ?).
Mammata (1050–1150): *Sangīta-ratna-mālā*.
Rudrasena (before Devendra).
Someshvara II (1131): *Mānasollāsa* or *Abhilāshārtha-chintāmani*.
Lochana Kavi (1160): *Rāga-tarangini*.
Paramardī (1165–1203 ?).
Devendra (after Bhoja): *Sangīta-muktāvali*.
Someshvara III (1174–1177): *Sangīta-ratnāvali*.

Sharadātanaya (c. 1200): *Bhāva-prakāsha.*

Nānya Bhūpāla or Nānya Deva (eleventh or twelfth century, between Abhinava Gupta and Sharngadeva): *Sarasvatī-hridayālamkāra* or *Bharata-bhāshya.*

Jaitra Simha (c. 1213? before Hammira): *Bharata-bhāshya.*

Sharngadeva (1210–1247): *Sangīta-ratnākara.*

There has been some speculation about the dates of Lochana Kavi. The *Rāga-tarangini* bears the date 1082 of the Shaka era. This would be A.D. 1160. Lochana Kavi, however, mentions the names of Jayadeva and Vidyāpati. The dates of Jayadeva are about A.D. 1116 but the known Maithili poet Vidyāpati is thought to have lived around the fourteenth century. Either Lochana lived after the fourteenth century, or this name refers to some other Vidyāpati. It appears that there is a local Shaka era in Eastern India according to which 1082 would be A.D. 1700 This would ascribe Lochana to a much later date. Against this supposition there is the fact that Lochana is quoted by Hridaya Nārāyana (c. 1667) who in turn is quoted by Bhava Bhatta (c. 1700).

The work of Lochana has therefore been dated either A.D. 1160, or fourteenth century (after Vidyāpati), or A.D. 1700.

Since the last date seems impossible, it is likely that the earlier of the remaining dates is the correct one and that, as some Bengali scholars assume, there was an earlier Vidyāpati.

II.   Jayasimha (before Hammira).
Ganapati (c. 1253? before Hammira).
Jayasena (c. 1253): *Nritta-ratnāvali.*
Hammira (1283 or 1364): *Sangīta-shringàra-hāra.*
Gopāla Nāyaka (1295–1315).
Pratāp (King?): *Sangīta-chūdāmani.*
Palkuriki Somanātha (thirteenth–fourteenth century): *Panditārādhyacharita, Bāsava Purāna.*
Vasanta Rājā (King Kumāragiri, before fourteenth century): *Vasanta-rājīya Nātya Shāstra.*
Digambara Suri (before Pārshvadeva).
Pārshvadeva (before Simha Bhūpāla, after Bhoja and Paramardī): *Sangīta-samaya-sāra.*
Sharngadhara (1300–1350): *Shārngadhara-paddhati.*
Haripāla (1309–1312): *Sangīta-sudhākara.*
Shrī Vidyā Chakravartin (early fourteenth): *Bharata-*

sangraha.
Sudhākalasa (1323–1349): *Sangīta-upanishad.*
Simhabhūpāla (c. 1330): *Sudhākara,* a comm. on *Sangīta-ratnākara.*
Vishveshvara (c. 1330).
Vidyāranya (1320–1380): *Sangīta-sāra.*
Vema Bhūpāla (late fourteenth–early fifteenth century): *Sangīta-chintāmani.*
Gopendra Tippa Bhūpāla (1423–1446): *Tāla-dīpikā.*
Kumbhakarna (1433–1468): *Sangīta-rāja, Sangīta-krama-dīpikā.*
Kallinātha (middle fifteenth century): *Kalānidhi,* a comm. on the *Sangīta-ratnākara.*
Kamala Lochana (c. fifteenth century ?): *Sangīta-chintā-mani, Sangītāmrita.*
Keshava (between 1240 and 1664): comm. on the *Sangīta-ratnākara.*
Rāmānanda Nārāyana Shiva Yogin (after thirteenth century): *Nātya-sarvasva-dīpikā.*

The most extensive work of the medieval period is the *Sangīta-ratnākara* of Shārngadeva (A.D. 1210–1247). It has several valuable commentaries, two of which—by Simha-bhūpāla (c. 1330) and by Kallinātha (fifteenth century)—have been published. The *Rāga-taranginī* of Lochana may also belong to this period.

In the first chapter of his *Sangīta-ratnākara,* Shārngadeva gives the following list of his chief predecessors:

"Sadāshiva, Shiva, Brahma, Bharata, Kashyapa Muni, Matanga, Yāshtika, Durgā-shakti, Shārdūla, Kohala, Vishā khila, Dantila (Dattila), Kambala, Ashvatara, Vāyu, Vish-vāvasu, Rambhā, Arjuna, Nārada, Tumburu, Ānjaneya, Mātrigupta, Rāvana, Nandikeshvara, Svāti, Guna, Bindurāja, Kshetra-rāja, Rāhala, Rudrata, Nānya Bhūpāla, and king Bhoja, Paramardī and Somesha the world emperor; then the commentators of Bharata: Lollata, Udbhata, Shankuka, Bhatta, Abhinava Gupta, the famous Kīrtidhara and many more in the past were experts in music."

The Fourth (Modern) Period

With the advent of foreign invasions musical theory quickly

decays, although musical practice maintains its standards. A few authors, however, attempt to re-establish the old theory and to re-shape it, so that it may agree with new ideas. Musicians had found many points of the reconstructed medieval theory irrelevant when confronted with the practice of their day. A series of attempts was therefore made to reconcile the theory with the facts. The chief works of this kind are the *Svaramela-kalānidhi* of Rāmāmātya (1549), the *Rāga-vibodha* of Somanātha (1610), the *Sangīta-darpana* of Dāmodara Mishra (1625) and especially the *Chaturdandī-prakāshikā* of Venkata Makhin (1620), the systematizer of South Indian music. Yet these efforts merely added to the confusion, for, in their attempt to explain apparent contradictions, the later authors often forced far-fetched interpretations upon ancient technical terms and theories.

A series of more recent works span the period between ancient and modern music. In Northern India the *Sangīta-pārijāta* of Ahobala (c. 1690) and the *Sangīta-dāmodara* of Shukambara (seventeenth century) are considered the most important.

The Chief Writers of the Fourth (Modern) Period

Harināyaka (c. 1500): *Sangīta-sāra*.

Meshakarna (before 1509): *Rāga-mālā*.

Madanapāla Deva (c. 1528): *Ānanda-sanjīvana*.

Lakshmī Nārāyana (first quarter of the sixteenth century): *Sangīta-sūryodaya*.

Lakshmīdhara (sixteenth century): *Bharata Shāstra-grantha*.

Rāmāmātya (1550): *Svaramela-kalānidhi*.

Pundarīka Vitthala (late sixteenth century): *Shadrāga-chandrodaya, Rāga-mālā, Rāga-manjarī, Nartana-nirnaya*.

Tanappāchārya (Tān-sen ?) (guru of Venkata Makhin. c. 1600).

Mādhava Bhatta (before 1610): *Sangīta-chandrikā*.

Somanātha (1610): *Rāga-vibodha*.

Govinda Dīkshita (1614): *Sangīta-sudhā*.

Govinda (?): *Sangraha-chūdāmani*.

Venkata Makhin (c. 1620): *Chaturdandī-prakāshikā*.

Dāmodara Mishra (1625): *Sangīta-darpana*.

Hridaya Nārāyana Deva (c. 1667): *Hridaya-kautuka, Hridaya-prakāsha.*

Bāsava Rājā (1698–1715): *Shiva-tattva-ratnākara.*

Ahobala (before Shrī Nivāsa and Bhava Bhatta; first half of seventeenth century or earlier): *Sangīta-pārijāta* (translated into Persian in 1724).

Shrī Nivāsa (late seventeenth century): *Rāga-tattva-vibodha.*

Abhilasa (seventeenth century): *Sangīta-chandra.*

Jagaddhara (fourteenth to seventeenth century): *Sangīta-sārasva.*

Kamalākara (later than 1600): *Sangīta-kamalākara.*

Kikarāja (seventeenth century): *Sangīta-sāroddhāra.*

Jagajjyotirmalla (seventeenth century): *Sangīta-sāra-sangraha, Sangīta-bhāskara.*

Raghunātha Bhūpa (seventeenth century): *Sangīta-sudhā.*

Nanga Rājā(?): *Sangīta-gangā-dharana.*

Veda or Mudaveda (during the reign of Shāhājī 1684–1712): *Sangīta-makaranda, Sangīta-pushpānjali.*

Vangamani (seventeenth century): *Sangīta-bhāskara.*

Shukambhara (before eighteenth century): *Sangīta-dāmodara.*

Somanārya (after 1609): *Nātya-chūdāmani.*

Bhāva Bhatta (alias Anushtupa Chakravartī, after Ahobala c. 1700): *Anupa-sangīta-ankusha, Anupa-sangīta-ratnākara, Anupa-sangīta-vilāsa.*

Tulajādhipa (ruled 1729–1735): *Sangīta-sārāmrita.*

Nārāyana (King) (late eighteenth century): *Sangīta-nārāyana.*

Kavi-ratna Nārāyana (eighteenth century): *Sangīta-sarani.*

Govinda (eighteenth century): *Sangīta Shāstra-sankshepa.*

Gopinātha Kavi Bhūshana (late eighteenth century): *Kavichintāmani.*

Pratāp Singh (1779–1804): *Sangīta-sāgara.*

Balarāma Varmā (ruled 1798–1810): *Bala-rāma-Bharata.*

Shrīkantha (late eighteenth century): *Rasa-kaumudī.*

The Authors of the Nineteenth and Twentieth Centuries are:

Rāma varmā Mahārāja: *Sangīta-kritayah.*

Appā Tulsi: *Abhinava-tāla-manjarī, Rāga-chandrikā, Rāga-kalpa-drumānkura, Sangīta-sudhākara.*

Krishnānanda Vyāsa: *Rāga-kalpa-druma* (1843).
Appalāchārya: *Sangīta-sangraha-chintāmani*.
Sourindra Mohan Sharmā (Rājā Tagore): *Sangīta-sāra-sangraha* (1875).
Vishnu Sharmā (Pandit Bhātkhande): *Abhinava-rāga-manjarī* (1921), *Shrīmallakshya-sangītam* (1921).

The Main Authors in North Indian Languages other than Sanskrit are:

Rāja Māna-simha Tomār (1486–1518): *Māna-kautūhala* (Hindi).
Tān-sen (c. 1549): *Rāga-mālā* (Hindi).
Shrī Rāma Malla: *Rāga-vichāra* (Hindi).
Harivallabha: *Sangīta-darpana* (Hindi) (mss. dated 1673).
Gangā Rām: *Setū* (comm. on *Sangīta-ratnākara*) (Hindi).
Deo Kavi: *Rāga-ratnākara* (1673) (Hindi).
Saiyid "Abd-al Wali" Uzlat: *Rāga-mālā* (1759) (Hindusthani).
Kavi Krishna: Rāga-kutuhala (1781) (Hindi).
Maharājā Sawai Pratāp Simha Deva of Jaipur (1779–1804): *Sangīta-sāra* (Hindi).
Muhammad Rezza: *Nāgmat-e-Asaphi* (1813) (Persian).
Rādhā Mohan Sen: *Sangīta-taranga* (1818) (Bengali).
Diwān Lacchirām: *Buddhi prakāsha-darpana* (1823) (Hindi).
Krishnānanda Vyāsa Deva: *Rāga Kalpa druma* (1842–1849) (Hindi and Bengali).
Chhatra Nripati: *Pāda-ratnāvalī* (1854) (Hindi).
Chunni Lāljī Gossain: *Nāda Vinoda* (1896) (Hindi).
Bhānu Kavi (Jagannāth Prasad): *Kāvya-prabhākara* (1909) (Hindi).

CHAPTER II

BASES OF MELODIC STRUCTURES

The Nature of Sound

"INTELLIGIBLE sound (Nāda) is the treasure of happiness for the happy, the distraction of those who suffer, the winner of the hearts of hearers, the first messenger of the God of Love. Easy of access, it is the nimble beloved of passionate women. May it for ever be honoured. It is the fifth approach to the Eternal Wisdom, the Veda." (*Sangīta Bhāshya.*)

In Indian musical theory it is said that there are two kinds of sound, one a vibration of ether, the other a vibration of air. The vibration of ether, which cannot be perceived in the physical sense, is considered the principle of all manifestation, the basis of all substance. It corresponds to what neo-Pythagoreans called "music of the spheres". It forms permanent numerical patterns which are the basis of the world's existence. This kind of vibration is not caused by a physical shock as are audible sounds. It is therefore called *anāhata*, "unstruck". The other kind of sound is an impermanent vibration of air, an image of the ether vibration. It is audible and always produced by a shock. It is therefore called *āhata* or "struck".

Thus the *Sangīta-makaranda* (I, 4–6) says:

"Sound is considered to be of two kinds, unstruck and struck; of these two, the unstruck will be first described.

"Sound produced from ether is known as 'unstruck'. In this unstruck sound the Gods delight. The Yogis, the Great Spirits, projecting their minds by an effort of the mind into this unstruck sound, depart, attaining Liberation."

"Struck sound is said to give pleasure, 'unstruck' sound leads to Liberation." (*Nārada Purāna.*)

But "this (unstruck sound) having no relation with human enjoyment does not interest ordinary men." (*Shiva-tattva-ratnākara, 6, 7, 12.*)

Not all audible vibrations are intelligible sounds. The sounds used in music are those whose mutual relationships form an image of the basic laws of the universe as represented by the unstruck sounds. Thus musical sounds have it in their power to reproduce the first creation of the Primordial Intellect. This creation is at the same time a rhythm and a thought. The main characteristic of musical sounds is that they convey ideas, emotions, and at the same time form simple harmonious relations. This is why, according to a symbolic etymology, musical sound is called "Nāda", "intelligible sound", and is said to result from the union of physical breath with the fire of intellect.

"The syllable 'Na' means breath, the syllable 'Da' the fire (of intellect). Born of the union of breath and fire, intelligible sound is called Nāda." (Sangīta-makaranda, 4, 18, reproduced in Sangīta-ratnākara, 1, 3, 6, and Sangīta-darpana, 1, 39.)

Three main elements are considered in musical sound— intensity, interval and timbre.

Intensity is the relative strength of the sound, whether soft or powerful.

The interval is defined by the relative pitch (shruti).

Timbre arises from the various possibilities of resonance which differentiate the sound of instruments and voices.

Musical sounds are classified into five main categories:

"Struck sounds are known to be of five kinds—produced by the nail (strings), by wind (flutes), from leather (drums), from metal (percussion instruments) or from the body (the voice)." (Sangīta-makaranda 1, 7.)

The Tonic or Drone

All music is based upon relations between sounds. These relations can be worked out in different ways, and thus give rise to varying musical systems, each of which has possibilities of expression peculiar to itself.

The modal group of musical systems, to which practically all Indian music belongs, is based on the establishment of relations between a permanent sound fixed and invariable, the "tonic" or Sa, and successive sounds, the notes.

Modal music is not merely melody without accompaniment, neither has a song or melody, in itself, anything to do with mode.

Indian music, like all truly modal music, is built on the independent relationship of each note to the tonic. The relationship to the tonic determines the meaning of any given sound. The tonic must therefore be constantly heard. It can either be sounded as a drone or repeated at frequent intervals, as is done on stringed instruments. It should be remembered that the drone is not merely intended to keep the singers on pitch, so that they can always attack at the correct pitch, but it is the key to all modal expression. As long as the hearer has not entirely identified himself with the tonic, but still perceives drone and melody as separate entities, it will remain impossible for him to follow or understand the meaning of modal music.

At different periods it appears that different notes were taken as the starting-point of the scale. But *Shadja* (Sa, C), the tonic of all modern music, seems to have been considered as such since medieval times.

"*Shadja* (Sa, C) is the first of all the notes and so it is the main or chief note." (Simhabhūpāla commentary on the *Sangīta-ratnākara*, 1, 4, 6–8.)

"Dattila explains that the *Shadja* (the tonic) may be established at will at any pitch (on any shruti) and that, by relation with it, the other notes should be established at the proper intervals." (Simhabhūpāla commentary on the *Sangīta-ratnākara*, 1, 4, 15–16.)

However, a common tonic is necessary so that the *rāga*-s may be easily compared. In the notations of *rāga*-s which form the second part of this book, the tonic is noted in every case as C, since C is usually considered the first note of the Western scale, just as *Sa* (in present-day music always the tonic) is the first note of the Indian scale.

With C as the tonic, the white keys of any keyboard instrument, such as the piano or organ, give approximately the major mode or unaltered (shuddha) scale, the scale of *Bilāval* in modern Indian music. The different modes can be visualized as modifications of this basic (shuddha) scale.

The fact that the tonic used by most singers is lower— often B flat—is not important. Once the real nature of each mode has been properly understood (and practice shows that

this is easier if the tonic is always noted as C) the modes can be
transposed so as to commence on any note that may be suit-
able for different voices or instruments.

The Three Main Octaves (Saptaka-s)

Music develops mainly within three octaves. In singing,
these correspond to the resonances of chest, throat and head.
These three octaves are called "low" (mandra), "medium"
(madhya) and "high" (tāra).

"In practice there are three [octaves in singing], the lower
one [resounding] in the chest, the middle one in the throat
and the higher one in the head. Each being the double of the
other." (*Sangīta-makaranda*, 4, 19, and *Sangīta-ratnākara*,
1, 3, 7.)

"[They are] in order: 'low octave' in the heart, 'middle
octave' in the throat, 'high octave' in the head." (*Sangīta-
darpana*, 1, 49.)

And:

"The lower octave has its place in the chest, the middle
octave in the throat, the high octave in the forehead. Although
they are similar, each is respectively the double of the preced-
ing one." (*Nārada Samhitā*.)

The Seven Notes (Svara-s)

The note (svara) is not only a definite pitch of sound. The
word *svara* means a sound plus an expression, so it would be
more correctly rendered as "expressive note".

Matanga says:

"The sound that generates an expression is called *svara*
(note)." (*Brihaddeshī*, comm. on 1, 63.)

"The word *svara* means 'that which shines of itself'— from
rājri (to shine) with the prefix *sva* (self)." (Matanga, *Brihaddeshī*, 1, 63.)

Ancient Indian music recognizes seven main and two
secondary *svara*-s. These notes represent definite intervals
and form the basic unaltered or "pure" (shuddha) scale. They
can be raised or lowered to form other scales. In that case they
are considered "altered" (vikrita). The notes that form the
basic scale are called pure (shuddha); notes lowered by half a

tone are said to be *komala* (soft—flat); notes raised by half a tone are called *tīvra* (sharp).

According to the mode, the notes can be slightly sharper or flatter, thus forming certain microtonal intervals which convey particular expressions. Hence the microtonal scale, or scale of the *shruti*-s, is considered to be the fundamental basis of musical scales, the notes or *svara*-s depending for their significance on the place they occupy in the microtonal scale.

Matanga says:

"*Shadja* (C) and the other notes (svara-s) are always manifested through the 'interval they form with the tonic', their *shruti*, just as a pitcher in the dark is made manifest by a lamp." (*Brihaddeshī*, 1, 36.)

The commentary on the *Rāga-vibodha* (1, 14) adds:

"What then constitutes a note, a *svara*? What is the particularity of these seven sounds? It is their intelligibility, their capacity to please the mind, to appeal to the consciousness of the hearer. They must do this of themselves, without external aid."

"The sound is first heard as an interval, a *shruti*; but the resonance that immediately follows, conveying of itself (without external aid) an expression to the mind of the hearer, is called a *svara*, a 'musical note'." (*Sangīta-ratnākara*, 1, 3, 24–25.)

And:

"The expressive sound, attractive and pleasing, which resounds immediately after the exact interval (the shruti) has manifested itself, is called a *svara* (note)." (*Sangīta-darpana*, 1, 57.)

The notes are seven in number.

"From the [twenty-two main] intervals (shruti-s) come the seven notes (svara-s) called *Shadja, Rishabha, Gāndhāra, Madhyama, Panchama, Dhaivata, Nishāda.*" (*Chatvārimshach'hata-rāga-nirūpanam*, 1, 18–19; *Sangīta-darpana*, 1, 167; *Shiva-tattva-ratnākara*, 6, 7, 22–23.)

"Others call them (for short): *Sa* (Do), *Ri* (Re), *Ga* (Mi), *Ma* (Fa), *Pa* (Sol), *Dha* (La), and *Ni* (Si)." (*Sangīta-darpana*, 1, 168.)

These notes, classified according to their relative importance, form the different parts of the "personality" of the "modal scale" (mūrch'hanā).

"The note *Sa* (C, the tonic) is said to be the soul, *Ri* (D) is called the head, *Ga* (E) the arms, *Ma* (F) the chest, *Pa* (G) the throat, *Dha* (A) the hips, *Ni* (B) the feet. Such are the seven limbs of the modal scale." (*Nārada Samhitā*, 2, 53-54.)

"These notes, which are seven as a rule, correspond, in the view of Matanga, with the seven basic elements of the physical body, and issue from the seven centres of the subtle body (chakra-s)." (Kallinātha commentary on the *Sangīta-ratnā-kara*, 3, 23.)

The *svara*-s or notes of the unaltered (shuddha) scale are associated with the cries of animals.

Although this association has been held to be symbolical, musicians claim that most animals have a distinct cry based on two notes. If we consider the lower note as the *Sa* (Do), the higher note may give us a second, a third, a fourth, etc.

"*Shadja* (the octave) is sounded by the peacock; the next note *Rishabha* (the major second) is uttered by the *chātaka* bird. The goat bleats *Gāndhāra* (the minor third), the heron (krauncha) cries *Madhyama* (the perfect fourth). In the season of flowers, *Panchama* (the perfect fifth) is softly sung by the cuckoo (kokila). *Dhaivata* (the natural sixth) is croaked by the frog in the season of rains. At all times, O Goddess! *Nishāda* (the minor seventh) is trumpeted by the elephant." (Kohala quoted in *Brihaddeshī*, commentary on 63.)

The ancient Indian natural scale, compared to the Western major mode, contains an E flat and a B flat (modern Ga komala and Ni komala).

A similar list of animal cries is given in the *Nārada Samhitā* (2, 55-56) and a slightly different one in the *Mānduki Shikshā* (1, 9) and in the *Nāradīya Shikshā* (I, V, 4-5) also reproduced in the *Shiva-tattva-ratnākara* (VI, 7, 33-35).

The peacock's octave starts from the upper note. Kālidāsa says:

"Both listened to the lovely cry of crested peacocks raising their heads at the sound of the axle of the chariot. In this cry resound two kinds of *Shadja svara*." (*Raghuvamsha*, 1, 39.)

The Intercalary Notes, Kākalī Ni and Antara Ga

In ancient music two accessory notes were added to the seven main notes dividing the major tones *Ni Sa* (B♭ C) and

Ga Ma (E♭ F) into half-tones. These two intercalary (sād-hārana) notes were called *Kākalī Ni* (the pleasing Si) and *Antara Ga* (intermediary Mi).

"When two *shruti*-s (half a tone) from Sa (C) pass into *Ni* (B♭), this is (called) *Kākalī* (B♮) The same from *Ma* (F) into *Ga* (E♭) is *Antaka* (E♮)." (Quoted in Simhabhūpāla comm. on the *Sangīta-ratnākara*, I, 3, 40, and in *Shiva-tattva-ratnākara*, VI, 7, 51.)

"The note called *Kākalī* is obtained by raising *Ni* (Si♭) by two *shruti*-s. The note called Antaıa is obtained from *Ga* (E♭) in the same way. They are not properly considered notes (svara-s) because they cannot be taken as tonic (amsha). So *Nishāda* (B♭) and *Gāndhāra* (E♭) are given prominence over them." (Dattila, 16–17, also quoted by Simhabhūpāla comm. on the *Sangīta-ratnākara*, I, 3, 56.)

The Intervals (Shruti-s)

The names and classification of the intervals, the *shruti*-s, as given in the ancient and medieval books, present many problems of interpretation. There are various reasons for this: (1) at different periods, different notes were taken as the t nic; (2) the more ancient treatises envisaged a descending scale, more recent ones an ascending scale; (3) the scale considered unaltered differed from one period to another. These difficulties will not surprise us if we remember that hundreds of years elapsed between the writing of many of the treatises.

As we have already seen, a note and its name depend upon its relationship to the tonic; it can be a fourth, a fifth (a Ma (F), a Pa (G), etc.) only through relationship to a basic sound (in modern Indian music, always the Sa).

Notes, therefore, depend upon intervals. The intervals from which the notes are produced are called *shruti*-s (audible), since it is only through hearing that the idea conveyed by the intervals can be grasped.

"It is grasped by the ear, hence it is called 'shruti' (audible)." " 'Shru', which means 'hearing', is the root of the word. To this is added the (feminine) suffix 'ktin' (denoting an abstract noun). In this way the term 'shruti' is defined by linguists (to represent) the 'means of expression'." (*Brihad-*

deshī, commentary on I, 26.)

The number of theoretically possible intervals in relationship to a given note is obviously limitless. Yet the number of intervals used in music is comparatively small. This is due to the limitations of the mental mechanism through which we can distinguish sounds.

Intervals do not merely produce pleasing or unpleasing sensations. Like words, they convey distinct and definite expressions to the mind of the hearer.

Indian musical theory considers that the ear can perceive sixty-six distinct meaningful intervals within the compass of an octave. We find, however, that among these intervals twenty-two are mainly used in music. These twenty-two which form well-defined ratios with the tonic are those which convey to our mind the most distinct meanings. In practice, we could say that within one octave it is possible to distinguish accurately twenty-two distinct expressions, and sixty-six distinct pitches of sound; beyond this we can naturally conceive of limitless relationships of sounds, but since we cannot distinguish them they have no reality in music.

"Some experts in the knowledge of intervals say that they number twenty-two. Others speak of sixty-six and some consider them numberless." (Kohala, quoted in *Brihaddeshī*, commentary on I, 28, and in both Simhabhūpāla's and Kallinātha's commentary on the *Sangīta-ratnākara*, I, 3, 8–9 and 10–16.)

The complete scale of the *shruti*-s is not a musical scale which can be directly used in a melodic form. It is merely the assemblage of the different intervals used in different modes; their ordered arrangement for purposes of study and comparison.

It is not possible to sing the scale of the *shruti*-s accurately in succession (as some singers pretend to do), but they can all be sung with perfect accuracy when they are embodied in melodic figures that have a definite expression. Hence Pārshvadeva says:

"The twenty-two sounds cannot be produced (in succession) by the throat. They should therefore be demonstrated on a stringed instrument." (Attributed to the *Sangīta-samaya-sāra*, though not found in the printed edition.)

The Measurement of the Shruti-s

According to the explanations given in the *Nātya Shāstra* and by Matanga in his *Brihaddeshī*, the interval, or *shruti*, used as the divisional basis of the octave appears to be the comma diesis 81/80, defined as the difference between *Pa* (modern Dha (A)), considered as the upper fourth from *Ri* (modern Ga (E)), and *Pa* as the lower fourth from *Sa* (modern Ri (D)). This comma is called the "measuring" or "standard" interval.

"The interval produced by the raising or lowering of *Panchama*, [which can also be envisaged as a] softening or [a difference in string-] length, is called the 'standard interval' (pramāna shruti)." (*Nātya Shāstra*, 28, 22; and *Brihaddeshī*, comm. on 1, 28.)

If we add the minor tone (G A, ancient Ma Pa) of 3 *shruti*-s to the perfect fourth (D G, ancient Sa Ma) of 9 *shruti*-s and then to another perfect fourth (A D, ancient Pa Sa) of 9 *shruti-s*, we find the octave from Ri to Ri (D to D) too short:

9 *shruti*-s $+ 3 + 9 = 21$ (i.e. $4/3 \times 10/9 \times 4/3 = 160/81$).

The difference between this and the real octave $(2/1)$ is one shruti or comma $(81/80)$. Thus: $21 + 1 = 22$, or $160/81 \times 81/80 = 2/1$.

To obtain a perfect octave, we must then either make the fourth *Dha Ri* (A D) too large $(27/20)$, or raise the harmonic *Dha* $(A = 5/3)$ into *Dha+* $(A+ = 27/16)$,[1] changing the minor tone *Pa Dha* $(G A = 10/9)$ into a major tone *Pa Dha+* $(G A+ = 9/8)$. But in this case the fourth *Ga Dha+* (E A+) becomes too large. To correct it, we may raise the *Ga* (E) into *Ga+* (E+); but this will destroy its consonance with *Ni* (B).

In this way we always have to choose between one perfect fourth or the other, the difference involved being in every case the interval of one comma $(81/80)$ or 5 savart-s which first appears on the *Dha* (A) (ancient Pa).

This comma was considered by the Greeks, the Arabs and the Hindus as the logical unit for any practical division of the scale.

The difference between important simple intervals can generally be expressed in terms of commas. For example, the difference between the major and minor tone 9/8 and 10/9 (Sa Ri and Ri Ga) is $9/8 \times 9/10 = 81/80$; the difference

[1] See notation signs on pp. 38-43

between the major half-tone (16/15) and the limma (256/243) is $16/15 \times 243/256 = 81/80$; the difference between the two minor thirds C E♭+ = 6/5 and C E♭ = 32/27 is $6/5 \times 27/32 = 81/80$; the difference between the harmonic major third C E (Sa Ga) = 5/4 and the Pythagorean third C E+ (Sa Ga+) = 81/64 is $81/64 \times 4/5 = 81/80$; etc.

This explains why a scale formed by adding twelve other notes, each raised by one comma, to the twelve notes of the basic scale and twelve more, each lowered by one comma, will give us practically all the intervals used in music.

The complete division of the octave is obtained by adding or subtracting either one or two commas from each of the twelve notes of the basic chromatic scale. This gives us a series of fifty-three intervals, which cannot all be used in modal scales though they may come into use through modulations (changes of tonic) or in certain forms of polyphony.

If we further divide the disjunctions of this scale which appear at each half-tone so as to form quarter-tones, we obtain the division of the octave (Sa to upper Sa) into sixty-five intervals—that is, counting the note that forms the octave itself, the scale of sixty-six intervals or *shruti*-s spoken of by Kohala.

It has been suggested that the sixty-six intervals of Kohala may refer to the twenty-two *shruti*-s in three octaves. But this is not usually accepted.

It should be noted that this scale makes use of only two kinds of intervals—commas of 5 savart-s and disjunctions of 8 savart-s. This is, in fact, besides the Pythagorean division into seven notes, the only possible complete division of the octave which uses only two sorts of intervals and which respects the fundamental consonances (fourth, fifth, etc.). All other divisions of the octave are either irregular or, as is the case with all tempered scales, never give perfect consonances.

The cycle of intervals gives us a division of the octave into fifty-three. This corresponds exactly to the number of letters in the complete phonetic alphabet of Sanskrit grammarians, in which the letters are arranged according to the five places of articulation, in each of which can be pronounced a vowel (short or long) and five consonants, a drawn unaspirate, a drawn aspirate, a thrown unaspirate, a thrown aspirate, and a nasal. Added to these, there are further vowels and consonants, using more than one place of articulation to form a total of fifty-two letters.

To these is added the sacred syllable (AUM) considered to be the origin and end of all articulate sounds and corresponding to the *Sa* (C) of music which has a similar function with regard to all the *shruti*-s. AUM is made of the guttural A, the labial U and the nasal M, the three extreme points of articulation, which form a triangle that includes all other letters. Thus, the laws that govern musical and articulate sound appear to the Hindu theorists strictly parallel and interdependent, both kinds of sound serving, though on different levels, to manifest ideas.

The Notation of the Shruti-s

To proceed with the theory of the *shruti*-s, we need an accurate and simple way of notating exact intervals. We have adopted the following method since it appeared to be the simplest and most convenient.

In order to notate the sixty-six intervals of the complete scale, we shall use conventional signs, placed beside the names of the notes within the frame of the harmonic form of the chromatic scale, which is the scale of modal music and which allows only one sort of accidental (either flat or sharp) for each note. Thus, the sign – – after the note means that the note is lowered by two commas; the sign – means that the note is lowered by one comma; the sign + means that it is raised by one comma, the sign ++ that it is raised by two commas.

We shall leave aside the quarter-tones that divide the disjunction into two approximately equal parts since they are never used in Indian musical practice.

For the notation we use the following symbols:

The notes of the diatonic series based upon C are written, as usual, ♩ . Notes lowered by one comma are written ♩ . Those raised by one comma are written ♩ . The rare notes raised by two commas are written ♩ , those lowered by two commas ♩ Thus the notation of the notes in ordinary use is:

The Sixty-six Shruti-s

Shruti-s	No.	Cents (interval)	Tempered Scale	Intervals with C (Sa)
Sa / C	1		x	1/1
		comma 20		
Sa+ / C+	2			81/80
		comma 20		
Sa++ / C++	3			(128/125)
		disjunction 32		
1/4	4			31/30
RiK-- / Db--	5			25/24
		comma 20		
RiK- / Db-	6		x	256/243
		comma 20		
RiK / Db	7			16/15
		comma 20		
RiK+ / Db+	8			27/25
		disjunction 32		
3/4	9			135/124
Ri-- / D--	10			(800/729)
		comma 20		
Ri- / D-	11			10/9
		comma 20		
Ri / D	12		x	9/8
		comma 20		
Ri+ / D+	13			256/225
		comma 20		
Ri++ / D++	14			125/108

33

Shruti-s														
	Ri++ D++	1/4	GaK- Eb-	GaK Eb	GaK+ Eb+	3/4	Ga--- E---	Ga- E-	Ga E	Ga+ E+	Ga++ E++	1/4	Ma--- P---	Ma- P-
	14	15	16	17	18	19	20	21	22	23	24	25	26	27
	disjunction	disjunction	comma	comma	disjunction	disjunction	comma	comma	comma	comma	comma	disjunction	comma	comma
Cents	32	32	20	20	32	32	20	20	20	20	20	32	20	20
Tempered Scale														
Intervals with C (Sa)	$(\frac{125}{108})$	$\frac{93}{80}$	$\frac{75}{64}$	$\frac{32}{27}$	$\frac{6}{5}$	$\frac{75}{62}$	$(\frac{243}{200})$	$\frac{100}{81}$	$\frac{5}{4}$	$\frac{81}{64}$	$\frac{32}{25}$	$\frac{31}{24}$	$(\frac{125}{96})$	$\frac{320}{243}$

34

Shruti-s	Ma- P-	Ma P	Ma+ P+	Ma++ P++	1/4	MaT-- P#--	MaT- P#-	MaT P#	MaT+ P#+	3/4	Pa-- G--	Pa- G-	Pa G	Pa+ G+	Pa++ G++
	27	28	29	30	31	32	33	34	35	36	37	38	39	40	41
Cents	comma 20	comma 20	comma 20	disjunction 32	disjunction 32	comma 20	comma 20	comma 20	disjunction 32	disjunction 32	comma 20	comma 20	comma 20	comma 20	comma 20
Tempered Scale	x					x						x			
Intervals with C (Sa)	$\frac{320}{243}$	$\frac{4}{3}$	$\frac{27}{20}$	$\frac{512}{375}$	$\frac{62}{45}$	$\frac{25}{18}$	$\frac{45}{32}$	$\frac{64}{45}$	$\frac{36}{25}$	$\left(\frac{45}{31}\right)$	$\frac{375}{256}$	$\frac{40}{27}$	$\frac{3}{2}$	$\frac{243}{160}$	$\frac{125}{81}$

35

Shruti-s		Cents	Tempered Scale	Intervals with C (Sa)
41	Pa++ / G++			(125/81)
		disjunction 32		
42	1/4		--- x	31/20
		comma 20		
43	DhaK- / Ab-			25/16
		comma 20		
44	DhaK / Ab		--- x	128/81
		comma 20		
45	DhaK+ / Ab+			8/5
		disjunction 32		
46	3/4			50/31
		comma 20		
47	Dha--- / A---			81/50
		comma 20		
48	Dha-- / A--			400/243
		comma 20		
49	Dha / A			5/3
		comma 20		
50	Dha+ / A+		--- x	27/16
		comma 20		
51	Dha++ / A++			128/75
		disjunction 32		
52	Dha++ / 1/4			31/18
		comma 20		
53	NiK-- / Bb---			125/72
		comma 20		
54	NiK- / Bb-			225/128

36

Shruti-s	54 NiK- Bb-	55 NiK Bb	56 NiK+ Bb+	57 3/4	58 Ni--- B---	59 Ni-- B--	60 Ni B	61 Ni+ B+	62 Ni++ B++	63 1/4	64 Sa--- C---	65 Sa- C-	66 Sa C
Cents	comma 20	comma 20	disjunction 32		disjunction 32	comma 20	comma 20	comma 20	comma 20	disjunction 32	comma 20	comma 20	comma 20
Intervals with C (Sa)	$\frac{225}{128}$	$\frac{16}{9}$	$\frac{9}{5}$	$\frac{29}{16}$	$(\frac{729}{400})$	$\frac{50}{27}$	$\frac{15}{8}$	$\frac{243}{128}$	$\frac{48}{25}$	$\frac{60}{31}$	$\frac{125}{64}$	$\frac{160}{81}$	$\frac{2}{1}$

Tempered Scale

Many of these theoretical intervals are seldom used in practice. The twenty-two (or twenty-five) most prominent intervals, which correspond to clearly perceptible and distinct expressions and which are used in the teaching of modal music, are usually considered to be the following:

Under no circumstances can these twenty-two divisions be considered equal. They refer only to twenty-two prominent intervals chosen out of the possible fifty-three (or sixty-six). In present day music a few other intervals are used, though seldom.

They are the rare F– and B♭– –

The remaining divisions, necessary only when the tonic is changed, are not considered in modal practice.

As we have already explained, if we raise and lower by one comma each of the twelve notes of the fundamental Pythagorean chromatic scale, we get a scale of thirty-six notes which contains practically all the intervals that are used in any form of music.

Thus, in this scale each of the twelve notes has three positions—low, middle and high. This mode of division of the scale seems to have been used by the celebrated Tumburu, a celestial musician, considered to be the originator of one of the chief ancient systems of music, who wrote a treatise now lost.

Tumburu expresses the strident character of all the raised notes and the mellowness of the lowered ones by connecting them to the four humours of the body whose relative predominance is said to bring similar tendencies. He says:

"A sound that is high is harsh (piercing). The wise know it to be born from the wind.

"A low sound, deep and mellow, should be known as born from the bile.

"The attractive (perfect) sound is born from the lymph. It

is sweet and tender.

"That which has the qualities of all three (the sound with vibrato) is known to be born from semen." (Attributed to Tumburu by Kallinātha, commentary on the *Sangīta-ratnā-kara*, I, 3, 10–16; and to Chatura in *Brihaddeshī*, commentary on, 27.)

The Expression of the Shruti-s

The division of the octave into sixty-six intervals is theoretical. Although we can clearly perceive the differences in pitch of the different intervals and rapidly train our ear to recognize them, some will not succeed in conveying a definite meaning. The types of expression attributed to some of the intervals have been carefully classified by ancient writers. Each *shruti* was given a name depicting its character. In the system of Pārshvadeva, the names of the individual *shruti*-s were different in each octave. These types of expressions were further classified into five main groups or "families" of intervals called *jāti*-s: "moderate, keen, broad, tender, and compassionate".

"*Dīptā* (keen), *Ayatā* (broad), *Karunā* (compassionate), *Mridu* (tender), *Madhyā* (moderate), these are the five families (jāti-s) of the *shruti*-s that are found in the notes." (*Sangīta-ratnākara*, I, 3, 27–28.)

Because of the confusion that has resulted from the changes in scale and tonic the exact interpretation of the ancient *shruti*-s presents a number of problems.

The safest way to interpret them is to start from the actual expression attributed to the intervals as found in musical practice today. The notation of these expressions given in the analysis of the *rāga*-s has been worked out by careful measurement of the intervals used by musicians playing different *rāga*-s and by noting the expression each particular note conveyed to the musician and to his audience. It was found that the same shade of meaning was always attributed to the same intervals occurring in *rāga*-s with quite different characters. The scale we give here is only the result of such experiments in a particular tradition and may therefore be subject to improvement.

In the following table we compare the *shruti*-s as given by Shārngadeva with the experimental ones. A few slight differences remain to be clarified. There is some difficulty in ascertaining which of the *shruti*-s of Shārngadeva really was the tonic. This has led to divergent interpretations. The three main interpretations have the scale starting from the *shruti*-s *Chhandovatī*, *Kshobhinī* or even *Ramyā*—corresponding to *Dha* (A), which is said to have been the ancient tonic of Nārada. The *Svaramela-kalānidhi* (A.D. 1549) takes *Chhandovatī* as *Sa* (tonic) but considers that *"Prasūnā"*, Nārada's first *shruti*, corresponds to *Kshobhinī*. On the other hand, Govinda in his *Sangīta Shāstra-sankshepa* (c. eighteenth century) places the tonic *Sa* on *Kshobhinī*.

The *shruti*-s given by Shārngadeva are as follows:

"Tīvrā, Kumudvatī, Mandā, Chhandovatī come within *Shadja*;

Dayāvatī, Ranjanī and *Raktikā* dwell in *Rishabha*,

Raudrī and *Krodhā* in *Gāndhāra*,

While the shruti-s *Vajrikā, Prasārinī, Prīti* and *Mārjanī* have their place in *Madhyama*.

Kshitih, Raktā, Sandīpanī and *Alāpinī* are in *Panchama*;

Madantī, Rohinī, Ramyā shelter in *Dhaivata*;

Both *Ugrā* and *Kshobhinī* rest in *Nishāda."* (*Sangīta-ratnākara*, I, 3, 35–39.)

I formerly followed the often admitted interpretation that starts the scale from *Kshobhinī*, but closer study of the expressions given by Shārngadeva seems to show beyond doubt that his scale starts from *Chhandovatī*, as seen in the following tables.

THE SCALE OF THE SHRUTI-S

Note	Actual expression	Ratio from C		Shārngadeva's Shruti-s (Name of shruti)	(Type of expression—Jāti-s)
Sa (C)	(base)	1/1	Sa	4 Chhandovatī (measuring)	Madhyā (moderate)
Sa+ (C+)	—	81/80			
Rik- (D♭-)	sad, pathetic	25/24		5 Dayāvatī (compassionate)	Karunā (compassion)
Rik (D♭)	tender, at peace	256/243			
Rik+ (D♭+)	loving, calm	16/15		6 Ranjanī (charming)	Madhyā (moderate)
Rik++ (D♭++)	enterprising	27/25			
Ri- (D-)	anxious, weak	10/9	Ri	7 Ratikā (sensuous)	Mriduh (tender)
Ri (D)	strong, confident	9/8			
Ri+ (D+)	fierce	256/225		8 Raudrī (fierce)	Dīptā (keen)
Gak- (E♭-)	sad	75/64	Ga	9 Krodhā (passionate)	Ayatā (large)
Gak (E♭)	loving	32/27			
Gak+ (E♭+)	passionate	6/5		10 Vajrikā (thundering)	Dīptā (keen)
Ga (E)	calm, pleasing	5/4	(Antara Ga)	11 Prasārinī (pervasive)	Ayatā (large)

THE SCALE OF THE SHRUTI-S—(contd.)

Note	Actual expression	Ratio from C		Shārngadeva's Shruti-s	
				(Name of shruti)	(Type of expression—Jāti-s)
Ga+ (E+)	awake, lively	81/64		12 Pritih (love)	Mriduh (tender)
Ga++ (E++)	hard, indifferent	32/25			
Ma− (F−)	doubt	320/243			
Ma (F)	moonlight, peace	4/3	Ma	13 Mārjani (purifying)	Madhyā (moderate)
Ma+ (F+)	intense	27/20			
MaT− (F♯−)	intense, grief	25/18		14 Kshitih (loss)	Mriduh (tender)
MaT (F♯)	uncertain, doubtful	45/32			
MaT+ (F♯+)	intense, active	64/45		15 Raktā (red)	Madhyā (moderate)
MaT++ (F♯++)	acute, interrogative	36/25		16 Sandīpani (inflaming)	Āyatā (large)
(Pa−) (G−)	inexpressive, self-contradictory	40/27	Pa	17 Alāpini (conversing)	Karunā (compassion)
Pa (G)	sunlight, joyful	3/2			
(Pa+) (G+)	confused, self-contradictory	243/160		18 Madanti (maddening)	Karunā (compassion)
Dhak− (A♭−)	deep sorrow	25/16			

THE SCALE OF THE SHRUTI-S—(contd.)

Note	Actual expression	Ratio from C		(Name of shruti)	Shārngadeva's Shruti-s (Type of expression—Jāti-s)
Dhak (Ab)	tender	128/81		19 Rohinī (adolescent)	Āyatā (large)
Dhak+ (Ab+)	loving, enterprising	8/5			
Dha− (A−)	uncertainty	400/243			
Dha (A)	soft, calm	5/3	Dha	20 Ramyā (restful)	Madhyā (moderate)
Dha+ (A+)	restless, playful	27/16		21 Ugrā (fearful)	Dīptā (keen)
(Dha++) (A++)	hard, active	128/75			
Nik− (Bb)	helpless, subdued	225/128			
Nik (Bb)	beauty, love	16/9	Ni	22 Kshobhinī (excited)	Madhyā (moderate)
Nik+ (Bb+)	desire, anxiety	9/5		1 Tīvrā (sharp)	Dīptā (keen)
(Ni− −) (B− −)	doubt	729/400			
(Ni−) (B−)	anguish, depression	50/27		2 Kumudvatī (lotus-like)	Āyatā (large)
Ni (B)	soft, voluptuous	15/8	(Kākali Ni)		
Ni+ (B+)	strong, sensuous	243/128		3 Mandā (low)	Mriduh (tender)
Ni++ (B++)	selfish, eager	48/25			
Sa− (C−)	—	160/81		4 Chhandovatī (measuring)	Madhyā (moderate)
Sa (C)	(base)	1/1	Sa		

The expression of a mode is the sum of the expressions of its different notes, defined by their relationship to the tonic. In each *rāga*, each of the different notes is attributed a definite meaning.

The expressions given in our notation for each note of each *rāga* have been compiled experimentally and verified over and over again, players and listeners always agreeing on the meaning of the notes.

There may, however, remain some inaccuracies in the accidental *shruti*-s used for particular notes in melodic figures. There are also other schools which hold different views on the expressive interpretation of the *rāga*-s. Only a very extensive comparison of the practice of different musicians would allow us to correct and perfect every detail in the use of the accidental *shruti*-s appearing in each *rāga*.

Some *rāga*-s have peculiarities in their scale or their tuning that modify their expression.

According to the theoretical explanation of the *shruti*-s, all the notes cannot have the same kind of expression and in a scale, therefore, there are necessarily contrasts. This is why the most intense *rāga*-s should be pentatonic, since in a pentatonic scale it is easier to eliminate the notes that would not support the predominant expression.

A very sad *rāga* will leave out the fifth (Pa) because a fifth always expresses sunshine, joy. A very passionate *rāga* will have no natural fourth (shuddha Ma) since that always expresses peace, serenity.

These contrasts between the notes provide a further reason why the *rāga*-s which were considered masculine in ancient music were always pentatonic, for a pentatonic scale can give a stronger and more coherent expression than a heptatonic scale which necessarily shows contrasts, indecisions, subtleties, and seems thus more feminine in character.

When sounds are used for creating ecstasy or for the treatment of mental or physical disease, the number of notes may be further reduced to a few sounds constantly heard, so as to create an overwhelming impression pulling in one direction only.

A Suggested Interpretation of the Families of Intervals (Shruti-Jāti-s)[1]

The scale of the *shruti*-s, as we here interpret it, is composed of several series of fifths, related to one another by harmonic thirds. Starting from C (Sa), we build five successive ascending fifths and five successive descending fifths. This gives us the series of intervals, generally known as Pythagorean.

The five ascending fifths are: G D A+ E+ B+.

The five descending fifths are: F B♭ E♭ A♭ D♭.

If now, starting again from C, we descend by a harmonic minor third (6/5), this gives us the A (Dha) which forms a sixth (5/3) with the lower C, and which is lower by one comma (81/80) than the Pythagorean sixth A+ (Dha+) = 27/16 which we obtained before.

If we build up ascending and descending fifths starting from this harmonic A, they will all naturally fall one comma below those of the basic series. This new series gives us: E B F♯ D♭ etc.

If we again take the harmonic minor third below A, we obtain F♯– = 25/18, the basis of a series of fifths two commas below those of the original series, thus: D♭– A♭– E♭– B♭–.

Starting again from C, if we ascend by a harmonic minor third to obtain the high E♭+ = 6/5, the basis of a series of fifths, all one comma higher than those of the basic series, thus: A♭+ D♭+ F♯+ B+.

Similarly, the harmonic minor third above E♭+ gives F♯++ = 36/25, the basis of a series of fifths, two commas higher than those of the basic series, thus: B++ E++ A++ D+.

Each of these series is based upon a particular type of ratio, and the notes of each series are seen to correspond to a definite type of emotion. Here there is a direct connection between intervals, determined by physical laws, and the emotions they arouse or express. This fact is the very foundation of music. Once we know the type of ratio that corresponds to a kind of emotion, we can tell at once what emotion a given interval must express by merely looking at the ratio to which it corresponds: we do not need to hear it.

[1] See the author's *"Sémantique Musicale"*, Hermann, Paris, 1966.

Starting from *Sa* (C) = $1/1$ which is neutral, the ascending fifths are all of the form $3^n/2^{n+}$, i.e. ratios formed by 3 and its multiples divided by multiples of 2. Thus: G (Pa) = $3/2$, D (Ri) = $9/8$ = $3^2/2^3$, A+ (Dha+) = $27/16$ = $3^3/2^4$, E+ (Ga+) = $81/64$ = $3^4/2^6$, B+ (Ni+) = $243/128$ = $3^5/2^7$.

These intervals represent an "active principle": they all express sunshine, strength and joy.

If we now take the descending fifths from *Sa* (C), these are all of the form $2^{n+}/3^n$. Thus F (Ma) = $4/3$ = $2^2/3$, B♭ (NiK) = $16/9$ = $2^4/3^2$, E♭ (GaK) = $32/27$ = $2^5/3^3$, A♭ (DhaK) = $128/81$ = $2^7/3^4$, D♭ (RiK) = $256/243$ = $2^8/3^5$.

These intervals represent a "passive principle"; they all express moonlight, beauty, peace.

The expression in these two basic series has an unpersonal character. Their ratios never use a prime number higher than three.

In the next series a new element appears, the prime number 5. We shall discover that whenever 5 appears as a constituent of the numerator, the interval whose ratio is so expressed conveys tenderness (that is, passive reaction to the outer world). Whenever it appears as a constituent of the denominator, the interval whose ratio is so expressed conveys passion (active reaction to the outer world).

The basic interval of this series is A (Dha) = $5/3$, which expresses sensitiveness, emotion. The ascending fifths will be E (Ga) = $5/4$ = $5/2^2$, B (Ni) = $15/8$ = $5 \times 3/2^3$, F♯ (MaT) = $45/32$ = $5 \times 3^2/2^5$, D♭ (RiK) = $135/128$ = $5 \times 3^3/2^7$. They all show the same character, though the growing influence of $3/2$ will bring in its own element of activity.

The descending fifths D− (Ri−) = $10/9$ = $5 \times 2/3^2$, G− (Pa) = $40/27$ = $5 \times 2^3/3^3$, C− (Sa−) = $160/81$ = $5 \times 2^5/3^4$, F− (Ma−) = $320/243$ = $5 \times 2^6/3^5$ should add to the already receptive, sensitive character of the series. In musical practice the passive character of the descending fifth, when added to that of the number 5 in the numerator, gives intervals so extremely negative and characterless that they are rarely used in music.

The basic interval of the series + (plus) is E♭+ (GaK+) $6/5$ = $2 \times 3/5$ which expresses passion, desire. The ascending fifths built upon it add their activity to the already active character produced by the number 5 in the denominator and thus create acute intervals which, except for the first one, where the element 2 does not appear, are rarely used in music.

$(B\flat+ (NiK+) = 9/5 = 3^2/5$, $F+ (Ma+) = 27/20 = 3^3/5 \times 2^2$, $C+ (Sa+) = 81/80 = 3^4/5 \times 2^4$, $G+ (Pa+) = 243/160 = 3^5/5 \times 2^5)$.

The descending series, on the other hand, combining passion ($\frac{n}{5}$) and beauty (descending fifths), is lively and charming. Its intervals are $A\flat+ (DhaK+) = 8/5 = 2^3/5$, $D\flat + (RiK+) = 16/15 = 2^4/5 \times 3$, $F\sharp+ (MaT +) = 64/45 = 2^6/5 \times 3^2$, $B+ (Ni+) = 256/135 = 2^8/5 \times 3^3$.

The five groups of sounds so obtained appear to correspond quite accurately to what was known in ancient Indian music as the *Shruti-jāti-s*, the families of intervals.

Shārngadeva gives them the following ancient names:

Madhyā (moderate): basic series ascending
Āyatā (large): basic series descending
Mriduh (tender): series –
Karunā (pathetic): series. – –
Dīptā (fiery): series +

The expression conveyed by these different classes of intervals is in no way arbitrary. It is related to psycho-physiological facts upon which all music depends. These intervals are used in all music more or less instinctively, by good singers and players of stringed instruments.

THE CLASSES OF SHRUTI-S (SHRUTI-JĀTI-S)

BASIC SERIES (COSMIC)

0 = C (Sa) 1/1 centre, earth, etc. (yellow)

I

Descending fifths (passive 2/3)

-1	F (Ma)	$4/3 = 2^2/3$	moonlight,peace,passivity (white)
-2	B♭ (NiK)	$16/9 = 2^4/3^2$	beauty,lovableness
-3	E♭ (GaK)	$32/27 = 2^5/3^3$	tender,loving,expectant
-4	A♭ (DhaK)	$128/81 = 2^7/3^4$	submissive,passive,expectant
-5	D♭ (RiK)	$256/243 = 2^8/3^5$	tenderness,charm,devotion

SERIES -
(passive emotion, enjoyment 5/n)

0 = A (Dha) 5/3 enjoyment, satisfaction

Descending fifths

-1	D- (Ri)	$10/9 = 5 \times 2/3^2$	weak,anxious
-2	G- (Pa-)	$40/27 = 5 \times 2^3/3^3$	
-3	C- (Sa-)	$160/81 = 5 \times 2^5/3^4$	
-4	F- (Ma-)	$320/243 = 5 \times 2^6/3^5$	
-5	B♭- (NiK-)	$1280/729 = 5 \times 2^8/3^6$	

Ascending fifths

1	E (Ga)	$5/4 = 5/2^2$	soft,pleasing
2	B (Ni)	$15/8 = 5 \times 3/2^3$	soft,voluptuous
3	F# (MaT)	$45/32 = 5 \times 3^2/2^5$	attractive,ambiguous
4	D♭ (RiK)	$135/128 = 5 \times 3^3/2^7$	tender,charming,devoted
5	A♭ (DhaK)	$405/256 = 5 \times 3^4/2^8$	_____

SERIES --
(depression, sadness 25/n)

0 = F#- (MaT-) $25/18 = 5^2/3^2 \times 2$ distressful

Descending fifths

-1	B- (Ni-)	$50/27 = 5^2 \times 2/3^3$	
-2	E- (Ga-)	$100/81 = 5^2 \times 2^2/3^4$	
-3	A- (Dha-)	$400/243 = 5^2 \times 2^4/3^5$	
-4	D-- (Ri--;)	$800/729 = 5^2 \times 2^5/3^6$	
-5	G--- (Pa---)	$3200/2187 = 5^2 \times 2^7/3^7$	

Ascending fifths

1	D♭ (RiK-)	$25/24 = 5^2/3 \times 2^3$	despair
2	A♭ (DhaK-)	$25/16 = 5^2/2^4$	intense sadness
3	E♭ (GaK-)	$75/64 = 5^2 \times 3/2^6$	sadness
4	B♭- (NiK-)	$225/128 = 5^2 \times 3^2/2^7$	helpless,subdued
5	F- (Ma-)	$675/512 = 5^2 \times 3^3/2^9$	doubt,melancholy

II

Ascending fifths (active 3/2)

1	G (Pa)	$3/2$	sunshine,joy,activity (red)
2	D (Ri)	$9/8 = 3^2/2^3$	strength,virility
3	A+ (Dha+)	$27/16 = 3^3/2^4$	confident,joyful,lively
4	E+ (Ga+)	$81/64 = 3^4/2^6$	independent,active,contented
5	B+ (Ni+)	$243/128 = 3^5/2^7$	boldness,desire,pleasure

SERIES +

(active emotion, passion n/5)

$0 = E♭+ (GaK+)\ 6/5 ≈ 2\times3/5$ passion, desire

Descending fifths

-1	A♭+ (DhaK+)	$8/5 = 2^3/5$	loving,passionate
-2	D♭+ (RiK+)	$16/15 = 2^4/5\times3$	loving,confident
-3	F#+ (MaT+)	$64/45 = 2^6/5\times3^2$	active,promising,intense
-4	B+ (Ni+)	$256/135 = 2^8/5\times3^3$	boldness,desire,pleasure
(-5)	E+ (Ga+)	$512/405 = 2^9/5\times3^4$	——

Ascending fifths

			passionate,intense,hopeful
1	B♭+ (NiK+)	$9/5 = 3^2/5$	passionate,intense,hopeful
2	F+ (Ma+)	$27/2o = 3^3/5\times2^2$	intense
4	C+ (Sa+)	$81/8o = 3^4/5\times2^4$	——
3	G+ (Pa+)	$243/16o = 3^5/5\times2^5$	——
5	D+ (Ri+)	$729/64o = 3^6/5\times2^7$	——

SERIES ++

(harshness,insensibility n/25)

$0 = F#++ (MaT++)\ 36/25 = 3^2\times2^2/5^2$ harsh, indifferent

Descending fifths

-1	B++ (Ni++)	$48/25 = 3\times2^4/5^2$	selfish,hard
-2	E++ (Ga++)	$32/25 = 2^5/5^2$	hard,indifferent
-3	A++ (Dha++)	$128/75 = 2^7/5^2\times3$	unconscious,insentient
-4	D+ (Ri+)	$256/225 = 2^8/5^2\times3^2$	insentient
(-5)	G+ (Pa+)	$1o24/675 = 2^{1o}/5^2\times3^3$	——

Ascending fifths

			harsh,enterprising
1	D♭++ (RiK++)	$27/25 = 3^3/5^2$	harsh,entersprising
2	A-- (Dha--)	$81/5o = 3^4/5^2\times2$	
3	E-- (Ga--)	$243/2oo = 3^5/5^2\times2^3$	
4	B-- (Ni--)	$729/4oo = 3^6/5^2\times2^4$	
5	F++ (Ma++)	$2187/16oo = 3^7/5^2\times2^6$	

Flats and Sharps

All the notes that differ from the seven notes of the basic scale are considered altered. Since there are several intermediary sounds between two notes, the alterations are of different kinds.

"When a note rises by one interval (shruti), it is called *tīvra* (sharp). If it rises by a further *shruti* it becomes *tīvratara* (very sharp). If the note rises by still one more *shruti*, it becomes *tīvratama* (extremely sharp), and when it is raised by four *shruti*-s, the sages say that it takes the name of *ati-tīvratama* (extra extremely sharp).

"If a note is lowered, it is called *komala* (flat); when it is lowered by one *shruti* it is *komala*, but if it is lowered by two *shruti*-s it is called *pūrva*." (Pūrv\ is now called ati-komala.) (*Sangīta-pārijāta*, 68–71.)

In most cases, this means that a note raised by a minor half-tone (25/24) is said to be sharp (tīvra), by a limma (256/243) "very sharp" (tīvratara); by a major half-tone (16/15) "extremely sharp" (tīvratama).

Similarly, a note flattened by a half-tone equal to one *shruti* (usually the minor half-tone, 25/24), is said to be *komala* (flat) and when it is flattened by a larger half-tone (the limma, 256/243, or the major half-tone, 16/15) it is said to be *ati-komala* (extremely flat).

Since this classification, though exact, may sometimes be misleading because of the different intervals represented by the *shruti*-s, we shall use here only the more general terms *komala* (flat) and *tīvra* (sharp); the tuning symbol, and the notation itself, will show which sort of flat or sharp is being used.

The classification of the *shruti*-s in Southern Indian music does not conform to these definitions. It appears that the reformers of the music of South India in the seventeenth and eighteenth centuries re-interpreted the theory of the *shruti*-s according to a particular system and this was introduced in musical practice. The North Indian musicians seem to follow the more ancient conception.

The Scale

"The scale (grāma) is the assemblage of the notes" (*Sangīta-makaranda* I, 49; *Sangīta-ratnākara*, I, 4, I; *Sangīta-darpana*, I, 95.)

A scale is not a group of sounds arbitrarily chosen. The building of any scale involves physical laws and a co-ordination of the *shruti*-s which are necessarily respected.

If we take the most consonant intervals, those composed of simple ratios involving prime numbers not higher than 5, to fill each of the tetrachords, we obtain the basic harmonic scale of seven notes:

C	D	E	F	G	A	B	C
$\dfrac{1}{1}$	$\dfrac{9}{8}$	$\dfrac{5}{4}$	$\dfrac{4}{3}$	$\dfrac{3}{2}$	$\dfrac{5}{3}$	$\dfrac{15}{8}$	$\dfrac{2}{1}$
Sa	Ri	Ga	Ma	Pa	Dha	Ni	Sa

There is, however, an alternative division. This consists of substituting for E (Ga) 5/4 and B (Ni) 15/8, E♭+ (Ga komala) 6/5 and B♭+ (Ni komala) 9/5 respectively. This gives the scale:

C	D	E♭+	F	G	A	B♭+	C
$\dfrac{1}{1}$	$\dfrac{9}{8}$	$\dfrac{6}{5}$	$\dfrac{4}{3}$	$\dfrac{3}{2}$	$\dfrac{5}{3}$	$\dfrac{9}{5}$	$\dfrac{2}{1}$
Sa	Ri	GaK	Ma	Pa	Dha	NiK	Sa

If both scales are taken together, we obtain the basic scale of nine notes as it was used in ancient Northern Indian music.

These divisions form the Diatonic divisions of the scale, so called because each tetrachord contains two whole tones.

There is another division, however, known to the Greek theorists as the Chromatic, which forms the basic scale of Southern Indian music. In this scale each tetrachord contains two semi-tones and one minor third:

	C	D♭+	D	F	G	A♭+	A	C
	$\dfrac{1}{1}$	$\dfrac{16}{15}$	$\dfrac{9}{8}$	$\dfrac{4}{3}$	$\dfrac{3}{2}$	$\dfrac{8}{5}$	$\dfrac{5}{3}$	$\dfrac{2}{1}$
Nortnern Indian:	Sa	RiK	Ri	Ma	Pa	DhaK	Dha	Sa
Southern Indian:	Sa	Ri	Ga	Ma	Pa	Dha	Ni	Sa

In this system the two additional notes Antara Ga and Kākali Ni, E (Ga) 5/4 and B (Ni) 15/8, give the complete scale of nine notes.

	C	Db	D		E	F	G	Ab	A		B	C
	$\frac{1}{1}$	$\frac{16}{15}$	$\frac{9}{8}$		$\frac{5}{4}$	$\frac{4}{3}$	$\frac{3}{2}$	$\frac{8}{5}$	$\frac{5}{3}$		$\frac{15}{8}$	$\frac{2}{1}$
Northern Indian:	*Sa*	*Rik*	*Ri*		*Ga*	*Ma*	*Pa*	*Dhak*	*Dha*		*Ni*	*Sa*
Southern Indian:	*Sa*	*Ri*	*Ant.Ga*		*Ga*	*Ma*	*Pa*	*Dha*	*Kāk,Ni*		*NiSa*	

This scale does not concern us here since it is never used as a basic scale in Northern Indian music. It may, however, be related to one of the ancient *grāma*-s.

The Sanskrit books do not generally define notes by string-lengths but rather by their expression, their *shruti*, which is the easiest way for trained musicians to recognize them.

The *Sangīta-parijāta* and the *Hridaya-kautuka* attempt to give the relative string-lengths of the different notes.

The unaltered scale of modern Northern Indian music is the basic harmonic scale of seven notes. It is approximately the scale of *Rāga Bilāval*, and is usually known by this name. It corresponds approximately to the major mode of Western music. *Rāga Bilāval* was first accepted as the unaltered scale in the *Sangīta-sāra*, compiled in Jaipur between 1779 and 1804, and in the *Nāgmat-e-Asaphi* of Muhammad Rezza in 1813.

In this scale the intermediary sounds are considered modifications of the seven main ones. These modifications are always conceived within the frame of the harmonic form of the chromatic scale in which each note can be altered only in one direction—either flattened or sharpened.

The harmonic form of the chromatic scale thus gives the twelve chromatic notes as follows:

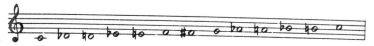

It should be remembered that the altered (vikrita) notes, and also certain of the unaltered (shuddha) ones, are susceptible to slight changes of pitch according to their expression or *shruti*.

The division of the octave into twenty-two or sixty-six *shruti*-s corresponds to what the ancient Greeks called the enharmonic division. They considered this division, as the Hindus also did, the fundamental division of the scale. Besides this basic division there exist in Indian music—indeed in all music—two main divisions of the octave one (diatonic) into seven notes, the other (chromatic) into twelve. Matanga says: "Modal scales (mūrch'hanā-s) are of two kinds—the scales of seven notes and the scale of twelve." (*Brihaddeshī*, commentary on I, 95.)

The Three Basic Scales (Grāma-s)

"There are two scales—that of *Shadja* (C) and that of *Madhyama* (F). Some also mention the scale of *Gāndhāra* (E) which is not, however, to be found in this world." (*Dattilam*, II.)

Three basic scales or *grāma*-s corresponding to different tunings of the harp, were used in ancient music. Each was named after its main note (which was not necessarily its tonic). A difference in the tonic was not and could not be their essential difference, for each of the notes in these scales could successively be taken as starting-point, thus forming plagal scales or *mūrch'hanā*-s which were further used as the basis of the modes. As we have already seen, the two main basic scales, the harmonic and the Pythagorean, are differentiated by the raising or lowering of the sixth note, the A (Dha) (ancient Panchama) by one comma. This is also the differentiation made in the *Nātya Shāstra* between the two main ancient basic scales, the *Shadja* and *Madhyama grāma*-s. For the ancient Hindus, the main scale seems to have been the one we call Pythagorean: in Indian music it is called *Shadja grāma*, or scale of C.

The second or harmonic scale was formed by lowering the A+ (Dha+) (ancient Pa) into A (Dha). This was known as the *Madhyama grāma*, or F scale.

The third basic scale known in ancient times, but already obsolete in the time of Dattila, was called *Gāndhāra grāma*. In the texts its nature is never explained in sufficient detail. It may have been the South Indian Chromatic.

The *Ga grāma* (scale of E; modern scale of F, Ma) was said to start from *Pa* (modern A, Dha).

"The modal scale (mūrch'hanā) of *Shadja grāma* is Sa, Ri, Ga, Ma, Pa, Dha, Ni.

"The modal scale of *Madhyama grāma* is Ma, Pa, Dha, Ni, Sa, Ri, Ga.

"The modal scale of *Gāndhāra grāma* is Pa, Dha, Ni, Sa, Ri,

Ga, Ma." (*Sangīta-dāmodara*, I, 40–41.)

The classification of the *grāma*-s has in practice, since medieval times, been abandoned. All the scales have since become modifications of the one *Shadja grāma*, particularly as the note *Shadja* itself became the universal tonic and the basic notes of the *grāma*-s were taken as their tonic. Hence:

"All worldly music (deshī) comes from the *Shadja grāma*." (*Svaramela-kalānidhi* 5, 17.)

"The basic scales (grāma-s) formed by the different arrangements of the svara-s are said to be three. They are known by the names *Shadja* (C), *Madhyama* (F) and *Gāndhāra* (E). They are the basis of modal scales (mūrch'hanā-s) and the *Shadja grāma* is the most perfect of the three. The modes obtained in the two other *grāma*-s are derived from the *Shadja grāma*." (Ahobala, *Sangīta-pārijāta*, 97–98.)

"The *Gāndhāra* and *Madhyama grāma*-s are considered to be no longer in use. Their definitions are given only so that they may not be mistakenly reinvented." (*Rāga-tattva-vibodha*.)

In fact the *grāma*-s correspond to the different tunings of the ancient harp. The harp was replaced after the sixth century by instruments of the lute type. The various modal scales depend on the lute on the arrangements of the frets and no longer on a basic tuning of the instrument. The classification of the *grāma*-s therefore lost its purpose.

"The modal scales begin from C (Sa) in the middle octave." (*Shiva-tattva-ratnākara* 6, 7, 47.)

The three notes chosen as the starting-points of the three *grāma*-s—C G F (Sa Pa Ma)—are never altered by one comma in modal music, as are all the other notes of the scale. These three, therefore, are fixed points in all scales and no confusion can arise when intervals are measured in relation to them. Matanga makes the following remark concerning the two of them:

"Why is it that the basic scales (grāma-s) are called by the names of *Shadja* (C) and *Madhyama* (F)? They are so called because these two notes are never altered. It is because they are never altered that they are said to belong to the kin of the Gods." (*Brihaddeshī* commentary on 92; also quoted by Simhabhūpāla, commentary on the *Sangīta-ratnākara* I, 4, 6–8.)

Modal Scales (*Mūrch'hanā-s*)

"That which spans (mūrcha) the scale of a mode is called *mūrch'hanā.*" (*Brihaddeshī,* 94.)

The term *mūrch'hanā* (modal scale) was used in medieval music for the different types of scales from which the modes are derived. There are three main types of such scales, thus three kinds of *mūrch'hanā-s.*

(1) The first use of the word *mūrch-hanā* refers to the classification of modes as plagal forms of the basic scale. This method of classification, which was probably of Greek origin, has in practice never completely replaced the "scale-types" or *thāta-s* of the Shivaite system still used by the musicians.

"The sequence of the seven notes in ascent or descent is called *mūrch'hanā.* There are seven in each of the two basic scales." (*Sangīta-makaranda,* 1–66, reproduced in *Chatvārim-shach'hata-rāga-nirūpanam,* 1, 22, *Sangīta-ratnākara,* 1, 4, 9, and *Shiva-tattva-ratnākara,* 6, 7, 32–33.)

(2) The name *mūrch'hanā* was also, in another system, given to the chromatic scale of twelve notes.

"The modal scale (mūrch'hanā) should be known to the wise as having twelve notes from which modal types can be built and melodies in the high as well as the low octave." (Nandi-keshvara quoted in *Brihaddeshī,* commentary on 118, and by Simhabhūpāla, commentary on the *Sangīta-ratnākara,*1 , 4, 15–16.)

(3) The term *mūrch'hanā* was further used for pentatonic, hexatonic, heptatonic and eight- or nine-note scales. This division is now usually known as *jāti.*

"The *mūrch'hanā-s* born of the seven notes are of four kinds: complete (heptatonic, pūrna), hexatonic (shādava), pentatonic (audava) and intercalary (sādhārana). In singing, a scale of seven notes is considered the complete scale (pūrna), a scale of six notes is called *shādava,* a scale of five notes *audava,* a scale of eight or nine notes, making use of the intercalary notes *Kākali Ni* (Bᵇ) and *Antara Ga* (Eᵇ), is called 'intercalary' (sādhārana)." (*Brihaddeshī,* commentary on 1, 95.)

The word *mūrch'hanā* is sometimes used in modern music, mostly by professional Mohammedan musicians, to designate melodic ornaments in the form of the mordents *tiripa* and *sphurita* ($\sim$ or $\rightsquigarrow$), more often called *hillola* or *gitkiri.*

Class (Jāti)

The Indian scale is divided into seven regions or sections ruled by the seven notes, or *svara*-s, of the diatonic scale and named after them.

As we have already seen, the mode is called "complete" (sampūrna) if one or more notes be used from each division in any mode. But if one division is not represented, whatever the number of notes in the other divisions, the mode is called hexatonic (shādava). If two divisions are not represented the mode is pentatonic (audava).

The classes obtained by grouping the modes according to the number of their notes are sometimes known as *jāti*-s. This term is still in use in the Eastern part of Northern India.

"Class (jāti), in *rāga*-s, is considered to be of three kinds— *audava* of five notes, *shādava* of six, *sampūrna* (complete) of seven notes." (*Nārada Samhitā* 2, 60; *Sangīta-darpana* 2, 6.)

Melodies comprising less than five notes cannot be called *rāga*-s (modes), but are mere "melodic figures" (tāna-s).

"Combinations of two or three or four pleasing notes form melodic figures (tāna-s): a *rāga* must have five or more [notes]." (*Hridaya-prakāsha.*)

Besides the three *jāti*-s, there are modes which, in addition to the main seven, make use of one or both of the two intercalary notes *Kākali Ni* and *Antara Ga*. In ancient music these eight- or nine-note modes were known as the "intercalary modes" (sādhārana).

Though Vishnu Digambar in his *Sangīta Tattva Darshaka* does not use the term *jāti*, he restates the ancient classification, adding the three kinds of *rāga*-s mentioned by Umāpati (quoted in *Rāga-vibodha*, commentary on 4, 3) and also by Matanga (mentioned by Kallinātha and quoted in *Sangīta-darpana*, 2, 5). These are called: *shuddha* (pure), *chhāyā-laga* (shadowed) and *sankīrna* (mixed).

They are defined as follows:

A *rāga* in which there are only unaltered notes is called "pure" (shuddha).

A *rāga* is called "shadowed" (chhāyā-laga) when it makes use of a few notes borrowed from another *rāga*, provided they do not alter the mood, but, on the contrary, enhance it.

A mixture of several *rāga*-s is called *sankīrna*.

"According to Umāpati, a 'pure' *rāga* charms by itself, a 'shadowed' *rāga* with the help of others, a 'mixed' *rāga* with the help of two." (*Rāga-vibodha*, 4, 3.)

"Sampūrna" means "complete", "shādava" means "of six". The word "audava" has given rise to some speculation: Fox-Strangways, for example, in his *Music of Hindostan* (p. 122) suggests that it may have come from the name of a province where the pentatonic scale was invented. But the *Sangīta-darpana* (commentary on 2–6), clearly explains the term:

"The derivation of the word 'audava' is as follows: Udava is where the planets move, hence the 'sphere of space' (vyoma). This is the fifth (space in Indian philosophy is a quality of ether) among the elements, thus it represents the number 5. From this it is clear that the number of notes of the *audava* (the ethereal scale) is five."

A similar explanation is given in the *Shiva-tattva-ratnākara*. There are rules for the use of the *jāti*-s, in accordance with the symbolism of numbers:

"For celebrating battle, charm and beauty, in separation, or in depicting a character, the hexatonic (shādava) [class of modes] is recommended.

"For destroying disease or enemies, dispelling fear or sorrow, in difficulty or in suffering, in forgiveness or when planets are unfavourable, auspicious words should be sung in the pentatonic scale." (*Shiva-tattva-ratnākara*, VI, 145–147.)

The term *jāti* was also used in ancient and medieval music for mode-types:

"The intervals (shruti-s), the initial note (tonic, graha) and the other notes (svara-s) combine to produce the resultant modal type, therefore they are called 'jāti-s' (results)." (*Brihaddeshī*, commentary on I, 194.)

"Jāti" in this sense has now been replaced by the term "thāta".

Mode-Types (*Thāta-s*)

Indian music, like Greek, Iranian and Arab music, divides the scale into two tetrachords or groups of four notes, ruled respectively by the "sonant" (vādī)[1] and the "consonant"

[1] See p. 57.

(samvādī): the lower tetrachord C D E F (Sa Ri Ga Ma) is called *pūrvānga* (first limb), the higher tetrachord G A B C (Pa Dha Ni Sa) *uttarānga* (higher limb). This is not an artificial division but corresponds to a physical fact, for, as we have said, there is great similarity of expression between the corresponding notes of the two tetrachords. In many *rāga*-s the division of the two tetrachords is identical.

In analysing each *rāga* we shall give the different intervals that arise between the notes of each tetrachord, together with their ratios.

Indian music envisages six main types of tetrachords spanned by a perfect fourth, and six secondary types spanned by an augmented fourth. These are obtained in the following ways:

If we take the twelve notes of the chromatic harmonic scale and divide them into lower and upper tetrachords (leaving between them F♯, Ma tīvra), we see that in each case six different types of tetrachords are available:

If we combine each of the possible lower tetrachords with each of the possible higher ones, we obtain thirty-six different scales of seven notes. If we then replace F (Ma) by F♯ (Ma tīvra) in each of these thirty-six scales, we obtain thirty-six further scales. The total number of theoretically possible basic scales is thus seventy-two. This classification is used in South India where such scales are called *mela*-s or *melakartā*-s. Its theory is explained by Pandit Venkata Makhin, the seventeenth-century systematizer of Southern Indian music who, in the fourth chapter of his *Chaturdandī-prakāshikā*, claims to have invented this system of classification though it is really an ancient system already mentioned in the *Sangīta-sāra* of Vidyāranya (1320–1380).

The term "mela" can, however, be used for any melody-type.

"A mela is a group of sounds from which *rāga*-s (modes) will be made manifest." (*Sangīta-pārijāta*.)

The artificial classification of the *mela*-s—musically inexact, for it neglects the differences in the *shruti*-s—merely helps the player to remember the approximate tuning of a mode. Many of the scales obtained by this system are not in use in Northern music, and this type of classification is only used in Southern India. In North India the modal bases are represented by a small number of mode-types or *thāta*-s (usually ten) which correspond to the approximate placing of the frets on the sitar.

The *Rāga-vibodha* says (commentary on I, 8):

"The particular arrangements of the notes (svara-s) into common scales (mela-s) under which modes (rāga-s) can be grouped, are spoken of as 'ghāta-s' (or thāta-s)."

These "thāta-s" or mode-types should not be mistaken for the *rāga*-s or modes that bear the same names, for the latter may have more or fewer notes and an accurate tuning, whereas the tuning of the mode-types is only approximate.

The ten *thāta*-s or mode-types are given as follows:

"The first is *Kalyānī* (Kalyāna) mela, the second *Velāvalī* (Bilāval), the third *Khammāja*, the fourth *Bhairava*, the fifth *Bhairavī*, the sixth *Āsāvarī* (our Yāvanapūrī), the seventh *Todī*, the eighth *Pūravi* (our Shrī), the ninth *Māravā*, the tenth *Kāfī*.

"Such are the ten mode-groups (mela-s) from which *rāga*-s arise." (Quoted in *Shrīmallakshya-sangītam*, II, I, 19–21.)

The *thāta*-s are as follows:

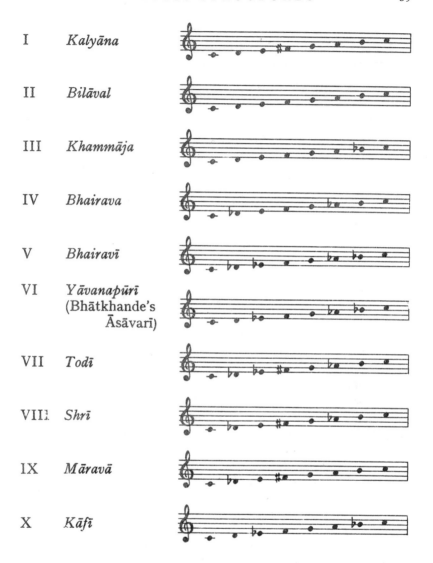

I	Kalyāna
II	Bilāval
III	Khammāja
IV	Bhairava
V	Bhairavī
VI	Yāvanapūrī (Bhātkhande's Āsāvarī)
VII	Todī
VIII	Shrī
IX	Māravā
X	Kāfī

The eighth *thāta*, *Shrī*, is given by Bhātkhande as *Pūravī*, but since the *Pūravī* in some traditions, such as the one we follow here, has an A natural (shuddha Dha), its name could not be given to a *thāta* containing an A flat (Dha komala). There is no divergence of opinion about the scale of *Shrī*.

Group

Some of the main *rāga*-s have, as their satellites, secondary modes with the same general characteristics and only minor differences. These are said to belong to the group of their parent *rāga*-s. For example, *Prabhāt, Bangāla, Rāmakalī*, etc., belong to the *Bhairava* group.

Some books consider the chief modes as masculine in character and call them "rāga-s", while the secondary modes, the "rāginī-s", are said to be their wives or even their "sons" (putra-s).

The male *rāga*-s, originally all pentatonic scales, are usually considered to be six in number, though some treatises mention seven, eight, or nine.

"*Bhairava, Mālakosha, Hindola, Dīpaka, Shrī rāga* and *Megha rāga*, these are the male *rāga*-s." (*Sangīta-darpana* and *Shiva-tattva-ratnākara*, 6, 8, 44.)

The *Sangīta-makaranda*, however, speaks of twenty-one male *rāga*-s. (3–53, etc.)

Graha, Amsha, Nyāsa

In ancient music, three notes are referred to under the names of *amsha, graha* and *nyāsa*.

"The note with which a *rāga* begins is called 'graha'. By 'nyāsa' is understood the note that ends a song. The note most often used while playing is called 'amsha'." (*Sangīta-darpana*, 163.)

The use of the terms *graha* and *amsha* is a little confusing, for their meaning is variously interpreted by authors of different periods. Some understand the "initial note" (graha) to be the first note of the mode, that is, the tonic; others consider it to be the first note of a melody, which may well be any note. But this last interpretation seems hardly justified.

Similarly the "main note" (amsha) is taken to mean sometimes the tonic and sometimes the predominant note, the "sonant" or *vādī*. The more ancient authors seem to have used the word in the first sense. Thus the *Nātya Shāstra* explains the word *graha* as being synonymous with *amsha* and meaning the tonic:

"In all the modal scales the initial note (graha) is equivale .t

to the main note (i.e. the tonic). The whole music takes its
significance from this main note (amsha) which is the same as
the initial note (graha)." (*Nātya Shāstra*, 28, 71; also quoted
in *Brihaddeshī*, comm. on 197.)

The *Brihaddeshī* also uses the term "amsha" (main note in
the sense of "tonic" (basic note, Sa):

The main note by relation with which a mode, a *rāga*, is mani-
cefted is the *amsha* (i.e. the tonic, Sa)." (*Brihaddeshī*,
somm. on 1, 196.)

"This *amsha-svara* is the vital note (Jīva-svara, the tonic)."
(*Chaturdandī-prakāshikā*.)

In the later music "Sa (C) is the initial (graha, i.e. the tonic)
of all the *rāga*-s." (*Rāga-mālā*.)

But Shārngadeva, on the other hand, identifies the "amsha",
the main note, with the "sonant", the *vādī*:

"Because it is most used during a performance, the *vādī*:
(sonant) is called *amsha* (main note)." (*Sangīta-ratnākara*,
1, 7, 34.)

This is also the view of Abhinava Gupta given in his commentary on the *Nātya Shāstra*:

"The *amsha svara* is the same as the *vādī*." (Abhinava
Gupta, comm. on the *Nātya Shāstra*, 28, 23.)

"The (note) that is most used is also called *amsha*." (*Brihaddeshī*, comm. on 1, 196.)

Yet the *Nātya Shāstra* definitely considers the *amsha* as the
tonic.

"The structure of the mode entirely depends on the *amsha*
(tonic), from which it begins, which separates the high and
low octaves, and from which its expression is derived. The
amsha is, further, the initial and final note (graha and nyāsa),
the phrase-final, part-final, and general-final note (apanyāsa,
vinyāsa, sannyāsa), the centre round which the mode revolves.
These are its ten characteristics." (*Nātya Shāstra*, also quoted
by Kallinātha, *Sangīta-ratnākara*, comm. on 1, 7, 29–34.)

The Predominant Note or Sonant (Vādī)

"The sonant (vādī) is the king of notes." (*Sangīta-makaranda*
2–7).

Besides the tonic (the Sa) which is always fixed, each *rāga*
has a predominant note from which all variations begin and

on which they end: it is always accentuated and bears long pauses. This main note is called *vādī* (that which speaks). The expression of the *vādī* is the predominant expression of the *rāga*: its character determines the mood.

"The chief element in which the power lies of bringing out a particular mood, a *rāga*, is the sonant (vādī)." (*Sangīta-darpana*, 1–68.)

"The sonant (vādī) is the note most used while playing; it is the king (of the melody)." (*Rāga-vibodha*, 1, 37.)

The commentary on the *Rāga-vibodha* adds: "the sonant (vādī), being constantly heard, dominates the melody. Because it explains and heralds the mode, it is called *vādī*, (that which speaks)."

The "Consonant" (*Samvādī*)

"The 'consonant' is like a minister." (*Sangīta-makaranda* 2, 7.)

Corresponding notes in the two tetrachords into which the octave is divided always have similar expressions. Another note a fourth or a fifth above the *vādī* will therefore be found that responds to it, playing in the upper tetrachord a similar, though secondary role. This note is called "samvādī" (consonant).

"The nature of the 'consonant' (samvādī) is to reinforce the 'sonant' (vādī) by which the expressiveness of the mode is engendered." (*Brihaddeshī*, comm. on 1, 63.)

Very rare exceptions apart, the *samvādī* is always a fifth or a fourth above the *vādī*. This corresponds to an interval of twelve or eight *shruti*-s.

"The notes that have between them an interval of twelve or eight *shruti*-s (perfect fifth and fourth) are called 'consonant' (samvādī). They are like ministers." (*Rāga-vibodha*, 1, 37.)

The commentary adds: "The *samvādī* . . . sustains the . . . impression created by the *vādī*, just as ministers carry out the order of the king."

"The notes between which there are eight *shruti*-s (perfect fourth) or twelve *shruti*-s (perfect fifth) are said, in relation with one another, to be consonant (samvādī). Such are *Ni* and *Ga* (B and E) or *Ri* and *Dha* (D and A)." (*Sangīta-darpana*, 1, 69–70.)

Rāga-s in which the *samvādī* is a fifth above the *vādī* are

called "panchama samvādī" (having a fifth as main consonance); those in which the *samvādī* is a fourth above the *vādī* are
called "madhyama samvādī" (having a fourth as main consonance). *Panchama samvādī rāga*-s have a clear, active, brilliant
expression; *madhyama samvādī rāga*-s are passive, dormant,
and soft.

The Assonant (*Anuvādī*)

"The 'anuvādī' is like a servant." (*Sangīta-makaranda* 2–7.)

The notes of a mode that are neither "sonant" nor "consonant" are called "assonant" (anuvādī):

"By those who see the subtle cause of things the note that is
neither the sonant nor the consonant and yet is not 'dissonant'
(vivādī) is called assonant (anuvādī)." (*Sangīta-pārijāta*,
81–83.)

The Dissonant (*Vivādī*)

"Dissonant (vivādī) notes are enemies." (*Sangīta-makaranda* 2–7.)

Notes that do not belong to a *rāga*, or, if they do, are used in
defiance of its rules are called "dissonant" (vivādī): They
destroy the expression.

"That which in a given mode breaks the charm is undoubtedly 'dissonant' (vivādī) from the notes of that mode. . .
This *vivādī* is like an enemy." (*Sangīta-pārijāta*, 83–84.)

"Melodic variations that would introduce a *vivādī* note
should always be avoided."

CHAPTER III

RHYTHM

Tempo (Laya)

"There are three tempos—fast, medium and slow." *(Dattilam,*
151.)

INDIAN music, theoretically, knows three main tempos (laya),
each being twice as quick as the previous one. These tempos
are:

Vilambita (slow), in which each beat (tālī) is said to last
about one second ($\bm{\mathsf{J}}$ = 60).

Madhya (medium), in which each beat is said to last about
half second ($\bm{\mathsf{J}}$ = 120).

Druta (fast), in which each beat is said to last about quarter
second ($\bm{\mathsf{J}}$ = 240).

The rhythmic beats, in the order of their duration, bear the
following names:

Chatasra	4 *mātrā*-s (units)	𝆸
Guru (long)	2 ,,	𝅝
Laghu (short)	1 ,,	𝅘𝅥
Druta (fast)	1/2 ,,	𝅘𝅥𝅮
Anu-druta (atom-fast)	1/4 ,,	𝅘𝅥𝅯
Anu-anu-druta	1/8 ,,	𝅘𝅥𝅰

In a more ancient system (see Svarup: *Theory of Indian
Music*, p. 106) the *mātrā*, or time-unit, is said to be the
shortest time in which a syllable can be pronounced. The
normal human pulse-beat lasts three *mātrā*-s. The usual musical
beat, or clap of the hand, is then called *laghu* (short) and is said
to last from 3 to 9 *mātrā*-s (usually 4).

The time-divisions, according to this system, are as follows:

♩   *Laghu* (short) lasts 4 *mātrā*-s.

♪   *Druta* (fast) lasts 2 *mātrā*-s.

♪   *Kalā* (portion) (or Anudruta, or Anu, or Virāma)
     lasts 1 *mātrā*.

Nimisha (wink) = 1/8th of a *mātrā*.
Kāshtha (limit) = 1/8th of a *Nimisha*.
Lava (fragment) = 1/8th of a *Kāshthu*.
Kshana (instant) = 1/8th of a *Lava*.

♩   *Guru* (long) = 8 *mātrā*-s.

♩. *Pluta* (extended) = 12 *mātrā*-s.

o   *Kākapada* (crow-foot) = 16 *mātrā*-s.

The tempos, like the scales, are connected with moods:
"In a laughing or a loving mood use a moderate tempo;
in disgust and fear, a slow one; in the heroic mood, in wrath
and in wonder, a fast tempo." (*Vishnu-dharmottara*, 3, 18.)

Rhythm (*Tāla*)

"The arising, enduring and disappearance of the three worlds
come from rhythm (tāla). From the worm onward, all animals
move by rhythm. All works in the world depend on rhythm. It is
by rhythm that the sun and the planets move." (Quoted in *Rāga-kalpa-druma*.)

"Song, dance and the playing of instruments depend upon
rhythm." (*Sangīta-ratnākara*, 5, 2; *Shiva-tattva-ratnākara*, 6, 9, 1.)

Indian music uses a large variety of rhythms or "tāla-s".

"The syllable 'ta' represents *Shankara* (Shiva) the 'Giver of
Happiness', the syllable 'la' the 'Lady of the Mountain'
(Pārvatī). Rhythm is called 'tāla', because it is the union of
the First Principle (Shiva) and his Energy (Shakti = Pārvatī).
Shiva and *Shakti* being its very nature, rhythm (tāla), one
with the life-breath, is meritorious, leads to fame, gives enjoyment and Liberation and so is cherished by Yogis." (Quoted in
Rāga-kalpa-druma and in *Shiva-tattva-ratnākara*, 6, 9, 3, in the
latter the first two sentences only.)

In the *Ālāpa*, the first exposition of the theme in slow tempo, there is no complex rhythm, though there are metric units (mātrā-s). Rhythmic formulae will be introduced only when, after the *Ālāpa*, the development of variations requires a rhythmic system. The thematic notation of the *rāga*-s is necessarily based on the first exposition of the theme in the *Ālāpa* and cannot, therefore, use any definite *tāla*.

Mnemonic monosyllabic names (bol-s) representing the different strokes on the drums (tablā or pakhāvaja) are used to memorize the basic rhythms. For the *tablā*, these basic rhythms are called "thekā". The syllables used to represent the strokes on the large drum (pakhāvaja) differ from those for the *tablā*: they are called "thapiyā".

A rhythm, or *tāla*, consists of three elements—an initial beat called "sama", other beats called "tāli", and empty beats or rests called "khāli". The middle point of a *tāla* is called "visama".

The first beat of each *tāla* (the "sama") is usually marked x or 1, the subsequent beats ("tālī-s") are marked 2, 3, 4, etc., the empty beats or rests ("khālī-s") are marked o (or ⨏).

Each of the equal time-units (represented here by distinct syllables) is called a *mātrā*.

The Main Rhythms (*Tāla-s*)

"The face is the main part of the body and the nose is the centre of the face. A song without rhythm is like a face without a nose." (*Sangīta Ratnākara, Nādārtha Rāga mālā.*)

Tāla Dādarā 6/4
6 *mātrā*-s (time-units), one main beat (Tablā bol-s).

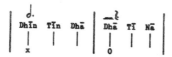

The alternate measure-bar can have the variation:

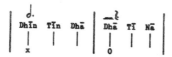

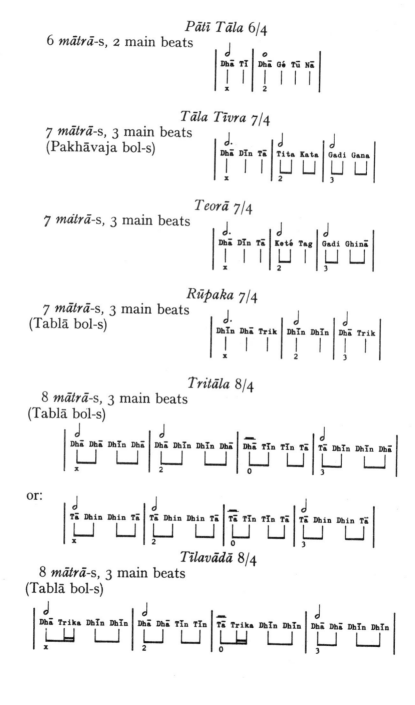

Pātī Tāla 6/4
6 mātrā-s, 2 main beats

Tāla Tīvra 7/4
7 mātrā-s, 3 main beats
(Pakhāvaja bol-s)

Teorā 7/4
7 mātrā-s, 3 main beats

Rūpaka 7/4
7 mātrā-s, 3 main beats
(Tablā bol-s)

Tritāla 8/4
8 mātrā-s, 3 main beats
(Tablā bol-s)

or:

Tīlavādā 8/4
8 mātrā-s, 3 main beats
(Tablā bol-s)

or:

Matta Tāla 9/4
9 *mātrā*-s, 6 main beats
(Tablā bol-s)

Kula Tāla 9/4
9 *mātrā*-s, 2 main beats

Chandrakrīdā Tāla 9/4
9 *mātrā*-s, 4 main beats

Jhapatāla 10/4
10 *mātrā*-s, 3 main beats

also given (tablā bol-s) as:

Or (pakhāvaja bol-s):

Sūla Tāla 10/4
10 *mātrā*-s, 3 main beats
(Pakhāvaja bol-s)

Suraphāktā 10/4
10 *mātrā*-s, 3 main beats

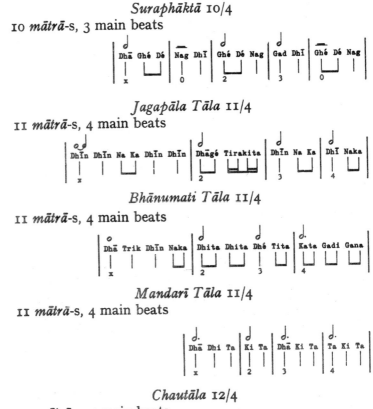

Jagapāla Tāla 11/4
11 *mātrā*-s, 4 main beats

Bhānumati Tāla 11/4
11 *mātrā*-s, 4 main beats

Mandarī Tāla 11/4
11 *mātrā*-s, 4 main beats

Chautāla 12/4
12 *mātrā*-s, 4 main beats
(Pakhāvaja bol-s)

Eka Tāla 12/4
12 *mātrā*-s, 4 main beats
(Tablā bol-s)

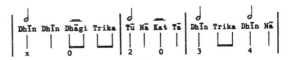

Or:

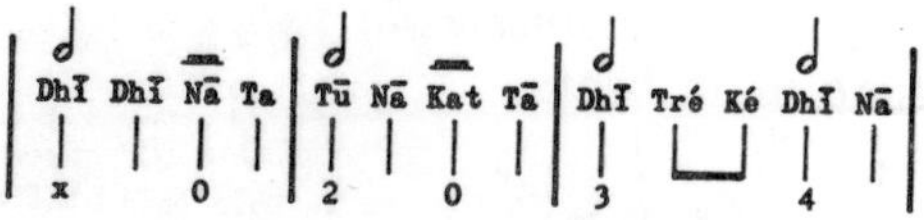

Udaya Tāla 12/4

12 *mātrā*-s, 3 main beats

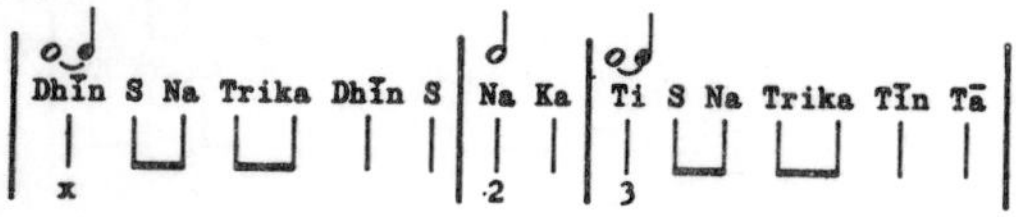

Pharodasta Panjā Tāla 14/4

14 *mātrā*-s, 5 main beats

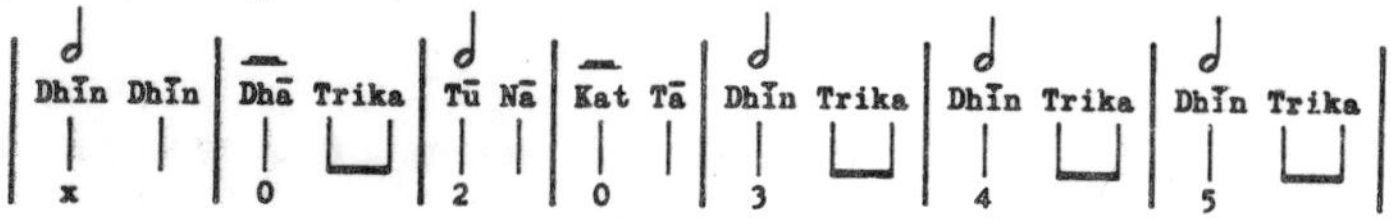

Ādā Chautāla 14/4

14 *mātrā*-s, 4 main beats
(Tablā bol-s)

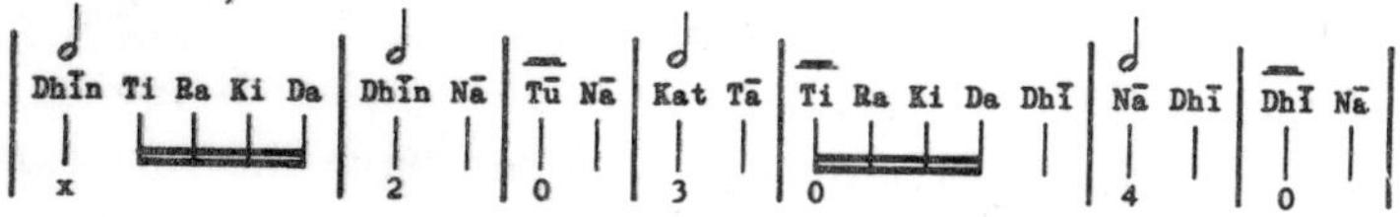

Or:

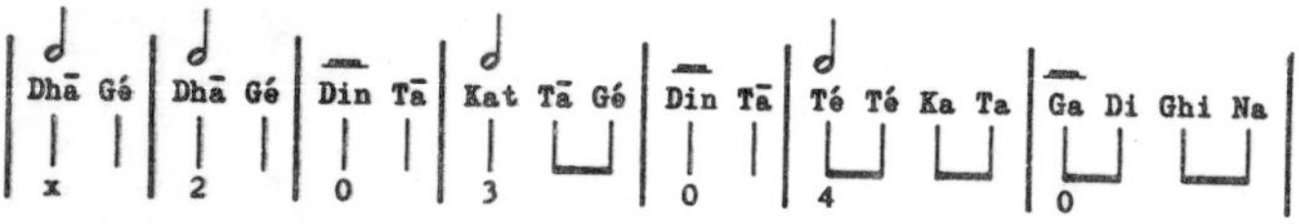

Dīpachandī 14/4

14 *mātrā*-s, 3 main beats
(Tablā bol-s)

Yata 14/4

14 *mātrā*-s, 3 main beats

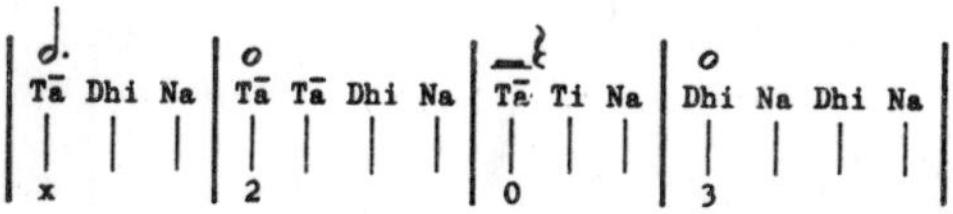

Brahma Tāla 14/4

14 *mātrā*-s, 10 main beats

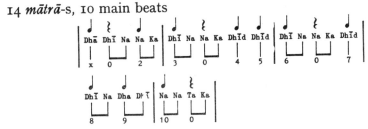

Jhūmarā Tāla 14/4

14 *mātrā*-s, 3 main beats
(Tablā bol-s)

DhĪn S Dhā Tri K	DhĪn DhĪn. Dhāgi Trik	TĪn S Tā Tri Kā

o
DhĪn DhĪn Dhāgi Trik
3

The alternative measure-bar can have the variation:

DhĪn DhĪn Nā Ka	DhĪn DhĪn Dhā Gi Trik	TĪn TĪn Nā Ka	DhĪn DhĪn Dhāgi Trik
x	2	0	3

Dhamār Tāla 14/4

14 *mātrā*-s, 3 main beats
(Pakhāvaja bol-s)

Kadh Ghi Ta Dhi Ta	Dhā S	Gat Ti Tā	Ti Ta Tā S
x	2	0	3

Or: 14 *mātrā*-s, 3 main beats

Ka Dhé Té	Dhé Té	Dhā S	Ga Di Na	Di Na	Tā S
x	0	2	0	3	0

Gaja Jhampa Tāla 15/4

15 *mātrā*-s, 3 main beats
(Tablā bol-s)

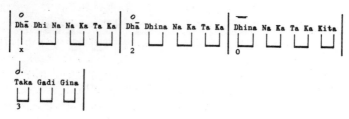

Panjā Sādhā Tāla 16/4

16 *mātrā*-s, 5 main beats

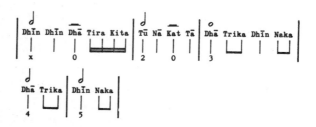

Chhakkā Tāla 16/4

16 *mātrā*-s, 6 main beats

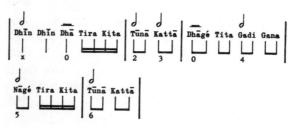

Udīrana Tāla 16/4

16 *mātrā*-s, 3 main beats

Shikhara Tāla 17/4

17 *mātrā*-s, 3 main beats

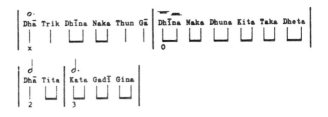

Syncopation

"From the point of view of rhythm, the attack of the sound can be of three kinds: 'on the beat' (sama), 'after the beat' (atīta) and 'before the beat' (anāgata).

"When the rhythm follows exactly the same timing as the song (dance, instruments), etc., and the stroke (of the drum) comes together with the rhythmic clap of the hands, this is known as the attack 'on the beat' (sama).

"When the attack (of the note) in the song comes after the clap of the hand, this is known as 'after the beat' (atīta).

"And when the note has a slight tendency to be attacked early, when the hand is just lifted to clap, this is known as the attack 'before the beat' (anāgata)." (*Sangīta-sārāmrita* (13th Chapter, p. 166, Madras ed.)

Played "after the beat", the note is said to express reluctance, doubt.

Played "on the beat", the note expresses precision, soberness.

Played "before the beat", the note is said to express joy, liveliness, vitality.

CHAPTER IV

MELODIC DEVELOPMENT

Melodic Movement (Varna)

ALL types of melodic forms or their variations through which a scale can be developed are called "melodic movement" (varna). There are three possible elements in melodic movement—ascending, descending and keeping to the same note. A mixture of these three is said to form a fourth kind of melodic movement, called "wandering" (sanchārī).

"The action of singing is called 'melodic movement' (varna). It is of four kinds, defined as: level, ascending, descending and wandering." (*Sangīta-ratnākara*, 1, 6, 1; *Sangīta-darpana*, 1–160.)

"Holding the same note continuously is called *sthāyī* (level); the two others are as their names indicate: ascending is called *āroha*, descending is called *avaroha*; a melodic movement combining all these features is called *sanchārī* (wandering)." (*Sangīta-ratnākara*, 1, 6, 2–3; *Sangīta-darpana*, 1, 160–161; *Shiva-tattva-ratnākara*, 6, 7, 82.)

The "level" (sthāyī) melodic movement is also described as follows:

"Where there are many intervals, this is called 'level' (sthāyī) melodic movement. And when a motive begins and ends on the same note this is also 'level' (sthāyī)." (*Shiva-tattva-ratnākara*, 6, 7, 84–85.)

"The singing of verses on one note only is called *sthāyī* (level) melodic movement." (*Dattilam*, 98.)

Tāna-s (Melodic Figures)

"The 490,000,000 tāna-s are divided into three categories."
(Nārada Samhita, 2, 64.)

Tāna-s are the melodic figures formed by combining the notes.

"The weaving together of the notes forms the tāna-s (melodic figures)." (Nāradīya Shikshā, 1, 2, 6.)

Originally the word tāna meant "tone" and is used in that sense in some of the earlier treatises. The meaning changed, however, before the Christian era and since then it signifies melodic figures.

Melodic figures are divided into two categories, those belonging to only one mode and those belonging to several modes, the first being known as pure (shuddha tāna-s), the second as deceitful (kūta tāna-s). Since a difference in any of the notes brings a change of mode, only figures that make use of all the notes of a mode can be said to really belong to it. Thus the shuddha tāna-s are usually said to be identical with plagal forms of the scales (the mūrch'hanā-s).

"The tāna-s (melodic figures) are of two kinds—pure (shuddha) or deceitful (kūta). A pure tāna is that through which the form of one rāga only can appear, while a deceitful tāna is one through which the forms of two or more different rāga-s may appear because it is common to several. For some unknown reason the ancient writers have not explained the use (of the pure tāna-s) in practical detail. But all agree that their number is eighty-four. In the opinion of some, they are developed from the mūrch'hanā-s (plagal scales)." (Chatur-dandī-prakāshikā.)

"The melodic figures by which a mode, a rāga, can be developed the wise call tāna-s (extensions). They are defined as of two kinds—pure (shuddha) or deceitful (kūta). The secret of the definition of the shuddha tāna-s is not to be developed here, so I need not speak of them." (Quoted in Shrīmallakshya-sangītam.)

The number of possible note-combinations that can be used to form melodic figures is theoretically very large.

"In each of the plagal scales (mūrch'hanā) there are five thousand and forty (possible) kūta tāna-s." (Sangīta-ratnākara, 1, 4, 33.)

"In these fifty-six *mūrch'hanā*-s are counted 282,240 complete (pure) and deceitful (kūta) *tāna*-s." (*Sangīta-ratnākara*, I, 4, 34–35.)

In present-day music the word "tāna" is often used for ornament (alamkāra). These ornaments form groups of notes or small melodic figures that repeatedly recur. When similar *tāna*-s follow one another in ascending sequence this is called *āhati* (rolling).

E.g.

The same, descending, is called *pratyāhati* (rolling down).

Ascent and Descent (*Aroha, Avaroha*)

The determining element in a mode, its ordered succession of notes, often differs in the ascending and descending forms. For example, many modes are pentatonic (audava) or hexatonic (shādava) ascending, and heptatonic (sampūrna) descending. Some have one or two of their notes natural (shuddha) ascending, and flattened (komala) descending, and so on. But the true scale of a mode, that which defines its full expression, is always the descending scale. In all ancient modal systems, the scale runs downwards from the upper tonic (Sa): to define a mode by giving its ascending scale first is a comparatively recent practice. Ascending scales always have an exploratory character, while descending scales, in any music, allow greater precision and clearer differentiation and should therefore always be taken as the standard.

In those parts of India where archaic forms of speech and song have been preserved (as, for example, in some of the valleys of the Himalayas), songs and the playing of instruments always start from the upper tonic in a descending scale.

Alamkāra (*Ornaments*)

"A melody without ornament is like a night without moon, a river without water, a vine without flowers, or a woman without jewels." (*Nātya Shāstra*, 29, 75.)

The *alamkāra*-s in the Indian systems are the melodic adornments, that is ornamental groups of notes, vocalisations, etc. They differ from the ornaments of notes, or *gamaka*-s, the

latter being the various ways of attacking and inflecting individual notes.
"An ornament (alamkāra) is a combination of several 'melodic movements' (varna-s)." (*Sangīta-ratnākara*, 1, 6, 3; *Shiva-tattva-ratnākara*, 6, 7, 44.)
The ornaments, now often confused with *tāna*-s (melodic figures), are vocalisations or groups of notes used to adorn the melody.
Alamkāra-s are divided into four types, like the *varna*-s from which they are derived. The *sthāyī alamkāra*-s (or level ornaments) are simple vocalisings which return to the note from which they start or to its octave; the *ārohi* (ascending) ornaments lead from one note to another higher note; the *avarohi* (descending) ornaments lead from one note to a lower one; and the *sanchārī* (wandering) ornaments are elaborate vocalisations combining the previous ones.
The *sthāyī* (level) *alamkāra*-s number seven:
"The seven *sthāyī alamkāra*-s are *prasanna-ādi*[1] (beginning low), *prasanna-anta* (ending low), *prasanna-ādi-anta* (beginning and ending low), *prasanna-madhya* (low in the middle); then, *krama-rechita* (orderly gallop), *prastāra* (the expanded) and *prasāda* (the serene)." (*Shiva-tattva-ratnākara*, 6, 7, 85–86.)
In the *Brihaddeshī* (comm. on 1, 120) these are defined as follows:
"*Prasanna-ādi* (beginning low) starts from below and ascends to the upper octave, thus:
Sa Ri Ga Ma Pa Dha Ni Sa."
Do Re Mi Fa Sol La Si Do
"*Prasanna-anta* (ending low) descends from above thus:
Sa Ni Dha Pa Ma Ga Ri Sa."
Do Si La Sol Fa Mi Re Do
"*Prasanna-ādi-anta* (beginning and ending low) is low in the beginning and the end and high in the middle, thus:
Sa Ri Ga MaPa Dha NiSa Ni Dha Pa MaGa Ri Sa."
Do Re Mi Fa Sol La Si Do Si La Sol Fa Mi Re Do
"*Prasanna-madhya* (low middle) is low in the middle or high at the beginning and the end, thus:
Sa NiDha Pa MaGa Ri Sa Ri Ga MaPa Dha Ni Sa."
Do Si La Sol Fa Mi Re Do Re Mi Fa Sol La Si Do

---

[1] The word *prasanna* ("pleasing") is used in music as a technical term synonymous with *mandra* ("low"): "The word *mandra* ("low") is used for a pleasing (prasanna) sound." (*Brihaddeshī*, comm. 1, 120.)

The span of the three other *alamkāra*-s is either less or more
than an octave, but their definitions in the *Shiva-tattva-ratnākara* are not clear.

Further "there are twelve ascending and twelve descending
melodic figures used as *alamkāra*-s." (*Shiva-tattva-ratnākara*
6, 7, 94.)

Among them the wandering (sanchārī) *alamkāra*-s are the
most numerous. "Seven are chiefly used by musicians. They
are: *tāra-mandra-prasanna* (high-low-low), *mandra-tāra-prasanna* (low-high-low), *āvartaka* (whirlpool), *sampradāna* (gift),
vidhuta (waved), *upalolaka* (rolling) and *ullāsita* (laughing)."
(*Shiva-tattva-ratnākara* 6, 7, 96–98.)

In the *Shiva-tattva-ratnākara* (6, 7, 101) these are defined:

(1) *Tāra-mandra-prasanna* (high-low-low) is like *prasanna-
ādi.*

(2) *Mandra-tāra-prasanna* (low-high-low) is like *prasanna-
anta.*

(3) *Āvartaka* (whirlpool):
Sa Sa Ri Ri Sa Sa Ri Sa; Ri Ri Ga Ga Ri Ri Ga Ri;
Ga Ga Ma Ma Ga Ga Ma Ga; etc.
Do Do Re Re Do Do Re Do; Re Re Mi Mi Re Re Mi Re;
Mi Mi Fa Fa Mi Mi Fa Mi; etc.

(4) *Sampradāna* (gift).
Sa Sa Ri Ri Sa Sa; Ri Ri Ga Ga Ri Ri;
Ga Ga Ma Ma Ga Ga; etc.
Do Do Re Re Do Do; Re Re Mi Mi Re Re;
Mi Mi Fa Fa Mi Mi; etc.

(5) *Vidhuta* (waved):
Sa Ga Sa Ga; Ri Ma Ri Ma; Ga Pa Ga Pa;
Ma Dha Ma Dha; etc.
Do Mi Do Mi; Re Fa Re Fa; Mi Sol Mi Sol;
Fa La Fa La; etc.

(6) *Upalolaka* (rolling):
Sa Ri Sa Ri Ga Ri Ga Ri; Ri Ga Ri Ga Ma Ga Ma Ga;
Ga Ma Ga Ma Pa Ma Pa Ma; etc.
Do Re Do Re Mi Re Mi Re; Re Mi Re Mi Fa Mi Fa Mi;
Mi Fa Mi Fa Sol Fa Sol Fa; etc.

(7) *Ullāsita* (laughing):
Sa Sa Ga Sa Ga; Ri Ri Ma Ri Ma; Ga Ga Pa Ga Pa;
Ma Ma Dha Ma Dha; etc.
Do Do Mi Do Mi; Re Re Fa Re Fa; Mi Mi Sol Mi Sol;
Fa Fa La Fa La; etc.

Grace (Gamaka)

"Graces (gamaka-s) are the ornaments of the notes." *(Sangīta-darpana, comm. 2–4.)*

"When, in singing, a note rises from its own pitch and moves toward another so that (something of the expression of) the second sound passes like a shadow over it, this is called a grace (gamaka)." *(Sangīta-samaya-sāra, 1, 47.)*

The ways in which notes can be attacked, ornamented or resolved are known under the general name of *gamaka*.

In Indian music these graces are very elaborate and present an endless variety. They may, however, be analysed: Shārngadeva and Nārada III consider that their constituent elements number fifteen. Pārshvadeva reduces them to seven, Nārada II extends them to twenty-one.

"*Gamaka*-s, also called 'roaming about' (charana), are said to be of twenty-one kinds." *(Sangīta-makaranda, 2, 17.)*

"The grace that pleases the mind of the hearer is a *gamaka*. These are of fifteen different kinds, called *tiripa* (flurry), *sphurita* (throb), *kampita* (shake), *līna* (melting away), *āndolita* (swing), *vali* (ripple), *tribhinna* (threefold), *kurula* (curl), *āhata* (struck), *ullāsita* (laughing), *plāvita* (overflow), *gumphita* (tied), *mudrita* (sealed), *nāmita* (obeisance), *mishrita* (mixed)." *(Sangīta-ratnākara, 2, 3, 87–89.)*

"Seven of the *gamaka*-s are more particularly known. They are *sphurita, kampita, līna, tiripa, āhata, āndolita* and *tribhinna*." *(Sangīta-samaya-sāra, 1, 48.)*

The Sanskrit definitions of the *gamaka*-s are not always clear. They are interpreted here in a way which presents the most likely results for the formation of the combined graces. Some of them may, however, have been misunderstood.

All definitions of the *gamaka*-s in the *Sangīta-ratnākara* are reproduced with a few minor variations in the *Shiva-tattva-ratnākara, 6, 7, 100–116.*

(1)   The Flurry (Tiripa) (or Tiripu)
       is now called *Hillola*

"A lovely quivering like a very gentle stroke on the drum, lasting only a quarter of a quaver (druta—i.e. one-eighth of a mātrā) is known as *Tiripa*." (*Sangīta-ratnākara*, 2, 3, 89–90.)

"When the intervals quickly move round like a whirl, this the connoisseurs of music know as *Tiripu*." (*Sangīta-samaya-sāra*, 1, 52.)

(2)   Throb (Sphurita)
       now called "Gitkiri"

"The speed of *sphurita* is exactly one-third of a quaver (i.e. one-sixth of a mātrā)." (*Sangīta-ratnākara* 1, 3, 90.)

(3)   The Shake (Kampita)
       now called "Khatkā"

"The *Kampita gamaka* lasts a semi-quaver (i.e. one-quarter mātrā)." (*Sangīta-ratnākara*, 2, 3, 91.)

"A shake of the note at twice the speed of a quaver (i.e. one-quarter mātrā) is known as *Kampita*." (*Sangīta Samaya-sāra*, 1, 50.)

(4)   Melting away (Līna)

"The speed of *Līna* is that of a quaver (druta = one-half mātrā)." (*Sangīta-ratnākara*, 2, 3, 91.)

"When a note at the speed of a quaver softly melts into another neighbouring note this is called Melting away (Līna)." (*Sangīta-samaya-sāra*, 1, 51.)

(5)   Swing (Āndolita)

"*Āndolita* lasts one crotchet (one mātrā)." (*Sangīta-ratnākara*, 2, 3, 91.)

"Whatever the speed of singing—fast, medium or slow—a swing lasting one crotchet (mātrā) constitutes the grace called

Āndolita.'' (Simhabhūpāla commentary on the *Saṅgīta-ratnākara*, 2, 3, 90.)

"When there is a rocking of the notes lasting one crotchet or *mātrā*, this grace is spoken of as a 'swing' by connoisseurs of music." (*Saṅgīta-samaya-sāra*, 1, 54.)

(6) The Overflow (Plāvita)

"When the shake of the notes lasts three crotchets (1 pluta = 3 mātrā-s) this is called an Overflow." (*Saṅgīta-ratnākara*, 2, 3, 94.)

(7) The Ripple (Vali)
now called *Mīda*

"Any kind of fast-sliding is called a Ripple (Vali)." (*Saṅgīta-ratnākara*, 2, 3, 92.)

(8) The Curl (Kurula)
now called *Ghasīta*

"*Kurula* is like *Vali* but performed softly with a contracted throat." (*Saṅgīta-ratnākara*, 2, 3, 93.)

(9) The Sealed (Mudrita)

"The *gamaka* called Sealed is produced by closing the mouth." (*Saṅgīta-ratnākara*, 2, 3, 95.)

(10) The Tied (Gumphita)

"A deep aspirate descending into the chest is called Tied (Gumphita)." (*Saṅgīta-ratnākara*, 2, 3, 95.)

(11) The Threefold (Tribhinna)

"The Threefold is a compact ornament running at one stroke through three notes without any rest." (*Saṅgīta ratnākara*, 2, 3, 92.)

"A grace that touches three distinct points and amalgamates

the qualities of all the three, turning round the note in a single flow, is traditionally known as the Threefold (Trib-hinna)." (*Sangīta-samaya-sāra*, 1, 55.)

The *Brihaddeshī* calls this ornament *Kuharita* (Cuckoo) in the middle octave and *Rechita* (the Gallop) in the higher octave.

(12) Struck (Āhata)

"Striking a neighbouring note and coming back is known as 'Struck' (Āhata)." (*Sangīta-ratnākara*, 2, 3, 93.)

"Striking the next highest note, touching it slightly, and quickly coming back is called 'Struck' (Āhata)." (Simhabhū-pāla comm. on the *Sangīta-ratnākara*, 2, 3, 93.)

Matanga calls this ornament the Point (Bindu):

"When, after remaining a long time on a note such as Sa (Do), one touches with the speed of fire a higher note, remains there but for a semi-quaver (Kalā $= \frac{1}{4}$ mātrā) and again comes down to the original *Sa*, this is the Point (Bindu)." (*Brihaddeshī*, comm. on 1, 120.)

A succession of *Āhata*-s makes a sort of sobbing trill called *Gadgadita* (Sobbing), often used in Indian music.

(13) Laughing (Ullāsita)

"When the notes follow one another in order this is called 'Laughing' (Ullāsita)." (*Sangīta-ratnākara*, 2, 3, 94.)

"In *Ullāsita* the notes ascend, one following another." (Simhabhūpāla comm. on the *Sangīta-ratnākara*, 2, 3, 94.)

(14) Obeisance (Nāmita)

"A bowing down of the notes the expert in music calls *Nāmita*." (*Sangīta-ratnākara*, 2, 3, 96.)

"*Nāmita* is an ornament in which the notes come down to a lower pitch as if bowing." (Simhabhūpāla comm. on the *Sangīta-ratnākara*, 2, 3, 95.)

(14a) Liberated (Nivritta) is the opposite of *Nāmita*.

"Touching another note for one semiquaver, as in Bindu, but stopping it without any tendency to come back is called *Nivritta* (Liberated)." (*Brihaddeshī*, comm. on 1, 120.)

* * *

Elaborate ornaments can be built from these elements. They are called the mixed *gamaka*-s.

(15) Mixed (Mishrita)

"Mixtures of these are known as the 'Mixed' (gamaka-s). They are of many kinds." (*Sangīta-ratnākara*, 2, 3, 96.)

Examples of mixed *gamaka*-s, given in the *Sangīta-ratnākara*, (3, 178–182):

(1) Flurry—swing
(Tiripa-āndolita)

(2) Melting away—shake
(Līna—kampita)

(3) Shake—struck
(Kampita—āhata)

(4) Flurry throb
(Tiripa—sphurita)

(5) Melting away—throb
(Līna—sphurita)

(6) Throb—struck
(Sphurita—āhata)

(7) Melting away—shake—melting away
(Līna—kampita—līna)

(8) Threefold—curl—struck
(Tribhinna—kurula—āhata)

(9) Overflow—laughing—ripple
(Plāvita—ullāsita—vali)

(10) Ripple—tied—sealed
(Vali—gumphita—mudrita)

(11) Obeisance—swing—ripple
(Nāmita—āndolita—vali)

(12) Ripple—obeisance—shake
(Vali—nāmita—kampita)

(13) Swing—overflow—much laughing—obeisance
(Āndolita—plāvita—samullāsita—nāmita)

(14) Flurry—swing—ripple—threefold—curl
(Tiripa—āndolita—vali—tribhinna—kurula)

(15) Threefold—melting away—throb—overflow—swing
(Tribhinna—līna—sphurita—plāvita—āndolita)

The modern *Bhelava*, a slow mordent at the end of a glissando, would be *Vali-sphurita*.

The Four Phases in the Development of a Rāga

A *rāga* is generally developed in four phases, called *Sthāyī, Antarā, Sanchārī* and *Ābhoga*.

I. The STHĀYĪ (The Pallavi of South Indian music) establishes the theme, starting from the middle tonic (middle Sa). It is focused on the predominant note (vādī) of the mode and though it never rises above the B (Ni) of the middle octave, it descends as deeply as possible into the lower octave.

II. ANTARĀ (the Anupallavi of South Indian music) starts from the middle of the middle octave and develops mainly towards the upper octave. It is focused on the consonant (samvādī), the secondary predominant note situated in the upper tetrachord.

III. SANCHĀRĪ (the Charanam of South Indian music) begins from the higher C (Sa) and moves freely in all three octaves.

IV. ĀBHOGA is a concluding variation, also starting, as a rule, from the higher C (Sa). In songs, the text of the *ābhoga* usually mentions the name of the composer.

In songs, the *sthāyī* is sung again after each part. In late medieval music, these four phases were rather differently divided. They were called *udgrāha* (prelude), *sthāyī* (theme), *sanchārī* (variation) and *muktāyī* (conclusion).

Shrī Nivāsa in his *Rāga-tattva-vibodha* describes them as follows:

"The melodic figures with which one begins are called *udgrāha* (prelude). The fixed melodic figures which do not as a rule appear at the beginning or the end are known to experts as *sthāyī* (the theme). The mixed theme, with ascending (and descending) vocalisation, is called *sanchārī* (variation). Where the mode comes to a rest is called *samāpti* (conclusion)."

Styles of Music

There are kinds of sound-relations intended merely to give pleasure, to evoke tender emotions and pleasing ideas. Only such kinds of sound come within the scope of secular or *deshī* music.

The chief terms used in ancient books to define the different kinds of music are as follows:

GĪTA (Music):

"A particular arrangement of sounds which is pleasing [to hear] is called music (gīta). It is of two kinds—sacred or celestial (gāndharva) and profane (gāna)." (*Sangīta-ratnākara*, 2, 4, 1, reproduced in *Svaramela-kalānidhi*, 2, 6.)

GĀNDHARVA (Sacred or Celestial Music):

"That [music] which, sung by celestial musicians or by those who know the theory of sacred music, which has come to them through the tradition, which knows no beginning, and which is the sure means of attaining Liberation, is known to the sages as Celestial (gāndharva)." (*Sangīta-ratnākara*, 2, 4, 2, and *Svaramela-kalānidhi*, 2, 7.)

This celestial music is also called the "path" (mārga) and is said to be composed in accordance with the cosmic laws of which physical harmony is but a reflection.

"That music, source of [all] development, which, in the beginning, was seen by the Creator in his contemplation and afterwards performed by Bharata and the other seers in the resplendent presence of Shambhu (Shiva), the Giver of Peace, is called the 'path' (mārga)." (*Chatvārimshach'hata-rāga-nirūpanam*, 1, 8–9; and *Sangīta-ratnākara*, 1, 1, 22–23.)

The derivation of the word *mārga* is given by Kallinātha: "*Mārga* means 'to contemplate'."

The relationships between spoken and musical sounds according to the *Mārga* theory are given in the *Rudra-dama-rūdbhava-sūtra-vivaranam*.

GĀNA (Profane Music):

"That [music] which is composed according to rules by experts, which is sung in the modes of secular or worldly music (deshī rāga-s), and which charms the people is *gāna*, 'profane music'." (*Sangīta-ratnākara*, 2, 4, 3 and *Svaramela-kalānidhi*, 2, 9.)

DESHĪ (Secular Music):

"The song, dance and playing of instruments, different from country to country and performed as people please, which charms the heart, is called *deshī* (secular)." (*Chatvārimshach'hata-rāga-nirūpanam* 1, 10; and *Sangīta-ratnākara*, I, 1, 23.)

Matanga believes that the word *deshī* (worldly) applies to all earthly music. "Sound (dhvani) goes everywhere in every place, hence it is called *deshī.*" (*Brihaddeshī*, 1, 2.)

"All the world, animate or inanimate, is subject to sound (dhvani). Sound is divided into two kinds—manifest and unmanifest. Manifest is the sound that comes to the lips in the form of a 'melodic movement' (varna), giving rise to *deshī* (secular) music". (*ibid.*, 1, 12.)

Styles of Singing or Playing

There are many distinct styles in which the variations of a *rāga* may be sung or played. Some of the most important are briefly described here.

A. STYLES OF SINGING

1. ĀLĀPA is the sober exposition of the theme in slow tempo, with portamentos but no elaborate ornaments.

2. SVARAMĀLIKĀ, OR SVARA-GRĀMA, or SA-RI-GA-MA is a form of *Ālāpa* which is sung using the names of the notes.

3. DHRUPADA is solemn and religious in style, usually sung in slow time and using only the more sober rhythms (tāla-s). It is the noblest and also the most difficult style of singing.

Bhāva Bhatta in his *Anupa Sangīta-ratnākara* defines *Dhrupada* as follows:

"*Dhruvapada* is a divine traditional style of singing that shines in the language and literature of the Middle Country. Composed of two or four sentences expressing the emotion of love, it is sung by both men and women. It consists of a poem set to the *ālāpa* of a *rāga* with repetition of final syllables and of groups of syllables conveying different meanings. It has a metrical introduction in two verses, a prelude, a chorus, and a final stanza of noble style." (*Anupa Sangīta-ratnākara*, 1, 65–67.)

Except for some minor developments in its style, the *Dhrupad* has remained very similar to the ancient *Dhruva pada*, and today it still represents the most austere and noble style in Indian vocal art. Vocalisations which belong to the *Khyāl*, and the slight variations of the *Thumri*, are not allowed here.

In the *Dhrupad* the expression of the *rāga*, the significance of the mode, is conveyed at its most profound level. A long prelude, the *ālāpa*, introduces the mode and the poem. The verses or individual words can be repeated several times and certain verses can recur like a refrain.

4. DHAMAR is a lighter form of *Dhrupad* sung always in the *Dhamar* rhythm. It is mainly used for singing love poems in a light vein.

5. JHORA is an *ālāpa* without portamentos. (Almost all Western vocal music would be considered as *Jhora*.)

6. TANJHORA is a fast *Jhora*.

7. KHĀNDĀRVĀNĪ DHRUPADA is a *Jhora* sung with each note repeated several times as if the voice were shaking.

8. In KHYĀL elaborate ornaments are used, particularly ascending and descending vocalisations, trills and grace notes (gamaka-s) and repeated groups of notes or melodic figures (tāna-s). *Khyāl* is charming and light, often used for love songs. It is usually sung in *madhya tāla* (moderate tempo). It is one of the most appreciated forms of Indian singing. We might compare it to bel canto.

9. TAPPĀ is a very elaborate style of singing in which each note of the *Dhrupada* prototype is delicately ornamented without, however, breaking or obscuring the general melodic line. It is usually sung in *madhya tāla*.

10. THUMRĪ combines *Khyāl* and *Tappā* in a very ornamental form (gamaka-s), and repeats each word or line in varied styles. It is very lively, and can be adapted to pantomime and dancing. It is usually sung in *madhya tāla*. It has only one *sthāyī* and one *antarā*.

11. TELLANĀ-S are sung rhythmically on the syllables (bol-s) used to represent the strokes of the drum.

12. DĀDRĀ-S were originally folk-songs in *Dādrā tāla* which developed into a lively style of classical singing.

13. GHAZAL-S (of Persian origin) are love-lyrics sung in a form similar to light popular *Thumrī*-s. They consist only of an *antarā* with a simple melody.

14. BHAJANA-S are religious popular songs with a fixed melody accompanied by rhythmic instruments. They are often sung in mixed *rāga*-s.

15. KĪRTANA-S are similar to *Bhajana*-s. Usually the *Kīr-*

tana-s form a succession of religious songs with changes of mood and *rāga*. This style is especially developed in Bengal.

B. STYLES OF PLAYING (ON STRING-INSTRUMENTS)

1. VILAMPAT is the development of the theme in slow tempo with portamentos, etc. It corresponds to *Ālāpa* in singing.

2. JHORA is played on the *vīnā* with the first two fingers only. It is the bare melody, each note separate, with neither portamento nor ornament.

3. JHALĀ is a rhythmic style in which each note of the melody is followed by a fixed number of rhythmic strokes on the tonic. For example:

4. THONK resembles *Jhora*, but is played loud and fast.

5. THONK-JHALĀ is a mixture of *Thonk* and *Jhalā*.

6. In TARPARAN the strings are struck by rapid forward and backward strokes of the finger or a metal nail.

CHAPTER V

THE RĀGA-S

"I do not dwell in heaven, nor in the heart of yogis. There only I abide, O Nārada, where my lovers sing." (*Nārada Samhitā*, 1, 7.)

"THAT which charms is a *rāga.*"

Indian music, like Arabian and Persian, always centres around one particular emotion which it develops, explains and cultivates, upon which it insists, and which it exalts until an impression is created on the listener which is almost impossible to resist. The musician can then, if his skill be sufficient, lead his audience through the magic of sound to a depth and intensity of feeling undreamt of in other systems.

The notes which are to convey particular emotions or ideas must be carefully selected from the twenty-two intervals of the shruti scale and then grouped to form a mode, a *rāga.* Any artificially constructed scale is not necessarily a *rāga*, for its meaning may be confused and without appeal. The essential feature of a *rāga* is its power of evoking an emotion that takes hold of the hearers like a spell.

"The word 'rāga', is obtained by adding the suffix 'ghan' (which indicates 'doing') to the root 'ranj', 'to please'." (*Sangīta-darpana*, comm. on 2–1.)

"That group of notes (svara-s) which charms is a 'rāga': so say the wise."

When all the notes that form a mode combine to express one coherent mood, the *rāga* appears more attractive and its magic more powerful. The mode must seize the mind and hold it as if enchanted. Then the mind "is charmed and becomes lost in it". (*Rāga-vibodha*, 1, 4.)

"A *rāga*, the sages say, is a particular arrangement of sounds in which notes and melodic movements appear like ornaments to enchant the mind." (*Sangīta-darpana*, 2–1.)

The Number of Rāga-s

In each of the seventy-two possible basic scales of seven notes we can have: one mode using seven notes in ascent and in descent; six different modes using seven notes in ascent and six notes in descent; fifteen different modes using seven notes in ascent and five notes in descent; six different modes using six notes in ascent and seven notes in descent; fifteen different modes using five notes in ascent and seven notes in descent; thirty-six different modes using six notes in ascent and six notes in descent; ninety different modes using six notes in ascent and five notes in descent; ninety different modes using five notes in ascent and six notes in descent; two hundred and twenty-five different modes using five notes in ascent and five notes in descent.

This gives a total of 484 modes in each scale, or 34,848 modes in the seventy-two scales.

If we now consider that there are modes in which the ascending and descending scales vary, modes which combine several scales, etc., we see that the number of possible modes is practically unlimited. It would be difficult in a life-time to hear them all, even once.

Ahobala speaks of 18,678 modes of seven notes, 31,050 modes of six notes and 17,505 modes of five notes in the *Ma grāma* alone.

Krishnānanda Vyāsa in his *Rāga Kalpa-druma* (Introduction, p.1) writes:

"For the sake of the 16,108 milkmaids, the Dark Lord, Krishna, took the same number of shapes. Each of the milkmaids for each of the Krishna-s sang a different *rāga* in a different rhythm, thus giving birth to 16,108 modes. These *rāga*-s and *rāginī*-s later became famous on earth."

In practice only a few hundred *rāga*-s are in general use, although as we have seen, their classification is often confused, the same *rāga*-s having different names in different provinces, and different *rāga*-s the same name.

Moods, Colours and Notes

Each of the notes of the scale has its own kind of expression and a distinct psychological or physical effect, and so it can be related to a colour, a mood, a metre, a deity or one of the subtle centres (chakra-s) of the body. These relationships are given an important place in all Sanskrit treatises on music. Since a complete list of them would be very lengthy, only the relationships of notes with moods and colours will be given here as an example.

"Love (shringāra), laughter (hāsya), compassion (karuna), heroism (vīra), wrath (raudra), fear (bhayānaka), disgust (bībhatsa), wonder (adbhuta) and peace (shānti) are the nine moods of dramatic art. . . "

Of these, for laughter and love, *Madhyama* (fourth) and *Panchama* (fifth) are used.

In the heroic mood, in wrath and wonder, *Shadja* (tonic) and *Panchama* (fifth) (or Rishabha, second):

"*Shadja* (tonic) and *Rishabha* (second) in the heroic mood in wrath and wonder." (*Brihaddeshī*, 1, 84.)

"For compassion, *Nishāda* (minor seventh) and *Gāndhara* (minor third);

in disgust and fear, *Dhaivata* (sixth);

in peace, *Madhyama* (fourth)." (*Vishnu-dharmottara*, 3, 18.)

"*Shadja* (C, the tonic) is bright like the petals of a lotus.

Rishabha (D) is like a parrot.

Gāndhāra (E♭) is golden.

Madhyama (F) is like jasmin.

Panchama (G) is dark (or, of the colour that attracts).

[That which attracts is called 'Krishna' (dark).]

Dhaivata (A) is yellow.

Nishāda (B♭) is of all colours."

(*Brihaddeshī*, 1, 77, and *Nāradīya Shikshā*, 4, 1–2.)

According to the *Sangīta-ratnākara* (1, 3, 54) *Rishabha* (D) is tawny (Pinjarah).

The Description of Rāga-s in Verses and Pictures

The relationship of the notes to colours, emotions, deities etc., makes a graphic representation of the modes possible. The *rāga* determines a state of feeling which can also be expressed in poems or in pictures. It should be remembered, however, that, since many *rāga*-s have changed their form, the ancient pictures and poems may no longer accurately represent the *rāga* after which they are named.

The poems are still known to the musicians, though they do not always know the books from which they are taken. Most of the verses, later reproduced in the *Sangīta-darpana*, the *Chatvārimshach'hata-rāga-nirūpanam*, the *Shiva-tattva-ratnā-kara*, the *Rāga-sāgara* and several other works, seem originally to have come from a work of Kohala now believed lost. Further verses are quoted, without reference, in the nineteenth-century encyclopedic work *Rāga-kalpa-druma*.

In several of the verses describing the *rāga*-s, we follow the quotations of the *Sangīta-darpana* given in the *Shiva-tattva-ratnākara* rather than the text of the available edition of the *Sangīta-darpana* itself, which seems corrupt.

Tuning of the Instruments

From a technical point of view a *rāga* is essentially a scale with a tonic and two axial notes, but which is endowed with further characteristics.

The frets of the stringed instrument must first be set to the proper intervals, the proper *shruti*-s. On some Indian stringed instruments the frets themselves are movable, to allow for this. On instruments such as the *vīnā*, where the frets are fixed, the exact notes have to be played by pulling laterally the string on the fret corresponding to a lower note. This renders the technique more difficult.

The true tuning, by which the expression of the *rāga* is defined, is always that of the descending scale. In *rāga*-s where there is a difference of *shruti*-s in ascent and descent the scale tuned for descending can be used for ascending by pulling or pressing the string, but the tuning of the ascending scale can never be used for the descending one.

It should be noted that there is a strict correspondence between the tuning of the different notes, the ascending and descending scales and other peculiarities of a *rāga*. Some *shruti*-s are mutually related by such intervals as prevent them from being played in succession. If, therefore, the expressions they represent have to be brought together to constitute the mood of a certain *rāga*, their use may require melodic artifices since they may never be taken in direct succession.

The tuning, the ascending and descending notes, the sonant and consonant, the theme and the expression form a homogeneous entity which very often, for arithmetical as well as acoustical reasons, simply cannot be other than it is. Therefore *rāga*-s should never be considered as the invention of an inspired artist; they can, at best, only be discovered as we discover a physical law that represents some aspect of the universe in which we live—a law, not in our power to modify.

Theme (Rūpa) and Outline

There are a few very typical groups of notes for each *rāga* by which it can at once be recognised. These form the main theme (rūpa).

It is impossible to write down in full the ever-changing development of a *rāga*. We have to limit ourselves to the first part of an average "exposition of the theme" (ālāpa) notated in its simplest form. From this, however, the musician is able to perceive the complete form of the *rāga* and, following the rules, proceed to the variations.

Time of Play

"One who sings knowing the proper time remains happy. By singing *rāga*-s at the wrong time one ill-treats them. Listening to them, one becomes impoverished and sees the length of one's life reduced." (*Sangīta-makaranda*, I, 23–24.)

The cycle of the day corresponds to the cycle of life which also has its dawn, its noon, its evening. Each hour represents a different stage of development and is connected to a certain kind of emotion. The cycle of sounds is ruled by the same laws as all other cycles. This is why there are natural relationships between particular hours and the mood evoked by musical modes. Musical modes played at the proper time develop naturally in favourable conditions. Orthodox musicians in India never play a *rāga* at any other than its proper time, for at the wrong hour it could never be developed so perfectly nor could it so greatly move an audience. The Western organist who would play a funeral march at a wedding would, to say the least, appear lacking in taste. In the same way the Indian musician who plays a morning mode in the evening disregarding the surroundings and the mood of his listeners appears utterly lacking in sensibility.

There are certain characteristics through which a *rāga*

shows at what time it should be played. *Rāga*-s to be played between midday and midnight have their predominant note (vādī) in the lower tetrachord (pūrva anga). They are called "Pūrva rāga-s". *Rāga*-s to be played between midnight and midday have their predominant note in the upper tetrachord (uttara anga). They are called "Uttara rāga-s". Modes that correspond to crucial moments (sunrise, sunset, midday, midnight, solstices, equinoxes, etc.) often use both F♯ and F♮ (Ma tīvra and Ma shuddha).

Besides these, Bhātkhande indicates the following time-characteristics, which are generally followed:

(1) Modes sung at sunrise and sunset are known as "samdhi-prakāsha (twilight) rāga-s." Most of them include *Ri* und *Dha komala* (D and A flat).

(2) Modes with *Ga* and *Ni komala* (E and B flat) usually belong to the middle of the day or night.

(3) Modes with *Ri, Ga, Dha* and *Ni shuddha* (D, E, A, and B natural) are usually played after twilight—in the first quarter of morning or night.

(4) Modes sung before twilight—in the last quarter of day or night—insist on the tonic, the fourth and the fifth (Sa Ma and Pa).

The *rāga*-s of evening twilight never omit Ga and Ni (E and B), and the *rāga*-s of morning twilight never omit Ri and Dha (D and A).

These rules, however, are not infallible.

PART II
NOTATION AND ANALYSIS OF THE RĀGA-S

"Even if he be an expert in the revealed and the traditional scriptures, in literature and all sacred books, the man ignorant of music is but an animal on two feet."

Notation

Shruti-s (intervals of one comma):

D♭--   D♭-   D♭   D♭+   D♭++

CHAPTER I
EARLY MORNING RĀGA-S

1. LALITĀ *at dawn*

This very fair and amiable yogi, anointed with divine fragrances, with tangled locks and a deer coming to his hand, is known as Lalita.

(Chatvārimshach'hata rāga nirūpanam p. 14)

Lalitā, charming in her innocence, is bright like gold. While she holds a lute, a cuckoo perches on her lotus hand. She is seated beneath the Wishing-tree, her breasts all unadorned, a thousand times desirable.

(idem p. 13)

A Vīṇā and a book in her hands, Lalitā appears, the Goddess of music. Charmingly playful she talks lightly, her eyes like red lotuses.

(Rāga-sāgara 3, 7)

Lalitā, young and fair, and garlanded with seven-fold flowers. Her long eyes like the petal of the lotus. Sighing, overwhelmed by fate—still, at dawn, dressed for a lovers' meeting.

(Chatvārimshach'hata-rāga-nirūpanam p. 20;
Sangīta-darpana 2, 63; *Shiva-tattva-ratnākara*, 6, 8, 90)

OR, IN ANOTHER READING

The young and fair Lord of Lalitā wears a garland of the sweet-scented seven-fold flowers. His lovely laughing eyes are long like the petal of the white lotus. It is dawn. Overwhelmed by fate, Lalitā sighs dressed for a lovers' meeting.

GROUP: independent

TUNING OF INSTRUMENT:

CLASS (*Jāti*):
Shāḍava (hexatonic)

Āroha Ascent   *Avaroha* Descent

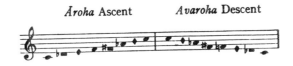

SONANT (*Vādī*): F(Ma)   CONSONANT (*Samvādī*): C(sa)

TIME OF PLAY: Early morning (before sunrise)

MODE TYPE (*Thāta*): Shrī   SCALE TYPE: Chromatic (plagal)

CHARACTERISTICS: No G (Pa); two F (2 Ma) [Bhātkhande gives Lalitā with a natural A (Dha shuddha).]

EXPRESSION:
Dawn
G (Pa) is sunshine, the absence of G (Pa) expresses the absence of Sun. The presence of both F (Ma) and F♯ (Ma tīvrǎ) is characteristic of critical moments. It is found at sunrise, sunset, midday and midnight, equinoxes, solstices, etc.

half-awake

dawn

absence of Sun dawn

Coming Sunrise
B+ (Ni+)

Night beauty and peace •
(no sharp F) (no tivra Ma)

SHRUTI-S: **Expression**

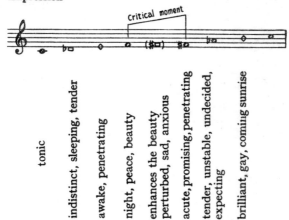

tonic

indistinct, sleeping, tender

awake, penetrating

night, peace, beauty

enhances the beauty
perturbed, sad, anxious

acute, promising, penetrating

tender, unstable, undecided,
expecting

brilliant, gay, coming sunrise

THEME (*Rūpa*):

OUTLINE

STHĀYĪ

ANTARĀ

2. VIBHĀSA *at sunrise*

Fair, and fair of face, with a white scarf. Bold like the cry of the cock at sunrise, his laughter sways the locks that brush his brow. Vibhāsa-rāga is lovely like the God of Love Himself.

(quoted in Rāga-kalpa-druma p. 30)

Vibhāsa is like Lalita.

(Sangīta-darpana 2, 136)

GROUP: independent

TUNING OF INSTRUMENT

CLASS (*Jāti*):
Audava (pentatonic)

Āroha Ascent   *Avaroha* Descent

SONANT (*Vādī*): A (Dha)   CONSONANT (*Samvādī*): E (Ga)

TIME OF PLAY: day at sunrise (after Lalita)

MODE TYPE (*Thāta*): Māravā   SCALE TYPE: Chromatic (defective)

CHARACTERISTICS: no Pa (G) and no Ni (B). This scale is similar to that of the mode of spring Panchama. (Bhātkhande, however, gives Vibhāsa with Ni (B) and Pa (G) in the descending scale.) In fact three different scales are known in Northern India under the name of Vibhāsa.

EXPRESSION:

night

    loveliness, early dawn, twittering of the birds. (In Panchama where D flat (Ri komal) is short and never accentuated, the Vādī and Samvādī are F sharp (Ma tīvra) and C (Sa), and the expression is energetic and challenging.)

tender
mysterious

SHRUTI-S: Expression

tonic

Subtlety, tenderness

lovely, lively

unstable, mysterious, critical time

(no G) (no Pa) no sun

joyful, loving

THEME (*Rūpā*):

OUTLINE

STHĀYĪ

ANTARĀ •

3. BHAIRAVA GROUP

(After Sunrise)

Yogiyā I
Yogiyā II
Prabhāt
Shiva Bhairava
Ānanda Bhairava
Bangāla Bhairava
Bhairava
Rāmakalī
Gunakalī

YOGIYĀ

"Holding trident, snake and lute, braids of matted hair falling about her limbs, whitened with ashes, violently furious in the heroic vein, she is a yoginī, adept in all the lore of yoga."

(quoted in *Rāga-kalpa-druma*, p. 31)

TUNING OF INSTRUMENT:

GROUP: Bhairava

CLASS (*Jāti*): Audava-shādava
(Pentatonic in ascent, hexatonic in descent)

SONANT (*Vādī*): C (Sa)   CONSONANT (*Samvādī*): F (Ma)

TIME OF PLAY: early morning just after dawn (before Bhairava)

Āroha Ascent   *Avaroha* Descent

MODE TYPE (*Thāta*): Bhairava

SCALE TYPE: Enharmonic in ascent—chromatic in descent

CHARACTERISTICS: Generally sung in the month of Chaitra (March) when everyone feels sleepy, lethargic. Yogiyā can be played with E+ (Ga+) or without E+ (Ga+) ; it is often played first without, the E+ (Ga+) being brought in later.

EXPRESSION: Half asleep, half willing, like a man disturbed in his sleep.

E+ (Ga+) means consciousness ; the absence of E+ (Ga+) therefore, creates an impression of vagueness, half-consciousness.

D♭ (RiK) is here lethargic.

peaceful contentment

SHRUTI-S: expression

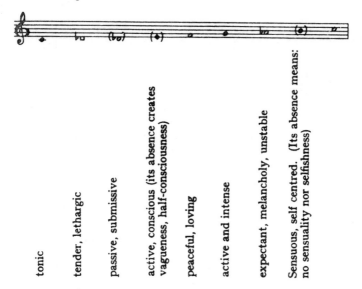

| tonic | tender, lethargic | passive, submissive | active, conscious (its absence creates vagueness, half-consciousness) | peaceful, loving | active and intense | expectant, melancholy, unstable | Sensuous, self centred. (Its absence means: no sensuality nor selfishness) |

THEME (*Rūpa*): (without E)

YOGIYĀ I (without E)
OUTLINE:

Scale

STHĀYĪ

Soft and dreamy (♩=40)

ANTARĀ

YOGIYĀ (II with E)
OUTLINE

STHĀYĪ

ANTARĀ

PRABHĀT

GROUP: Bhairava

CLASS (*Jāti*):
Sampūrna (Heptatonic)

Āroha Ascent   *Avaroha* Descent

SONANT (*Vādī*): Sa (C)

CONSONANT (*Samvādī*): F (Ma)

TIME OF PLAY: morning,
before Bhairava (between
Lalitā and Bhairava)

MODE TYPE (*Thāta*):
Bhairava

SCALE TYPE: Chromatic

CHARACTERISTICS: Bhairava played in Lalitā style (the G (Pa) replacing the
F♯ (MaT) of Lalitā).
The lower tetrachord is augmented by one comma: C F+ (Sa Ma+) = 27/20.

EXPRESSION: E+ (Ga+) and F+ (Ma+) indicate extreme contentment. Lalitā
is still sleepy, Prahbāt is the fully awakened and joyful morning.

SHRUTI-S: expression

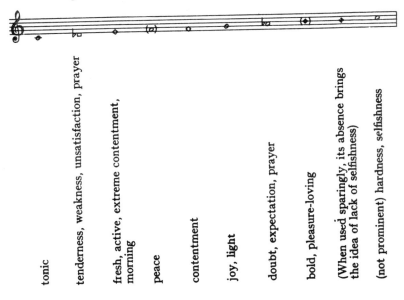

tonic

tenderness, weakness, unsatisfaction, prayer

fresh, active, extreme contentment, morning

peace

contentment

joy, light

doubt, expectation, prayer

bold, pleasure-loving

(When used sparingly, its absence brings the idea of lack of selfishness)

(not prominent) hardness, selfishness

THEME (Rūpa):

OUTLINE

Scale

STHĀYĪ

ANTARĀ

SHIVA BHAIRAVA

GROUP: Bhairava

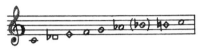

CLASS (*Jāti*):
  Sampūrna (Heptatonic)

Āroha Ascent   *Avaroha* Descent

SONANT (*Vādī*): A flat (Dha komal)   CONSONANT (*Samvādī*):
                                                D flat (Re komal)

TIME OF PLAY: day, first quarter (from sunrise)

MODE TYPE (*Thāta*): Bhairava   SCALE TYPE: Pythagorean Chromatic
                                        (with additional diatonic tetrachord)

CHARACTERISTICS: Use of both B and B♭ (Ni and Ni komal)

EXPRESSION: The flat B (Ni komal) changes the sex of Bhairava (as if were
  felt the presence of Gaurī the consort of Shiva. The use of both B and B♭
  (Ni and NiK) gives the idea of a couple.

  B+ (Ni+) is manly, but light and pure (while B (Ni) would appear worldly
  and material). B♭ (NiK) is modest, quiet and kind (while B♭– (NiK–)
  would be heavy and impure).

sadness

weeping

very light and slow trill

NOTE: Bhātkhande gives also both E and E♭ (Ga and GaK.), the ascending notes being then those of Bhairava and the descending notes those of Bhairavī. But this changes so much the appearance of the rāga that, in the opinion of other teachers, it can no longer be said to belong to the Bhairava group.

SHRUTI-S: expression

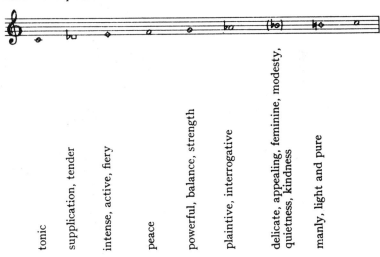

THEME (*Rūpa*)

OUTLINE

STHĀYĪ

ANTARĀ

ĀNANDA BHAIRAVA

"Seated under a wood-apple tree, the joyful Ānanda Bhairava holds a hautboy and a peacock's plume. His hair is tied in a knot."

(*Rāga-sāgara* III, 84)

GROUP: Bhairava

TUNING OF INSTRUMENT:

CLASS (*Jāti*): Sampūrna (Heptatonic)

Āroha Ascent   *Avaroha* Descent

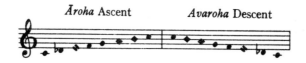

SONANT (*Vādī*): C (Sa)   CONSONANT (*Samvādī*): F (Ma)

TIME OF PLAY: Day, first quarter (from sunrise)

MODE TYPE (*Thāta*): Māravā with F natural (Ma shuddha)

SCALE TYPE: The lower tetrachord is chromatic and the upper one diatonic

CHARACTERISTICS: Bhairava with A natural (Dha shuddha)

EXPRESSION: Joyful, energetic, loving
  B+ (Ni+) is high, airy, it expresses joy which the B (Ni) does not bring out.

activity, acuteness (B+, Ni+)
together with emotion and
love (D♭, RiK)

contentment
happiness,
peace

SHRUTI-S: expression

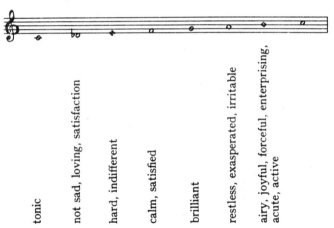

THEME (*Rūpa*):

OUTLINE

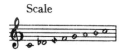

Scale

STHĀYĪ

ANTARĀ

BANGĀLA BHAIRAVA

Dark, in a dark robe, determined, brazen, eager for lust, with big breasts and in her hand a lute, Bangālī, dear to rogues.
(Chatvārimshach'hata-rāga-nirūpanam p. 18)

Bāngālī is described as a young woman large-eyed, bright golden like the sun. Smeared with ashes, her hair matted and tightly bound, with a sword under her arm, in her left hand she bears a blazing trident.
(Sangīta-darpana 2, 49;
Shiva-tattva-ratnākara 6, 8, 61)

His sacred lock, bound on one side, shines like black sapphire. Ever shall my heart dream of Bangāla, greatest of rāga-s, red like the China rose. Holding a sword and shield, honoured by men, he worships the feet of Shiva on whose brow the crescent moon shines.
(Rāga-sāgara 3, 25)

GROUP: Bhairava

TUNING OF INSTRUMENT:

CLASS (*Jāti*):
Shādava (hexatonic)

Āroha Ascent   *Avaroha* Descent

SONANT (*Vādī*): C(sa)   CONSONANT (*Samvādī*): F(Ma)

TIME OF PLAY: day, first quarter, (from sunrise)

MODE TYPE (*Thāta*): Bhairava   SCALE TYPE: Chromatic-Enharmonic

CHARACTERISTICS: No B(Ni); E(Ga) very light [Bhātkhande gives the Vādī-
Samvādī as A♭(Dha k.) and D♭(Ri k.)]

EXPRESSION:
B natural (Ni shuddha)
and also E natural (Ga
shuddha) indicate self-con-
trol, will and independence;
their absence leaves room
only for dreaming, half-
consciousness.

the Rāga often begins
with a swing

E+(Ga+) should
be used only in
appoggiatura

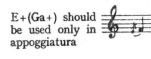

characteristic
figure at the
end of each
motive

SHRUTI-S: expression

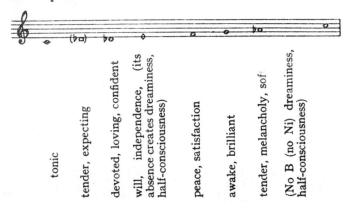

THEME (*Rūpă*):

OUTLINE

STHĀYĪ

ANTARĀ

BHAIRAVA

His limbs smeared with ashes (that lovely body), his brow lustrous with the cool rays of the moon, trident in hand and mounted on a bull, such is Bhairava, and so the sages tell.

(Chatvārimshach'hata-rāga-nirūpanam p. 13)

Upholding Gangā, the crescent moon upon his brow, three-eyed, wrapped in the skin of an elephant and adorned with snakes, his scarf white, his garland of human skulls, armed with a burning trident—so triumphs Bhairava, the first of rāga-s.

(Sangīta-darpana 2, 46
Shiva-tattva-ratnākara 6, 8, 54)

We praise Bhairava, the hero, the source of life, the measure of rhythm, pervading the ocean of notes and intervals. A skull in his hand, the crescent moon upon his matted hair, he worships Shiva, Lord of Sleep. His body is smeared with sandal paste.

(Rāga-sāgara 3, 1)

TUNING OF INSTRUMENT

GROUP: Bhairava

CLASS (*Jāti*):
Sampūrṇa (heptatonic)

Āroha Ascent   *Avaroha* Descent

SONANT (*Vādī*):   CONSONANT (*Samvādī*):
  A flat (Dha komal)   D flat (Ri komal)

TIME OF PLAY: day first quarter (from sunrise)

MODE TYPE (*Thāta*): Bhairava   SCALE TYPE: Chromatic

CHARACTERISTICS: The tender D♭– (Ri k--) can become, in ascending, D♭n
(Ri kn) it gives then an idea of action

EXPRESSION: Morning invocation, soft, tender, melancholy

Ri kn (D♭n) and Ga+ (E+) are sometimes used, although in ascent only:

This tuning is found in the
  following example:

SHRUTI-S expression

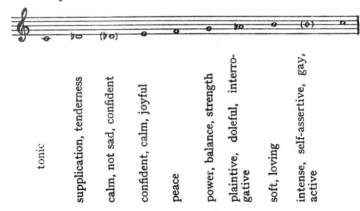

THEME (*Rūpă*):

OUTLINE

STHĀYĪ

ANTARĀ

RĀMAKALĪ[1]

Sylph with the lotus face, for fauns and centaurs hard to win, lute in hand and standing on a mountain, the wise have called her Rāmakrī.

(Chatvārimshach'hata-rāga-nirūpanam p. 10)

Bright like gold, her robe deep blue, Rāmakalī wears a garland and rich ornaments. Haughty and pretending anger, yet when her lover is near her voice grows sweeter.

(Sangīta-darpana 2, 60;
Shiva-tattva-ratnākara 6, 8, 83)

A shining woman in the posture of heroes, thus should Rāmăkriyā be seen. Dark like the jambu fruit she holds a bow and an arrow.

(Rāga-sāgara 3, 18)

TUNING OF INSTRUMENT

GROUP: Bhairava

CLASS (*Jāti*): Audava-sampūrna
(Pentatonic in ascent, heptatonic in descent)

Āroha Ascent   *Avaroha* Descent

[1] Sometimes called Rāmakrī or Rāmakirī.

SONANT (*Vādī*): G(Pa)　　　　　CONSONANT (*Samvādī*): C(Sa)

TIME OF PLAY: day, first
　quarter (from sunrise)

MODE TYPE (*Thāta*): Bhairava　　SCALE TYPE: (Pythagorean) Chromatic
　　　　　　　　　　　　　　　　　　(with enharmonic ascent)

CHARACTERISTICS: No D (Re) and no B (Ni) in ascending (Bhātkhande
gives Rāmakalī with an additional F♯ (Ma tīvra) and B♭ (Ni komal)

EXPRESSION: fully awake, joyful, active, without the anguish of desire,
B+(Ni+) being sparingly used. Sa and Pa(C and G) as Vādī and Samvādī
denote activity

SHRUTI-S **expression**

　tonic

　(never accentuated), tender

　active

　contentment, peace

　active, awake

　tender, interrogative

　Ni+ (B+) (selfishness, desire)
　absent or sparingly used,
　means no selfishness, nor
　desire

THEME (*Rūpa*):

OUTLINE

STHĀYĪ

ANTARĀ

GUNAKALĪ[1]

Faithful, dear to cowherds, adorned wtih a golden pigment taken from the cow, mysterious in her movements, Gunakriyā is said to know of hidden treasures.

(Chatvārimshach'hata-rāga-nirūpanam p. 15)

Her head bowed low, lovely tresses dishevelled about her form, once famous for her beauty; since her lover went away Gunakirī is in a pitiable state. Her reddened eyes are desperate, her sorrow-shrunken limbs are soiled with mud.

(Sangīta-darpana 2, 56 ;
Chatvārimshach'hata-rāga-nirūpanam p. 10 ;
Shiva-tattva-ratnākara 6, 8, 75)

I remember Gundakriyā playing in a garden of sandal trees. Her silken garment is yellow her hips are beautiful. With her left hand she holds the neck of a Vīnā.

(Rāga-sāgara 3, 23)

TUNING OF INSTRUMENT

GROUP: Bhairava

CLASS (*Jāti*): Audava (Pentatonic)

Āroha Ascent   *Avaroha* Descent

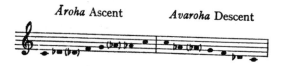

---

[1] Sometimes called Gunakriyā or Gunakirī or Gaudakrī.

SONANT (*Vādī*): A flat (Dha komal)   CONSONANT (*Samvādī*): D flat (Re komal)

TIME OF PLAY: morning

MODE TYPE (*Thāta*): Bhairavī   SCALE TYPE: Enharmonic

CHARACTERISTICS: Typical enharmonic having in each tetrachord a major third or ditone completed by a half tone, itself subdivided into two

EXPRESSION: Sadness and renunciation, melancholy and emptiness in the first stages of renunciation

SHRUTI-S expression

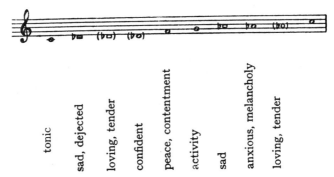

tonic / sad, dejected / loving, tender / confident / peace, contentment / activity / sad / anxious, melancholy / loving, tender

THEME (*Rūpă*):

OUTLINE

Scale

STHĀYĪ

ANTARĀ

4. TODĪ GROUP I

(First quarter of the day)

Gurjarī
Mukhārī
Lāchārī Todī
Todī
Vilāsakhānī Todī

GURJARĪ

"A Southern girl, dusky, with splendid hair, Gurjarī sits smiling upon a bed made from the tenderest sandal-trees of the Malaya mountain. Knowing all the secrets of music, she plays, cheek leaning upon the lute."

(Sangīta-darpana 2, 80 ;
Shiva-tattva-ratnākara 6, 8, 123)

"Praised be Ghurjarī whose cheeks are rosy like the young Lodhra tree. A ball in her hand, she plays with girl companions. Her limbs are hidden by a white garment."

(Rāga-sāgara 3, 23)
GURJARĪ

GROUP: Todī

TUNING OF INSTRUMENT:

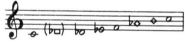

CLASS (*Jāti*):
    Shādava (Hexatonic)

Āroha Ascent   *Avaroha* Descent

SONANT (*Vādī*): A♭ (DhaK)   CONSONANT (*Samvādī*): D♭ (RiK)

TIME OF PLAY: Day, first
    quarter (from sunrise)

MODE TYPE (*Thāta*): Todī with F natural   SCALE TYPE: Chromatic
(Ma shuddha)

CHARACTERISTICS: No G (no Pa). Resembles Vilāsakhānī except for the F♮ (Ma shuddha).

EXPRESSION: Remembrance of pleasant thoughts ; melancholy remembering of lovely times.

No G (Pa) means absence, mental depression, sadness.

F (Ma) is lovely, quiet and joyful, peaceful and spiritual.

remembrance of joy

SHRUTI-S: expression

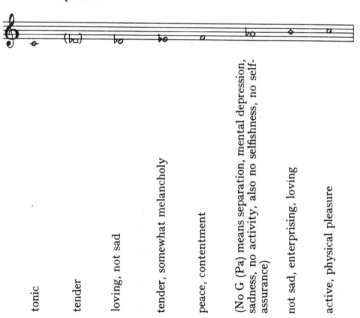

| tonic | tender | loving, not sad | tender, somewhat melancholy | peace, contentment | (No G (Pa) means separation, mental depression, sadness, no activity, also no selfishness, no self-assurance) | not sad, enterprising, loving | active, physical pleasure |

THEME (*Rūpa*):

OUTLINE

Scale

STHĀYĪ

ANTARĀ

MUKHĀRĪ

"His lotus face adorned with coral-flowers, his melody inspiring happiness, Mukhāri shines, depicted by the sages."

(*Chatvārimshach'hata-rāga-nirūpanam*, p. 21)

"I ever see Mukhārī drunk with wine and pleasure. She draws near, supported by two maidens, a garland of corals round her neck."

(*Rāga-sāgara* 3, 15)

GROUP: Todī

TUNING OF INSTRUMENT:

CLASS (*Jāti*):
Sampūrna (Heptatonic)

Āroha Ascent   *Avaroha* Descent

SONANT (*Vādī*): A♭ (DhaK)

CONSONANT (*Samvādī*): D♭ (RiK)

TIME OF PLAY: day, first quarter (from sunrise)

MODE TYPE (*Thāta*): Shrī scale (i.e. Todī with E natural, Ga shuddha)

SCALE TYPE: Chromatic

CHARACTERISTICS: The scale of Shrī played in Todī style.

EXPRESSION: Very active. She tries to be nice and pleasant but her real character appears with E+ (Ga+) which means self-satisfaction (I know best, I only am wise, etc.); it shows impertinence and vanity, therefore cruelty and crudeness.

(Flat E (Ga komal), as in Todī, would be dependant, polite and appealing.) E+ (Ga+) should anyhow never be accentuated in this rāga as it would bring in the appearance of the evening rāga Pūravī. It should be passed over lightly.

SHRUTI-S: expression

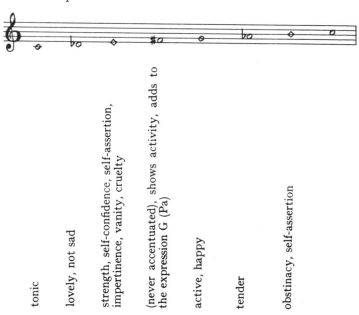

tonic

lovely, not sad

strength, self-confidence, self-assertion, impertinence, vanity, cruelty

(never accentuated), shows activity, adds to the expression G (Pa)

active, happy

tender

obstinacy, self-assertion

THEME (*Rūpa*):

OUTLINE

Scale

STHĀYĪ

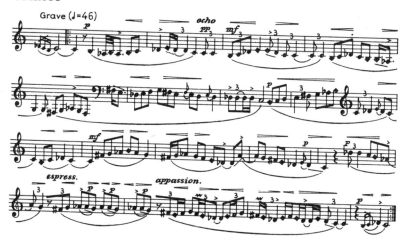

ANTARĀ

LĀCHĀRĪ TODĪ

GROUP : Todī

TUNING OF INSTRUMENT:

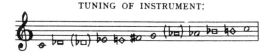

CLASS (*Jāti*):
Sampūrna (Heptatonic)

Āroha Descent   *Avaroha* Descent

SONANT (*Vādī*): G (Pa)

CONSONANT (*Samvādī*): C (Sa)

TIME OF PLAY: day, first quarter (from sunrise)

MODE TYPE (*Thāta*):
Mixed Shrī and Todī

SCALE TYPE: Chromatic
with a diatonic variation

CHARACTERISTICS: Lāchārī is Todī with both E and E♭ (Ga and GaK)
and both B and B♭ (Ni and NiK). B♭ (NiK) is used only as an ornament
from Pa (G) provided there is no touch of F (Ma) in the melodic figure.
Any other use of B♭ (NiK) would create confusion in the expression of the
mode.
E+ (Ga+) should be used only in ascending, preferably without touching
the D♭ (RiK). E+ (Ga+) should always be accentuated ; used in any
other way, it changes the expression of the mode.
As a rule, in any rāga, whenever both E (Ga) and E♭ (GaK) or B (Ni)
and B♭ (NiK) are used, it is necessary, after playing one of them, to
come back respectively to C (Sa) and to G (Pa) before playing the other,
as both have harmonious relations with the tonic and the fifth respectively,
but generally no direct relation with one another. They represent different
paths for the melody, and when entering into one, it is necessary to come
back to the starting point before entering the other.
(Bhātkhande uses also A♮ (Dha shuddha) and D♮ (Ri shuddha) in this
rāga.)

EXPRESSION: Appeal with hope of success. This hope fails, thus despair. Double-edged, both angry and sober, both ordering and appealing, asking with red angry eyes (♮ shuddha notes) and then with eyes full of tears (♭, komal notes).

Ga+ and Ni+ (E+ and B+) mean command, order.

B+ Ni+ means imperious desire ("I wish you to do it"), while B♭ (NiK) means helplessness ("as you will").

"You promised it, you must do it."

Tears, appeal

SHRUTI-S: expression

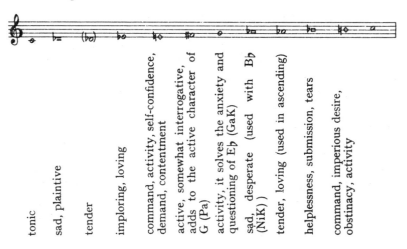

THEME (*Rūpa*):

OUTLINE

Scale

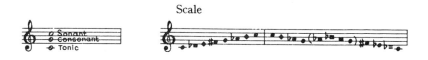

STHĀYĪ

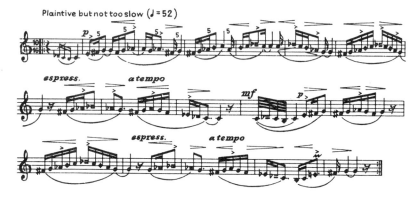

TODĪ

Her slender body anointed with saffron and camphor gleams white like the jasmin-flower. The woodland deer are spellbound at the sight of Todī splendid, holding a lute.

(Sangīta-darpana 2, 53 ; Chatvārimshach'hata-rāga-nirūpanam p. 15 ; Shiva-tattva-rat-nākara 6, 8, 69)

Never shall my heart forget Todī, one hand supporting her charming face, the other clasping the edge of her lover's garment. Her crystal cup is filled with the wine of Kadamba.

(Rāga-sāgara 3, 45)

TUNING OF INSTRUMENT

GROUP: Todī

CLASS (*Jāti*):
Sampūrna (heptatonic)

Aroha Ascent   *Avaroha* Descent

SONANT (*Vādī*): Ab-(Dha komal-) CONSONANT (*Samvādī*): Eb-(Ga komal-)

TIME OF PLAY: day, first quarter (from sunrise)

MODE TYPE (*Thāta*): Todī   SCALE TYPE: Enharmonic-chromatic

CHARACTERISTICS: A very typical and attractive type of enharmonic scale

EXPRESSION: Very tender and loving appeal.   Ga k– (E♭–) is dependent, appealing, sad. (Note the E+ (Ga+), impertinent vanity, in Mukhārī Todī)

Ma T+ (F♯+) is clear, manly, at ease, stern and strong.

masculine:　　　　　　　　　　*feminine:*

weeping.

SHRUTI-S: expression

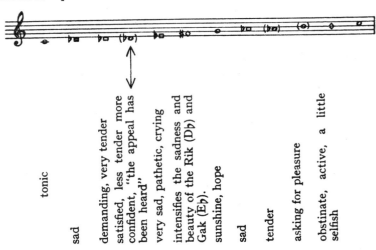

tonic

sad

demanding, very tender

satisfied, less tender more confident, "the appeal has been heard"

very sad, pathetic, crying

intensifies the sadness and beauty of the Rik (D♭) and Gak (E♭).

sunshine, hope

sad

tender

asking for pleasure

obstinate, active, a little selfish

THEME (*Rūpa*):

OUTLINE

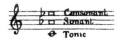

STHĀYĪ

ANTARĀ

VILĀSAKHĀNĪ TODĪ

This rāgă is the creation of Vilāsa Khan, a musician of the Moghul Court. There is no Sanskrit poem depicting its mood.

TUNING OF INSTRUMENT

GROUP: Todī

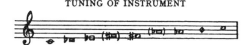

CLASS (*Jāti*):
Shadava (hexatonic)

Āroha Ascent   *Avaroha* Descent

SONANT (*Vādī*): A♮- (Dha k-)   CONSONANT (*Samvādī*): E♭- (Ga k-), but D♭-- (Ri k--) is also very prominent

TIME OF PLAY: day, first quarter (from sunrise)

MODE TYPE (*Thāta*): Todī _

SCALE TYPE: Chromatic in the lower tetrachord and usually chromatic in the upper one, which only accidentally becomes Enharmonic (B++; Ni++)

CHARACTERISTICS: No G (no Pa). Resembles Gurjarī but with F♯-- (Ma t--). (Under the name of Vilāsakhānī Bhātkhande gives another rāga with B♭ (Ni komal) and G (Pa))

EXPRESSION:

The absence of G (Pa) creates an impression of great sorrow, that of an irreparable loss mourned. Very sorrowful, intense grief and misery (like the death of a very dear friend)

There is no trace of harshness or selfishness

F♯-- (Ma T--) gives sadness, which without G (Pa), in the melancholy surroundings of Todī, brings out the burning intensity of grief (while F natural (Ma shuddha) in Gurjarī expresses quiet and peaceful resignation). G (Pa) in Todī, brings forth a radiant sunshine in which sorrows are dissolved

melancholy

The very sharp B++ (Ni++) further intensifies the sadness

SHRUTI-S **expression**

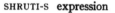

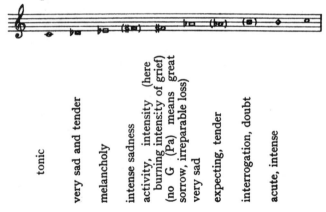

THEME (*Rūpa*):

OUTLINE

STHĀYĪ

ANTARĀ

5. TODĪ GROUP II (Yāvanapūrī)
(First quarter of the day)

Gāndhārī
Deshī
Pathamanjarī
Yāvanapūrī
Āsāvarī

GĀNDHĀRĪ

"Her two hands clasping a Vīnā, Gāndhārī is seen ever seated near the temple of Shiva, Lord of Sleep. Her crown is of gold set with precious stones."

(Rāga-sāgara 3, 47)

GROUP: (Yāvanapūrī) Todī

TUNING OF INSTRUMENT:

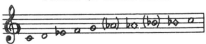

CLASS (*Jāti*): Audava-sampūrna
(Pentatonic in ascent and heptatonic in descent)

Āroha Ascent   *Avaroha* Descent

SONANT (*Vādī*):
Ab (DhaK.)

CONSONANT (*Samvādī*):
Eb (GaK.)

TIME OF PLAY: day, first quarter (from sunrise)

MODE TYPE (*Thāta*): Yāvanapūrī   SCALE TYPE: Diatonic (but in the ascent the first tetrachord is chromatic and the second enharmonic).

CHARACTERISTICS: Yāvanapūrī scale played in Āsāvarī style.

EXPRESSION: Tender, calm, but with love and charm. No B (Ni) in ascending shows purity.

appeal, "I need"   *asking*

SHRUTI-S: expression

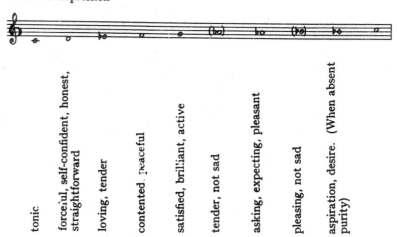

| tonic | forceful, self-confident, honest, straightforward | loving, tender | contented, peaceful | satisfied, brilliant, active | tender, not sad | asking, expecting, pleasant | pleasing, not sad | aspiration, desire. (When absent purity) |

THEME (*Rūpa*):

OUTLINE

Scale

STHĀYĪ

ANTARĀ

DESHĪ

"Tall and amorous, with lovely limbs, her skin prickling in the rapture of the heroic mood, forcing away the passionate arms that bind her, Deshī shines, beloved of Hindola."

(Chatvārimshach'hata-rāga-nirūpanam, p. 20)

"This is the famous Deshī, fair, charming, decked with parrot-plumes. Eager for pleasure, her heart full of desire she tries to awaken her lover who pretends to be asleep."

(Sangīta-darpana 2, 67 ;
Shiva-tattva-ratnākara 6, 8, 79)

"Her hand caressing a young woman I see Deshī, wrapped in a spotless veil, in a hut made of fragrant grass. Her limbs are pale, garlands of flowers entwine her arms."

(Rāga-sāgara 3, 14)

GROUP: (Yāvanapūrī) Todī

TUNING OF INSTRUMENT:

CLASS (*Jāti*): Audava-sampūrna
(Pentatonic in ascent, heptatonic in descent)

Āroha Ascent   *Avaroha* Descent

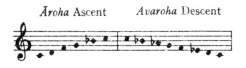

SONANT (*Vādī*): G(Pa)   CONSONANT (*Samvādī*): D (Ri)

TIME OF PLAY: day, first quarter (from sunrise)

MODE TYPE (*Thāta*): Yāvanapūrī   SCALE TYPE: Diatonic (but chromatic
                                                                           in ascent)

CHARACTERISTICS: Jump from D (Ri) to G (Pa).

Each
motive
ends:

EXPRESSION: Happiness without ambition, goodness. Morning gaiety
(dominant notes G and D, Pa and Ri), lively and active, without com-
plexities, nor depth.
More radiant than Yāvanapūrī, and also more childish (no A♭, DhaK) in
ascent.

SHRUTI-S: expression

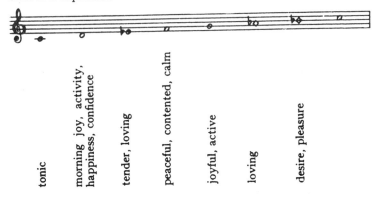

THEME (*Rūpa*):

OUTLINE

Scale

STHĀYĪ

ANTARĀ

PATHAMANJARĪ

"Grown lean and tarnished sundered from her lover, Pathamanjarī decks with flowers her withered beauty. Her friend is trying to comfort her."

(Saṅgīta-darpaṇa 2, 62 ;
Shiva-tattva-ratnākara 6, 8, 87)

"I ever see Rāga Phalamanjarī seated in a bower of grape vines with young women on his sides. Magnificent, he wears a crown and armlets set with precious stones."

(Rāga-sāgara 3, 13)

TUNING OF INSTRUMENT:

GROUP: (Yāvanapūrī) Todī

CLASS (*Jāti*): Audava-sampūrna
(Pentatonic in ascent, and heptatonic in descent)

Āroha Ascent   *Avaroha* Descent

SONANT (*Vādī*): G (Pa)   CONSONANT (*Samvādī*): C (Sa)

TIME OF PLAY: day, first quarter (from sunrise)

MODE TYPE (*Thāta*): Kāfī   SCALE TYPE: Diatonic (chromatic in ascent)

CHARACTERISTICS: Somewhat resembles Deshi but its samvādi is C (Sa). A+ (Dha+) is high, there is no E (Ga), no A (Dha) in ascent.

EXPRESSION: Joyful, playful but ambitious. G and C (Pa and Sa) give an expression graver than Deshi. This rāga is akin to Āsāvarī in spite of the D natural (Ri shuddha).

Joyful, active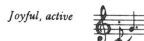

SHRUTI-S: expression

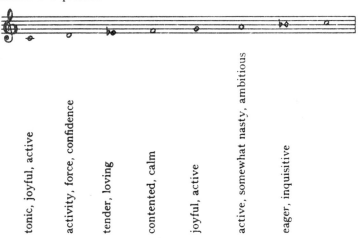

THEME (*Rūpa*):

OUTLINE

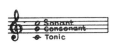

Scale

STHĀYĪ

ANTARĀ

YĀVANAPŪRĪ

Yāvana Todī is fully ripe, a foreign girl. Richly dressed, her hair plaited upon her brow, she wears golden ear-rings shaped like flowers and set with precious stones. Skilful, she plays in the morning languidly, sipping the wine of grapes, letting her white limbs and lovely form be seen.

(Rāga-mālā of Pundarika Vitthala)

TUNING OF INSTRUMENT:

GROUP: Todi

CLASS (*Jāti*): Shādava-sampūrna (hexatonic in ascent and hepta-tonic in descent)

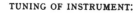

Āroha Ascent   *Avaroha* Descent

SONANT (*Vādī*): A♭ (Dha k.)   CONSONANT (*Samvādī*): E♭ (Ga k.)

TIME OF PLAY: morning first watch (6 to 9)

MODE TYPE (*Thāta*): Yāvanapūrī

SCALE TYPE: Pythagorean diatonic. Plagal mode of A(Dha) in the natural scale

CHARACTERISTICS: combination of Deshī and Gāndhārī (Bhātkhande calls this rāga Āsāvarī)

EXPRESSION: Tender, loving and active appeal. Sensuous but with depth of feeling; daring and childish (D, Ri), but, at the same time, grown-up and serious (Ab, Dha k.), with grace and beauty

D (Ri) manly, commanding, childish, stubborn.   (In Āsāvarī Db (Ri k.) is wise and melancholy)

Ab (Dha k.) is mature

Bb+ (Ni k.+) is impure, selfish

Request with selfish motives

SHRUTI-S: expression

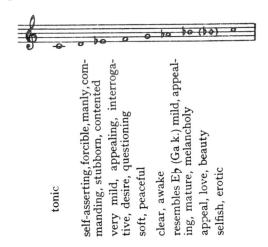

THEME (*Rūpā*):

OUTLINE

STHĀYĪ

ANTARĀ

ĀSĀVARĪ

Her breast adorned with saffron, embraced by her man of expert taste in music, so shines Asāverī, in the mind of the sages.

(Chatvārimshach'hata-rāga-nirūpanam p. 22)

I remember Asāverī, all clad in red, eating pomegranates. Fair, with lovely nails, her arm supports her heavy breasts. Holding a cushion she bends her body and shows her face, loosening her garments in her eagerness for pleasure.

(Rāga-sāgara 3, 65)

On the peak of a mountain, Āshāvarī of shining blackness, adorned with peacock feathers and a rare necklace of splendid pearls, drags forth the serpent from the sandal-trees and wears it as a zone.

(Sangīta-darpana 2, 75 ; *Shiva-tattva-ratnākara* 6, 8, 113)

GROUP: Todī

CLASS (*Jāti*): Audava-sampūrna
(pentatonic in ascent and heptatonic in descent)

Āroha Ascent   Avaroha Descent

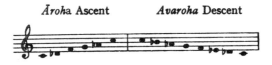

TUNING OF INSTRUMENT:

SONANT (*Vādī*): Ab (Dha k.)   CONSONANT (*Samvādī*): Db (Ri k.)

TIME OF PLAY: morning first watch (6 to 9)

MODE TYPE (*Thāta*): Bhairavī

SCALE TYPE: enharmonic in ascent, and diatonic in descent

CHARACTERISTICS: resembles Gāndhārī or Yāvanapūrī but with B♭ (Ri k.)

EXPRESSION:
Renunciation, grave and dignified. Ascent always by thirds.

Similar to Gāndhārī but more pathetic because of D flat (Ri komal) which makes it more feminine and deeper than Yāvanapūrī, it introduces melancholy but also wisdom and soberness. (The D natural (Ri shuddha) of Yāvanapūrī is manly, commanding, childish, stubborn.) Much use of A flat (Dha komal) makes this rāga very expressive and tender.

feminine

SHRUTI-S expression

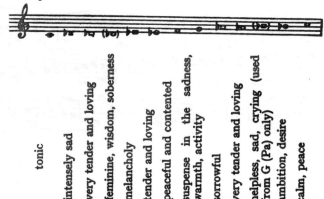

tonic

intensely sad

very tender and loving

feminine, wisdom, soberness

melancholy

tender and loving

peaceful and contented

suspense in the sadness, warmth, activity

sorrowful

very tender and loving

helpless, sad, crying (used from G (Pa) only)

ambition, desire

calm, peace

THEME (*Rūpa*):

OUTLINE

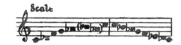

STHĀYĪ

ANTARĀ

CHAPTER II
LATE MORNING RĀGA-S

—

6. BHAIRAVĪ GROUP
(Second quarter of the day)

Rewā
Dhānī
Shat
Bhairavī
Bhūpālā
Sāmanta

REWĀ

GROUP: Bhairavī

TUNING OF INSTRUMENT:

CLASS (*Jāti*):
Audava (Pentatonic)

Āroha Ascent   *Avaroha* Descent

SONANT (*Vādī*): Sa (C) (Bhātkhande gives the Vādī as Ga (E), or RiK (B♭).)

CONSONANT (*Samvādī*): Pa (G)

TIME OF PLAY: day, second quarter

MODE TYPE (*Thāta*): Bhairava

SCALE TYPE: Defective chromatic in the lower tetrachord, enharmonic in the upper one.

CHARACTERISTICS: No F (Ma) and no B (Ni). The tuning D♭ (RiK) and A♭ (DhaK) is the real tuning of the rāga, giving its chief expression. D♭ (RiK) and A♭+ (DhaK+) are only incidentally used. Vādī and samvādī Sa Pa (C G) express activity, energy. The absence of F (Ma) means absence of calm, thus restlessness.

EXPRESSION: Tender and loving appeal. Resembles Shrī or Dīpaka.

SHRUTI-S: expression

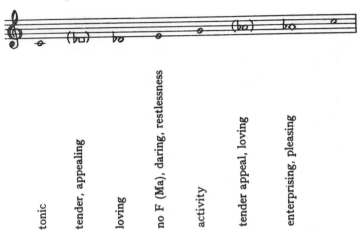

tonic

tender, appealing

loving

no F (Ma), daring, restlessness

activity

tender appeal, loving

enterprising, pleasing

THEME (*Rūpa*):

OUTLINE

Scale

STHĀYĪ

ANTARĀ

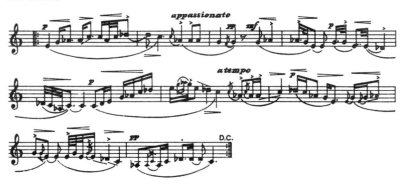

DHĀNĪ

GROUP: Bhairavī

TUNING OF INSTRUMENT:

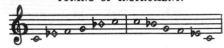

CLASS (*Jāti*): Audava (Pentatonic)

Āroha Ascent   *Avaroha* Descent

SONANT (*Vādī*):
  B♭ (NiK)

CONSONANT (*Samvādī*):
  E♮ (GaK)

TIME OF PLAY: day, second quarter (9 to 12)

MODE TYPE (*Thāta*): Kāfī

SCALE TYPE: Chromatic

CHARACTERISTICS: No D (Ri), no A (Dha).
  Ga (E) like in Mālakosha slightly trembling. Dhānī is the morning equivalent of the evening rāga Mālakosha ; the difference being that the A♭ (DhaK) of Mālakosha is replaced here by G (Pa), which is sunlight.

EXPRESSION: Love of Nature, green fields ; contemplation of the forest or the mountains, happy and poetic, but with some daring and strength.

The interval C G (Sa Pa)
expresses Nature, life.

SHRUTI-S: expression   all the notes are light and spontaneous without sadness ;

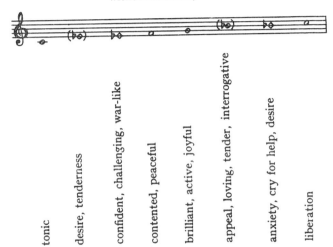

- tonic
- desire, tenderness
- confident, challenging, war-like
- contented, peaceful
- brilliant, active, joyful
- appeal, loving, tender, interrogative
- anxiety, cry for help, desire
- liberation

THEME (*Rūpa*):

OUTLINE

Scale

STHĀYĪ

ANTARĀ

SHAT

On the blessed summit of Mount Kailāsa dwells the Greatest of Sages. With matted locks, His body white with the ash of funeral pyres, sweetly and tenderly He smiles. Ever in Him, Shat rāga, at dawn, are sung majestic odes worthy of meditation. In Him there dwells the music of the Gods, its sweetness and its meaning. *(Rāga-kalpa-druma* p. 30)

TUNING OF INSTRUMENT:

GROUP: Bhairavī

CLASS (*Jāti*): Audava-sampūrna (pentatonic in ascent, heptatonic in descent)

Āroha Ascent   *Avaroha* Descent

SONANT (*Vādī*): G (Pa)   CONSONANT (*Samvādī*): C (Sa)

TIME OF PLAY: day, second quarter (9 to 12)

MODE TYPE (*Thāta*): Bhairavī   SCALE TYPE: Chromatic in ascending; and Pythagorean diatonic in descending.

CHARACTERISTICS: all flat notes

EXPRESSION: (resembling Āsāvarī but in male character). Misery, helplessness, loving and sad

male   compare with female shape of Bhairavī

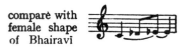

characteristic motive of the male shape of Shat

compare with female shape in
Āsāvarī; where Ab (Dha k.)
gives a female character

SHRUTI-S: expression

THEME (*Rūpă*):

OUTLINE

STHĀYĪ

ANTARĀ

BHAIRAVĪ

She whom poets in their vision see as great-eyed Bhairavī, golden consort of Bhairava, throned on carven crystal at the peak of Kailāsa, with cymbals in her hands, worships Him with the leaves and flowers of the lotus.

(Rāga-kalpadruma p. 17 ; *Sangīta-darpana* 2-48
Chatvārimshach'hata-'rāga-nirūpanam p. 13 ;
Shiva-tattva-ratnākara 6, 8, 59)*

TUNING OF INSTRUMENT

GROUP: Bhairavī

CLASS (*Jāti*):
Sampūrna (heptatonic)

Āroha Ascent   *Avaroha* Descent

SONANT (*Vādī*): C (Sa)   CONSONANT (*Samvādī*): F (Ma)

TIME OF PLAY: day, second   MODE TYPE (*Thāta*): Bhairavī
quarter (9 to 12)

SCALE TYPE: Pythagorean diatonic

CHARACTERISTICS: accidental use of D natural (shuddha Ri) and of F♯ (Ma tīvra)

EXPRESSION: very tender, loving, and melancholy. Sadness mixed with passion and pleasure.

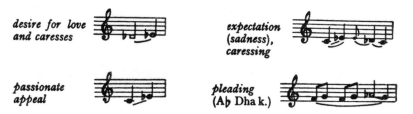

desire for love and caresses

expectation (sadness), caressing

passionate appeal

pleading (A♭ Dha k.)

F♯ (Ma tīvra) and D natural
(Ri shuddha) express in-
tensity, pleasure.
F♯ (Ma tīvra denotes tension
D natural (Ri shuddha)
shows lack of shyness.

satiation,
satisfaction      *question*

compare the feminine shape of Bhairavī with the
similar expression in the male character of
Mālakośha:

SHRUTI-S: **expression**

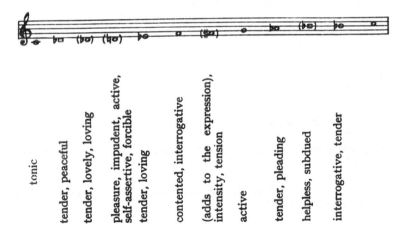

THEME (*Rūpā*):

OUTLINE

STHĀYĪ

ANTARĀ

BHŪPĀLA

I see Bhūpāla comfortably seated on a lion's throne, his huge family around him. Young women, their eyes like those of deer, fan him with a whisk.

(*Rāga-sāgara* 3, 5)

GROUP: Bhairavī

CLASS (*Jāti*): Audava (pentatonic)

TUNING OF INSTRUMENT.

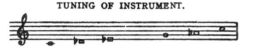

Āroha Ascent   *Avaroha* Descent

SONANT (*Vādī*): A♭ (Dha k.)   CONSONANT (*Samvādī*): A♭ (Ga k.)

TIME OF PLAY: day, first quarter (from sunrise)

MODE TYPE (*Thāta*): Bhairavī   SCALE TYPE: Enharmonic (plagal)

CHARACTERISTICS: no F (Ma) and no B.(Ni); all the mobile notes are flat.

EXPRESSION: great sadness but borne with calm. Sad, tender and loving

No F(Ma): *dejected unsatisfied, unreal*   *like a story told of love rejected*

pleading 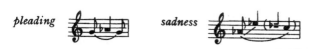 *sadness*

some satisfaction 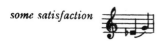   *but sink again into despair*

Very sad and depressed (the dominant notes being A♭ and E♭ (Dha k-Ga k-). Every note expresses sadness but this sadness may come either from saturation, helplessness, or devotion. G(Pa) gives the strength to endure it.

SHRUTI-S: **expression**

tonic

very sad, despair

crying, melancholy, sadness

(No F(Ma): dejection, un-satisfied, unreal)

contentment, sympathy in pain, strength to bear great sadness

THEME (*Rūpá*):

OUTLINE:

STHĀYĪ

ANTARĀ

SĀMANTA

GROUP: Bhairavī

TUNING OF INSTRUMENT:

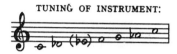

CLASS (*Jāti*): Audava-shādava
(Pentatonic in ascent and
hexatonic in descent)

Āroha Ascent   *Avaroha* Descent

SONANT (*Vādī*): F (Ma)   CONSONANT (*Samvādī*): C (Sa)

TIME OF PLAY: noon

MODE TYPE (*Thāta*): Bhairavī

SCALE TYPE: Enharmonic in ascending but the lower tetrachord becomes diatonic in descending by the addition of E♭ (GaK).

CHARACTERISTICS: By its structure this rāga should belong to Sandhi-prakāsha (conjunction of day and night) but it is actually played in the middle of the day because of the predominance of the interval C F (Sa Ma). Never stop nor insist on A (Dha).

EXPRESSION: Contentment and quiet pleasure, calm and powerful, no anguish, nor anxiety. Sāmanta has been said to represent the creation of the universe.

Sa Ma (C F) expresses *contentment*

F G Ab (Ma Pa DhaK) *pleasure*

no pleading, no animal passion (no Bb or Eb) (no NiK nor GaK)
Eb (GaK) in descending (Avaroha) brings joy.

SHRUTI-S: expression

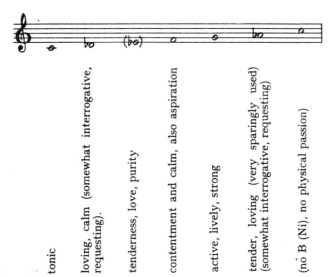

THEME (*Rūpa*):

OUTLINE

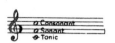

Scale

STHĀYĪ

ANTARĀ

7. BILĀVAL GROUP
(Second quarter of the day)

Bilāval
Lach'hā Bilāval
Kakubha Bilāval
Alhaiyā Bilāval

BILĀVAL

Velāvali has the lustre of the blue lotus. Arranging jewels upon her body she makes secret signs to her lover. How can she forget for one moment her chosen deity, the God of Love?

(*Sangīta-darpana* 2, 59 ; *Chatvārimshach'hata-rāga-nirūpanam* ; *Shiva-tattva-ratnākara* 6, 8, 81)

GROUP: Bilāval

CLASS (*Jāti*): Audava-shādava (Pentatonic in ascent and hexatonic in descent)

TUNING OF INSTRUMENT:

Āroha Ascent *Avaroha* Descent

SONANT (*Vādī*): A(Dha)   CONSONANT (*Samvādī*): E(Ga)

TIME OF PLAY: day, second quarter (from 9 to 12)

MODE TYPE (*Thāta*): Bilāval

SCALE TYPE: Diatonic (but defective in ascent) in the lower tetrachord; and chromatic (minor tone and minor third) in the upper tetrachord. This explains the sometimes very pathetic expression of this apparently major mode

CHARACTERISTICS: resembles the Western diatonic scale and was taken as basic scale for the first time in 'Nagmat e Asaphi' (1813) by Muhammad Rezza. B(Ni) is used sparingly and only as a grace note to A (Dha)

EXPRESSION: active and tender, inquisitive, mixing joy and affection. D(Ri) and G(Pa) are clear and joyful. E (Ga) and A(Dha) are soft and gentle. F-(Ma–) is uncertain and grave, tender and affectionate

SHRUTI-S: **expression**

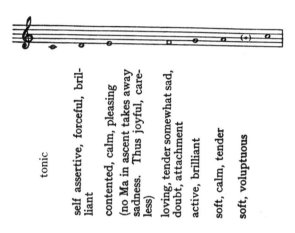

tonic

self assertive, forceful, bril-liant

contented, calm, pleasing

(no Ma in ascent takes away sadness. Thus joyful, care-less)

loving, tender somewhat sad, doubt, attachment

active, brilliant

soft, calm, tender

soft, voluptuous

THEME (*Rūpă*):

OUTLINE

STHĀYI

ANTARĀ

LACH'HĀ BILĀVAL

GROUP: Bilāval

TUNING OF INSTRUMENT:

CLASS (*Jāti*): Shādava-sampūrna (Hexatonic in ascent, heptatonic in descent)

Āroha Ascent   *Avaroha* Descent

SONANT (*Vādī*): B (Ni)

CONSONANT (*Samvādī*): E (Ga)

TIME OF PLAY: day, second quarter (9 to 12)

MODE TYPE (*Thāta*): Khammāja

SCALE TYPE: Diatonic

CHARACTERISTICS: Similar to Ālhaiyā Bilāval but with vādī B (Ni) and samvādī E (Ga).

EXPRESSION: Pleasant, joyful morning, deep and sincere, spiritual and contented, for songs of devotion, love and happiness.

The upper tetrachord resembles Kkammāja, the lower tetrachord resembles Bilāval.

E (Ga) with the sparingly-used D (Ri) gives the expression of prayer and shyness, soft and tender.

B♮ (Ni shuddha) is clear and joyful.

SHRUTI-S: expression

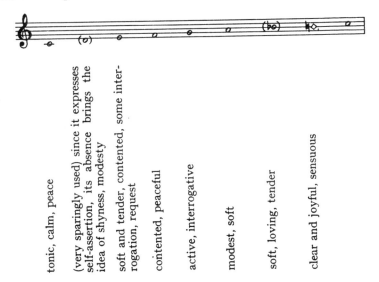

tonic, calm, peace

(very sparingly used) since it expresses self-assertion, its absence brings the idea of shyness, modesty

soft and tender, contented, some inter-rogation, request

contented, peaceful

active, interrogative

modest, soft

soft, loving, tender

clear and joyful, sensuous

THEME (*Rūpa*):

Allegro

OUTLINE

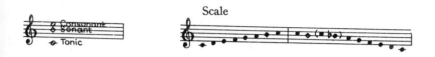

STHĀYĪ

ANTARĀ

KAKUBHA BILĀVAL

"With a garland of champaka, her face like the moon, plump, showy, generous, adorned for love, Kakubha with her enticing glances is charming."

(*Sangīta-darpana* 2, 57;
Shiva-tattva-ratnākara 6, 8, 78)

GROUP: Bilāval

TUNING OF INSTRUMENT:

CLASS (*Jāti*): Sampūrna (Heptatonic)

Āroha Ascent   *Avaroha* Descent

SONANT (*Vādī*): B (Ni)
(sometimes G (Pa))

CONSONANT (*Samvādī*): E (G.
(sometimes D (Ri))

TIME OF PLAY: late morning towards midday (like Sāranga)

MODE TYPE (*Thāta*): Khammāja

SCALE TYPE: Pythagorean diatonic (with ornamental diminished 7th) (Ni komal).

CHARACTERISTICS: Use of both B and B flat (Ni komal).

EXPRESSION: Glory (sung at the time of coronation, etc.). Very joyful

SHRUTI-S: expression

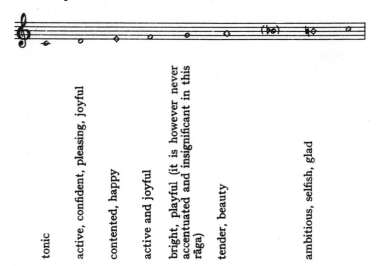

tonic

active, confident, pleasing, joyful

contented, happy

active and joyful

bright, playful (it is however never accentuated and insignificant in this rāga)

tender, beauty

ambitious, selfish, glad

THEME (*Rūpa*):

Lively

OUTLINE

STHĀYĪ

ANTARĀ

ALHAIYĀ BILĀVAL

GROUP: Bilāval

TUNING OF INSTRUMENT:

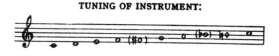

CLASS (*Jāti*): Sampūrna
(Heptatonic)

Āroha Ascent   *Avaroha* Descent

SONANT (*Vādī*): G(Pa)   **CONSONANT** (*Samvādī*): D (Ri)

TIME OF PLAY: day, second quarter (9 to 12)

MODE TYPE (*Thāta*): Khammāja   **SCALE TYPE:** Diatonic

CHARACTERISTICS: use of B♭ (Ni k.) as an ornament from G(Pa) and rarely of an accidental F♯ (Ma t.) as an ornament of G (Pa). [According to Bhātkhaṇḍe, Dha(A) and Ga(E) are the Vādī and Samvādī]

EXPRESSION:
pleasing, lovely. B♭ (Ni k.) is tender and submissive, gently praying with folded hands. In relation with D(Ri), the samvādī, F-(Ma-) forms a minor third and thus has a melancholy expression.

demand

all depends upon your mercy

weeping, the head on the master's feet

SHRUTI-S: **expression**

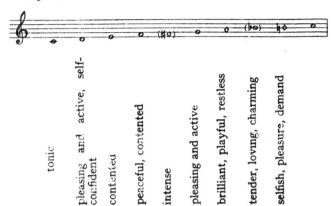

tonic

pleasing and active, self-confident

contented

peaceful, contented

intense

pleasing and active

brilliant, playful, restless

tender, loving, charming

selfish, pleasure, demand

THEME (*Rūpā*):

OUTLINE

STHĀYĪ

ANTARĀ

CHAPTER III
NOON AND AFTERNOON RĀGA-S

8. SĀRANGA GROUP
(Noon rāga-s)

Sāranga
Madhyamādi
Brindābani
Gauda

SĀRANGA

His sombre limbs mighty in armour are covered with a yellow robe. Armed with discus, mace and bow and bearing a shield, his gleaming quiver full, holding a lotus and a conch, adorned with sumptuous ornaments, Sāranga rides upon the bird-form Garuda.

(Rāga-mālā of Pundarika Vitthala)

Sāranga, the young hero, pride of the god of love, drinks the liquor of honey. He delights in bouquets of flowers.

(Chatvārimshach'hata-rāga-nirūpanam p. 16)

GROUP: Sāranga

CLASS (*Jāti*): Audava
(Pentatonic)

TUNING OF INSTRUMENT:

Āroha Ascent   *Avaroha* Descent

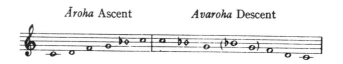

SONANT (*Vādī*): G(Pa)   **CONSONANT** (*Samvādī*): D(Ri)

TIME OF PLAY: midday

MODE TYPE (*Thāta*): Khammāja   **SCALE TYPE:** Chromatic

CHARACTERISTICS: no A(Dha) and no E(Ga)

EXPRESSION: pleasing and charming. The subject of all Sāranga-s is lovely forms, no pathos, but only tenderness. Among Sāranga-s, Shuddha Sāranga is like a motherly woman, who expresses herself in soft, moderate and affectionate terms. She is gentle, soft and selfless.

SHRUTI-S: expression

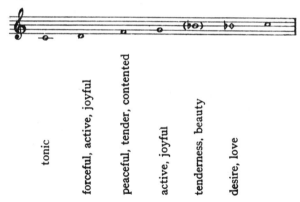

tonic

forceful, active, joyful

peaceful, tender, contented

active, joyful

tenderness, beauty

desire, love

THEME (*Rūpā*):

OUTLINE

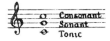

STHĀYĪ

ANTARĀ

MADHYAMĀDI SĀRANGA

"Madhyamādi, lotus-eyed, her golden skin smeared with saffron, laughingly embraced by her husband, kisses and is kissed by him, the sages tell, after her heart's desire."

(Sangīta-darpana 2, 47 ; *Chatvārim-shach'hata-rāga-nirūpanam,* p. 9 ; *Shiva-tattva-ratnākara* 6, 8, 57)*

GROUP: Sāranga

TUNING OF INSTRUMENT:

CLASS *(Jāti)*: Audava (Pentatonic)

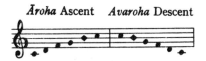

Āroha Ascent   *Avaroha* Descent

SONANT *(Vādī)*: G (Pa)

CONSONANT *(Samvādī)*: D (Ri)

TIME OF PLAY: midday

MODE TYPE *(Thāta)*: Bilāval

SCALE TYPE: Pythagorean chromatic in the lower tetrachord and Pythagorean enharmonic in the upper tetrachord.

CHARACTERISTICS: No A (Dha) and no E (Ga)

EXPRESSION: Pleasing ; all-brilliant midday.   Forceful, childish, hungry. Among Sāranga-s she is a child, or a woman of pleasure. All notes are self-confident, even F (Ma) is not soft.

SHRUTI-S: expression

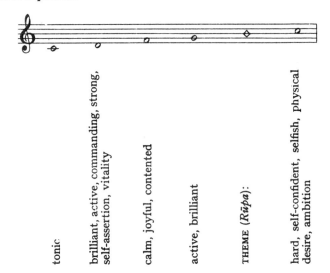

tonic

brilliant, active, commanding, strong, self-assertion, vitality

calm, joyful, contented

active, brilliant

THEME (*Rūpa*):

hard, self-confident, selfish, physical desire, ambition

THEME (*Rūpa*):

OUTLINE

Scale

STHĀYĪ

Moderate but rhythmical (♩ = 56)

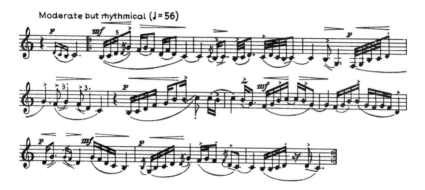

ANTARĀ

BRINDĀBANI SĀRANGA

GROUP: Sāranga

TUNING OF INSTRUMENT:

CLASS (*Jāti*): Audava (Pentatonic)
with both B (Ni) and B♭ (NiK)

Āroha Ascent   *Avaroha* Descent

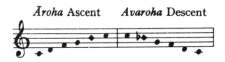

SONANT (*Vādī*): G (Pa)

CONSONANT (*Samvādī*): D (Ri)

TIME OF PLAY: midday

MODE TYPE (*Thāta*): same scale as Mallār (Khammāja thāta)

SCALE TYPE: Chromatic (the upper tetrachord being enharmonic in ascent)

CHARACTERISTICS: No E (Ga), no A (Dha).
B (Ni) is natural (shuddha) in ascent and flat (komal) in descent.

EXPRESSION: A young woman, passionate, pleasing, loving and tender. She has both force and charm.
B♭ (NiK) closed eyes,
B natural (Ni shuddha), open eyes.

B+ (Ni+) demands. Speaking clearly, without dissimulation. It makes the rāga childish, gay and clear.

B♭ (NiK) brings in more delicate emotions, no demands but love and affection. Among Sāranga-s, Brindābanī seems more grown up. Already a woman, she shows deeper understanding, is more moving, she will also obtain more.

SHRUTI-S: expression

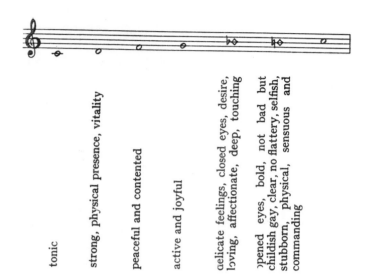

tonic

strong, physical presence, vitality

peaceful and contented

active and joyful

delicate feelings, closed eyes, desire, loving, affectionate, deep, touching

opened eyes, bold, not bad but childish gay, clear, no flattery, selfish, stubborn, physical, sensuous and commanding

THEME (*Rūpa*):

OUTLINE

Scale

STHĀYĪ

ANTARĀ

GAUDA SĀRANGA

Seated beneath the wishing Tree his body white as snow, his long hair tightly bound, Gauda Sāranga is seen in the afternoon playing upon a lute. The sages tell that he has the voice of a nightingale. (*Rāga-kalpa-druma* p. 29)

TUNING OF INSTRUMENT:

GROUP: Sāranga

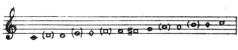

CLASS (*Jāti*): Shādava-sam-
    pūrna (Hexatonic in
    ascent, pentatonic in
    descent)

Āroha Ascent   *Avaroha* Descent

SONANT (*Vādī*): E(Ga)   CONSONANT (*Samvādī*): B(Ni)

TIME OF PLAY: midday

MODE TYPE (*Thāta*): Kalyāna   SCALE TYPE: Diatonic

CHARACTERISTICS: similar to Bihāga (a midnight rāga). In all Sāranga-s, D, F and G (Ri Ma and Pa) are predominant, this is a characteristic of midday.

EXPRESSION: contentment, faith, very tender and loving prayer, more restful, lovely, peaceful and contented than other Sāranga-s.
The two F(2 Ma) (natural and sharp) represent midday (or midnight).
E_+ (Ga_+) denotes satisfaction, contentment, faith; E (Ga) relief, consolation.

SHRUTI-S: **expression**

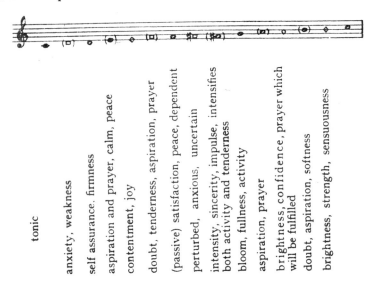

tonic

anxiety, weakness

self assurance. firmness

aspiration and prayer, calm, peace

contentment, joy

doubt, tenderness, aspiration, prayer

(passive) satisfaction, peace, dependent

perturbed, anxious, uncertain

intensity, sincerity, impulse, intensifies
both activity and tenderness

bloom, fullness, activity

aspiration, prayer

brightness, confidence, prayer which
will be fulfilled

doubt, aspiration, softness

brightness, strength, sensuousness

THEME (*Rūpā*):

OUTLINE

STHĀYĪ

ANTARĀ

9. SHRĪ GROUP
(Last quarter of the day)

Dhanāshrī
Mālavashrī
Shrī
Bhīmapalāshrī
Multānī

DHANĀSHRĪ

"Charming is Dhanāshrī, her body sombre like the durvā grass. Her cheeks are pale with the torment of separation. The tear drops falling on her breast, she is writing to her beloved."

(*Sangīta-darpana* 2, 74 ; *Chatvārim-shach'hata-rāga-nirūpanam*, p. 9 ; *Shiva-tattva-ratnākara* 6, 8, 110)

"Beautifully dark at the side of her lord Dhanyāsī lies on a bed in a charming mountain hut. A lute presses against the nipple of her breast. I ever think of her."

(*Rāga-sāgara* 3, 43)

GROUP: Shrī

TUNING OF INSTRUMENT:

CLASS (*Jāti*): Audava-sampūrna
(Pentatonic in ascent, hepta-tonic in descent)

Āroha Ascent   *Avaroha* Descent

SONANT (*Vādī*): C (Sa)   CONSONANT (*Samvādī*): F (Ma)

TIME OF PLAY: second part of the afternoon

MODE TYPE (*Thāta*): Bhairavī   SCALE TYPE: Diatonic (with chromatic ascent)

CHARACTERISTICS: Sister of Bhīmapalāshrī A♭ (DhaK) is always used lightly and sparingly.
Never stop on Ri♭ (D♭), which must be soft and lightly used.

EXPRESSION: Softness (while Bhīmapalāshrī has a noble appearance), loving and tender but with desire ; voluptuous, contented but with shyness. A sadness is latent in the background (the Db (RiK) and Ab (DhaK) never stopped upon); its vague presence gives more value to the tenderness expressed.

physical satisfaction

SHRUTI-S: expression

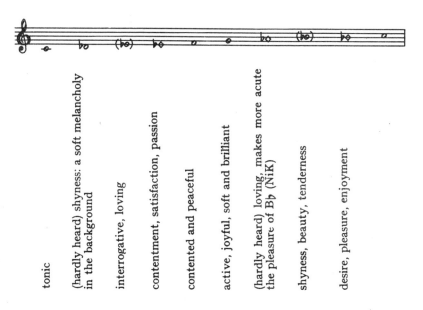

tonic

(hardly heard) shyness: a soft melancholy in the background

interrogative, loving

contentment, satisfaction, passion

contented and peaceful

active, joyful, soft and brilliant

(hardly heard) loving, makes more acute the pleasure of Bb (NiK)

shyness, beauty, tenderness

desire, pleasure, enjoyment

THEME (*Rūpa*):

OUTLINE

STHĀYĪ

ANTARĀ

MĀLAVASHRĪ

"Slender, sitting at the foot of a mango-tree, with a dreamy smile she holds in the palm of her hand a red lotus. So they describe Mālavashrī."

(Sangīta-darpana 2, 73 ; *Shiva-tattva-ratnākara* 6, 8, 108)*

GROUP: Shrī

TUNING OF INSTRUMENT:

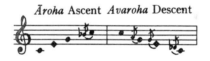

CLASS (*Jāti*): Three main notes with ornaments

Āroha Ascent *Avaroha* Descent

SONANT (*Vādī*): C (Sa)   CONSONANT (*Saṁvādī*): G (Pa)

TIME OF PLAY: second part of the afternoon, before twilight

MODE TYPE (*Thāta*): Pūravī   SCALE TYPE: Overtones

CHARACTERISTICS: The ornamental notes should be short and light.

EXPRESSION: Manlike; pleasure, readiness for work. A tender and joyful call, commanding and inspiring.

SHRUTI-S: expression

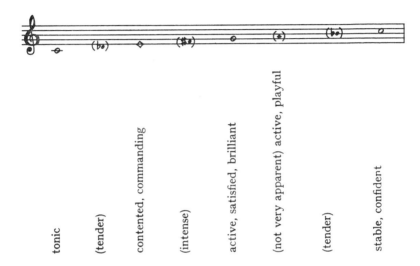

tonic · (tender) · contented, commanding · (intense) · active, satisfied, brilliant · (not very apparent) active, playful · (tender) · stable, confident

THEME (*Rūpa*):

OUTLINE

Scale

STHĀYĪ

SHRĪ

Shrī-rāga is eighteen. With tender leaves quivering at his ears, he is the alluring image of the God of Love. Robed in red, he looks like a king. Sa and all the other notes are his slaves.

(Sangīta-darpana 2, 70 ; *Chatvārimshach'hata-rāga-nirūpanam* 1, 68 ; *Shiva-tattva-ratnākara* 6, 8, 103)

My heart worships Shrī Rāga, whom lovely women surround. His hand resting on a lion's head, he sits in the posture of heroes. His sceptre is laden with precious stones.

(Rāga-sāgara 3, 9)

TUNING OF INSTRUMENT:

ʒROUP: Shrī

ϽLASS (*Jāti*): Audava-sampūrna (pentatonic in
ascent, heptatonic in
descent)

Āroha Ascent   Avaroha Descent

SONANT (*Vādī*): D♭ (Ri k.)   CONSONANT (*Samvādī*): G(Pa)

TIME OF PLAY: second part of the afternoon

MODE TYPE (*Thāta*): Pūravī   SCALE TYPE: Chromatic

CHARACTERISTICS: no E(Ga) and no A(Dha) in
ascent. The higher A♭ (Dha k.) is used only
in the following figures:

EXPRESSION: lethargy, melancholy, half awake, tender, loving, sad but spiritual, as a call for evening prayer.

half awake   *melancholy*

Contentment, peace   *inner joy*

SHRUTI-S:

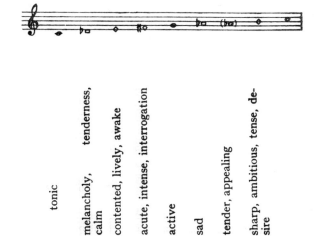

tonic

melancholy, calm

tenderness,

contented, lively, awake

acute, intense, interrogation

active

sad

tender, appealing

sharp, ambitious, tense, desire

THEME (*Rūpă*):

OUTLINE

STHĀYĪ

ANTARĀ

BHĪMAPALĀSHRĪ

With wide lotus eyes and fragrant with celestial flowers, Bhīmapalāshrī, the sages tell, sings with her deep voice to the lute. Her lovely form is the embodiment of art.

(Ragā-kalpa-druma p. 22)

GROUP: Shrī

TUNING OF INSTRUMENT:

CLASS *(Jāti)*: Audava sampūrna (pentatonic in ascent, heptatonic in descent)

Āroha Ascent   *Avaroha* Descent

SONANT *(Vādī)*: F (Ma)   **CONSONANT** *(Samvādī)*: C(Sa)

TIME OF PLAY: 2nd part of the afternoon

MODE TYPE *(Thāta)*: Kāfī   **SCALE TYPE:** diatonic (with chromatic ascent)

CHARACTERISTICS: Kāfī played in Multānī style, F (Ma) is always **accentuated**

EXPRESSION: peaceful, tender and pleasing, with some ambition

SHRUTI-S: **expression**

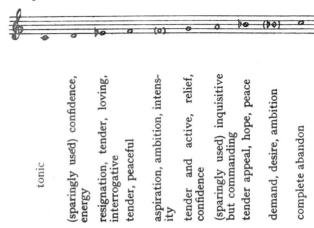

tonic

(sparingly used) confidence, energy

resignation, tender, loving, interrogative

tender, peaceful

aspiration, ambition, intensity

tender and active, relief, confidence

(sparingly used) inquisitive but commanding

tender appeal, hope, peace

demand, desire, ambition

complete abandon

THEME (*Rūpă*):

OUTLINE

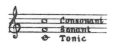

STHĀYĪ

ANTARĀ

MULTĀNĪ

GROUP: Shrī

TUNING OF INSTRUMENT:

CLASS (*Jāti*): Audava-sampūrna (pentatonic in ascent, heptatonic in descent)

Āroha Ascent   *Avaroha* Descent

SONANT (*Vādī*): E♭ (Ga k.)   CONSONANT (*Samvādī*): B$_+$ (Ni$_+$)

TIME OF PLAY: 2nd part of the afternoon

MODE TYPE (*Thāta*): Todī   SCALE TYPE: Chromatic

CHARACTERISTICS: Todī scale

EXPRESSION: Tender and melancholy, but also pleasing and lovely. More clear, more contented, more manly, less mild than Todī. No sadness, (F♯$_+$ (Ma T$_+$) and A♭ (Dha k.) do not bring sadness). D♭ (Ri k.) is never used in the ascending scale and is very light in the descending one.

SHRUTI-S: **expression**

tonic

tender and loving, its very sparing use creates a veiled melancholy

passionate

adoration, adds to the ex-pression of E♭(Ga k.) and of G (Pa)

active, calm and confident

tender, loving and interro-gative but contented

selfish and pleasure-loving, forcible, active

THEME (*Rūpă*):

OUTLINE

STHĀYĪ

ANTARĀ

10. NATA

(In the afternoon)

"Valorous, his golden body smeared with blood, his arm upon the neck of his stallion he wanders about the battlefield. So the ancients imaged Nata-rāga."

(Sangīta-darpana 2, 69 ; *Shiva-tattva-ratnākara* 6, 8, 101)

"Ever shall I praise Nata rāga proudly riding a large horse through the battle field. Wearing a high crown, he carries a sword and a shield and a bow in his hand. The crescent moon on his forehead, he appears kind and gentle surrounded on all sides with beheaded bodies."

(Rāga-sāgara 3, 29)

GROUP: Nata

TUNING OF INSTRUMENT:

CLASS *(Jāti)*: Sampūrna-audava
(Heptatonic in ascent, pentatonic in descent)

Āroha Ascent   *Avaroha* Descent

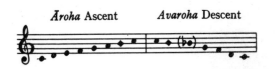

SONANT (*Vādi*): F (Ma)   CONSONANT (*Samvādi*): C (Sa)

TIME OF PLAY: afternoon, second half.
(Some, however, place it in the second quarter of the night)

MODE TYPE (*Thāta*): Bilāval   SCALE TYPE: Diatonic

CHARACTERISTICS: Nata mixes easily with other rāga-s, hence there is Nata-Bihāga, Kāmoda-Nata, Kedāra-Nata, etc.

EXPRESSION: Pleasing and joyful

SHRUTI-S: expression

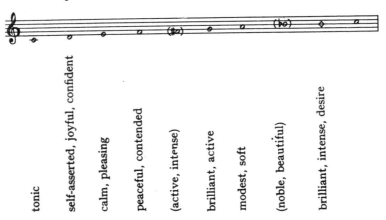

tonic

self-asserted, joyful, confident

calm, pleasing

peaceful, contended

(active, intense)

brilliant, active

modest, soft

(noble, beautiful)

brilliant, intense, desire

THEME (*Rūpa*):

OUTLINE

Scale

STHĀYĪ

Lively (♩=84)

ANTARĀ

NATA BIHĀGA

KĀMODA NATA

KEDĀRA NATA

CHAPTER IV
EVENING RĀGA-S

11. PILŪ

GROUP: Pilū.

TUNING OF INSTRUMENT:

CLASS (*Jāti*): Sampūrna (heptatonic)

Āroha Ascent   *Avaroha* Descent

SONANT (*Vādi*): E♭ (Ga k.)   **CONSONANT** (Samvādī): B$_+$ (Ni$_+$)

TIME OF PLAY: fourth quarter of the day (late afternoon before sunset)

MODE TYPE (*Thāta*): Pilū

SCALE TYPE: the twelve chromatic notes. The regular descent is equivalent to the Western minor mode.

CHARACTERISTICS: Pilū uses all the chromatic notes. F♯ (Ma t.) is only used as an ornament of G (Pa). In ascent for each note, the inferior half tone should be used as ornament, in descent the superior half tone.

EXPRESSION: she does not know herself what she wants, she is satisfied yet longing for something else, sometimes gay and sometimes sad, ever changing.

SHRUTI-S: expression

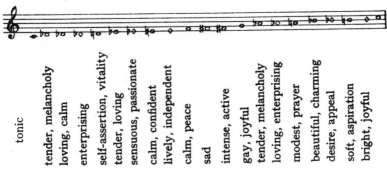

tonic
tender, melancholy
loving, calm
enterprising
self-assertion, vitality
tender, loving
sensuous, passionate
calm, confident
lively, independent
calm, peace
sad
intense, active
gay, joyful
tender, melancholy
loving, enterprising
modest, prayer
beautiful, charming
desire, appeal
soft, aspiration
bright, joyful

THEME (*Rūpā*):

OUTLINE

STHĀYĪ

ANTARĀ

12. PŪRAVĪ GROUP
(At the end of the day)

Māravā
Pūravī
Rāt Pūriyā

MĀRAVĀ

First among the daughters of the Rajput desert, this stately moon-faced girl with her long tresses, tender eyed like a young deer. Her golden limbs are robed in red and richly adorned with flowers. Smiling, she praises the knights assembled on the battle-field. Thus, ever, is Māravā, with Ni and Ga like fire, Ri and Dha like elephants.

(Rāga-mālā of Pundarika Vitthala)

I see Māravā who playfully holds a many coloured discus. Beneath a sweet-mango tree she stands near to Shiva, the three-eyed Lord of Sleep. *(Rāga-sāgara 3, 37)*

TUNING OF INSTRUMENT:

GROUP: Pūravī

CLASS (*Jāti*): Shadava (hexatonic)

Āroha Ascent   *Avaroha* Descent

SONANT (*Vādī*): E(Ga)   CONSONANT (*Samvādī*): A(Dha)

TIME OF PLAY: late afternoon before sunset.

MODE TYPE (*Thāta*): Māravā

SCALE TYPE: Chromatic

CHARACTERISTICS: no G(Pa), D(Ri) and B(Ni) sparingly used in ascent

EXPRESSION: uncomfortable time, when something is expected to happen. Somewhat warlike, but with tender D♭ (Ri k.) ; rough, unfinished, uncomfortable, uneasy.
No G (no Pa) means that something essential is missing.
E_+ (Ga$_+$) and A_+(Dha$_+$) are active energetic. D♭ (Ri K.) is reluctant, tender.

SHRUTI-S: expression

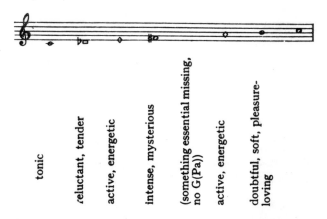

tonic

reluctant, tender

active, energetic

intense, mysterious

(something essential missing, no G(Pa))

active, energetic

doubtful, soft, pleasure-loving

THEME (*Rūpā*):

OUTLINE

STHĀYĪ

ANTARĀ

PŪRAVĪ

Pūravī, her deceitful body so charmingly beautiful is filled with the pain of separation. Her lotus eyes heavy with sleep, still, at the end of the day she is thinking of her lover.

(*Rāga-kalpa-druma* p. 23)

Strong, of many colours, with a floating white veil, Pūrvikā, skilled in archery, comes riding on an elephant.

(*Chatvārimshach'hata-rāga-nirūpanam* p. 8)

Intoxicated with wine and with praise, Pūrvikā is restless like a young deer. Her moonlike body is clad in a garment thinly woven with gold. Her hands hold a parrot and a cup of wine. The head of her lover rests upon her lap.

(*Rāga-sāgara* 3, 49)

GROUP: Pūravī

TUNING OF INSTRUMENT:

CLASS (*Jāti*):
Sampūrna
(heptatonic)

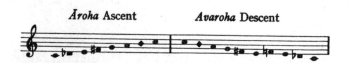

Āroha Ascent   *Avaroha* Descent

SONANT (*Vādī*): E (Ga)   CONSONANT (*Samvādī*): $B_+(Ni_+)$

TIME OF PLAY: end of the day (last quarter of the day)

MODE TYPE (*Thāta*): Māravā   SCALE TYPE: mixed chromatic and diatonic

CHARACTERISTICS: both F natural (Ma shuddha) and F♯ (Ma tīvra)

EXPRESSION: sunset, prayer, request.
     The abundant use of E (Ga) gives strength.
     The use of both F(Ma) and F♯ (Ma t.) brings about a good natured and energetic expression.
     (The use of both F (Ma) and F♯ (Ma t.) always accentuate the expression) the D♭– (Ri k.–) is very tender.

SHRUTI-S: **expression**

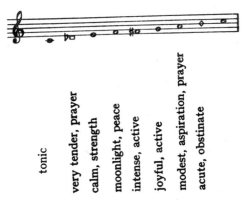

tonic

very tender, prayer

calm, strength

moonlight, peace

intense, active

joyful, active

modest, aspiration, prayer

acute, obstinate

THEME (*Rūpā*):

OUTLINE

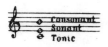 

STHĀYĪ

ANTARĀ

RĀT PŪRIYĀ

GROUP: Pūravī

TUNING OF INSTRUMENT:

CLASS (*Jāti*): Shādava (Hexatonic)

Āroha Ascent   *Avaroha* Descent

SONANT (*Vādī*): E (Ga)

CONSONANT (*Samvādī*): B (Ni)

TIME OF PLAY: early night (first quarter)

MODE TYPE (*Thāta*): Māravā

SCALE TYPE: Chromatic

CHARACTERISTICS: No Pa (Ga), C (Sa) very rarely used and only at the end of variations.

EXPRESSION: Anarchy, a country without a king, disorder in feelings, instability.

(Because of the absence of fifth (Pa) and the rarity of the tonic (Sa).)

SHRUTI-S: expression

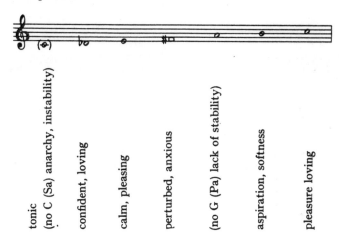

- tonic
- (no C (Sa) anarchy, instability)
- confident, loving
- calm, pleasing
- perturbed, anxious
- (no G (Pa) lack of stability)
- aspiration, softness
- pleasure loving

THEME (*Rūpa*):

OUTLINE

STHĀYĪ

ANTARĀ

13. DĪPAKA
(The Fire rāga)
(After sunset)

"For a lustful end having put out the lamp, Dīpaka, king of rāga-s, draws near to his beloved in the darkened house. But he is made bashful by the brilliance of her jewelled diadem."

(Sangīta-darpana 2, 64 ; *Chatvārimshach'hata rāga-nirūpanam,* p. 21 ; *Shiva-tattva-ratnākara* 6, 8, 92)*

GROUP: Dīpaka

TUNING OF INSTRUMENT:

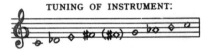

CLASS (*Jāti*): Shādava
(Hexatonic)

Āroha Ascent   *Avaroha* Descent

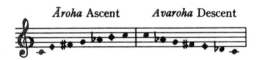

SONANT (*Vādī*): G (Pa)   CONSONANT (*Samvādī*): C (Sa)

TIME OF PLAY: sunset, when lamps are lighted at the end of twilight

MODE TYPE (*Thāta*): Shrī   SCALE TYPE: Chromatic

CHARACTERISTICS: No D (Ri) in ascent and no B (Ni) in descent.

EXPRESSION: Fire, vigorous and manly.

The scales of Dīpaka and Shrī are similar, the one being masculine, the other feminine.

The A♭+ (DhaK+) is clear, expressive (not soft and sad like the A♭ (DhaK) of Todī).

SHRUTI-S: expression

THEME (*Rūpa*):

OUTLINE

Scale:

STHĀYĪ

(♩=68)

ANTARĀ

CHAPTER V
RĀGA-S OF THE EARLY NIGHT

14. KALYĀNA GROUP
(Night, first watch)

Yaman-Kalyāna
Tilaka Kāmoda
Gopi Kāmbhojī
Yaman
Kāmoda
Chhāyānata
Kedārā
Bhūpālī

YAMAN-KALYĀNA

"I see Yamanā Kalyānī in her blue royal robes gently rocking on a swing. Women hold her lovely hands."

(Rāga-sāgara 3, 57)

"With her dim moon-fair body, her lovely breasts, and a lotus in her hand, her skin chilling with an exquisite emotion, Kalyānī of the lovely voice is riding on a deer."

(Chatvārimshach'hata-rāga-nirūpanam, p. 11)

"Lovely lotus of the forest Kalyānī, the giver of boons, strikes with a plectrum the strings of her lute. Yellow as turmeric, her neck is loaded with garlands of golden champak flowers. The she-parrot, the Shārī bird, the swan, enhance her music with their cries. For her each day is the season of love."

(Rāga-sāgara 3, 26)

TUNING OF INSTRUMENT:

GROUP: Kalyāna

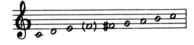

CLASS (*Jāti*): Sampūrna (Heptatonic)

Āroha Ascent *Avaroha* Descent

SONANT (*Vādī*): E (Ga)

CONSONANT (*Samvādī*): B (Ni)

TIME OF PLAY: first quarter of the night

MODE TYPE (*Thāta*): Yaman

SCALE TYPE: Diatonic

CHARACTERISTICS: Both F natural (Ma shuddha) and F♯ (MaT).

EXPRESSION: Softer than Yaman, peaceful joy with a veiled melancholy.

SHRUTI-S: expression

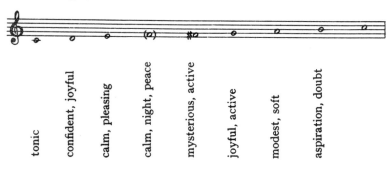

tonic — confident, joyful — calm, pleasing — calm, night, peace — mysterious, active — joyful, active — modest, soft — aspiration, doubt

THEME (*Rūpa*):

OUTLINE

Scale

(all like Yaman except):

TILAKA KĀMODA

GROUP: Kalyāna

TUNING OF INSTRUMENT:

CLASS (*Jāti*): Audava-sampūrna
(Pentatonic in ascent, heptatonic in descent)

Āroha Ascent   *Avaroha* Descent

SONANT (*Vādī*): D (Ri)

CONSONANT (*Samvādī*): G (Pa)

TIME OF PLAY: first quarter of the night

MODE TYPE (*Thāta*): Khammāja

SCALE TYPE: Diatonic (chromatic-enharmonic in ascent).

CHARACTERISTICS: Both B natural (Ni shuddha) and B♭ (NiK) ; no E (Ga) nor A (Dha) in ascent.

EXPRESSION: Graceful and lovely.

SHRUTI-S: expression

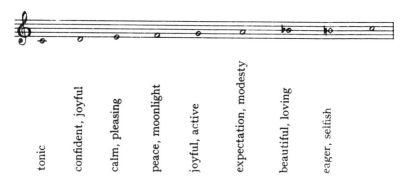

tonic   confident, joyful   calm, pleasing   peace, moonlight   joyful, active   expectation, modesty   beautiful, loving   eager, selfish

THEME (*Rūpa*):

OUTLINE

Scale

STHĀYĪ

ANTARĀ

GOPI KĀMBHOJĪ

"I think of Gopi Kāmbhojī who loves children. In one hand she holds a jug of curds taking out the cream with her other hand." *(Rāga-sāgara* 3, 91)

GROUP: Kalyāna

TUNING OF INSTRUMENT:

CLASS *(Jāti)*: Sampūrna
(Peptatonic)

Āroha Ascent   *Avaroha* Descent

SONANT *(Vādī)*: E (Ga)   CONSONANT *(Samvādī)*: A (Dha)

TIME OF PLAY: first quarter of the night

MODE TYPE *(Thāta)*: Bilāval   SCALE TYPE: Diatonic

CHARACTERISTICS: As it is used mostly in Kīrtan (devotional song) the rules of ascent and descent are not very rigorous.

EXPRESSION: Prayer, selflessness.

SHRUTI-S: expression

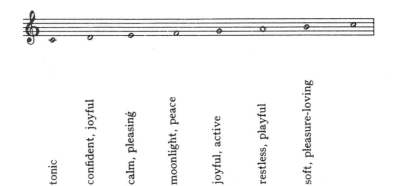

tonic

confident, joyful

calm, pleasing

moonlight, peace

joyful, active

restless, playful

soft, pleasure-loving

THEME (*Rūpa*):

OUTLINE

Scale

STHĀYĪ

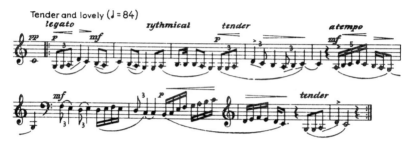

ANTARĀ

YAMAN

Holding a drum Yamunā, mother of voluptuousness rests in the arms of the vanquisher of demons. How could I forget her radiance that puts to shame the blue Jumnā.[1]

(*Rāga-sāgara* 3, 56)

Blood-red, sword in hand, his forehead marked with sandal paste, he enters the battle robed in gold. The sages speak of Kalyāna-rāga as the embodiment of fury [2]

(*Rāga-kalpa-druma* p. 32 ;
Sangīta-darpana 2, 82)

TUNING OF INSTRUMENT:

GROUP: Kalyāna

CLASS (*Jāti*): Sampūrna (heptatonic)

Āroha Ascent   *Avaroha* Descent

---

[1] ' Yamunā ' is a Sanskritised form of the word ' Yaman '.
[2] Kalyāna rāga is a form of Yaman.

K

SONANT (*Vādī*): E (Ga)   CONSONANT (*Samvādī*): B(Ni)

TIME OF PLAY: night first quarter

MODE TYPE (*Thāta*): Kalyāna

SCALE TYPE: Pythagorean diatonic

CHARACTERISTICS: F♯ (Ma t.)

EXPRESSION: joyful and contented

SHRUTI-S: expression

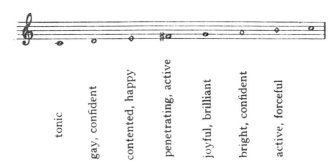

tonic

gay, confident

contented, happy

penetrating, active

joyful, brilliant

bright, confident

active, forceful

THEME (*Rūpā*):

OUTLINE

STHĀYĪ

ANTARĀ

KĀMODA

In the forest, dressed in yellow and with lovely hair,
Kāmodī looks about on every side in terror. Thinking of her
lover, even the cuckoo's happy cry fills her with desperation.

(*Sangīta-darpana* 2, 68)

TUNING OF INSTRUMENT:

GROUP: Kalyāna

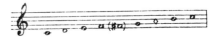

CLASS (*Jāti*): Sampūrna (8 notes)

Āroha Ascent   Avaroha Descent

SONANT (*Vādī*): D (Ri)   CONSONANT (*Samvādī*): G(Pa)

TIME OF PLAY: first quarter of the night

MODE TYPE (*Thāta*): Kalyāna   SCALE TYPE: diatonic

CHARACTERISTICS: additional ornamental F♯ (Ma t.)

EXPRESSION: pleasing, contented

SHRUTI-'S: expression

tonic	confident, joyful	calm, pleasing	night, calm, loving	intense, mysterious	joyful, active	restless, playful	soft, pleasure loving

THEME (*Rūpa*):

OUTLINE

STHĀYĪ

CHHĀYĀNATA

Chhāyānata, fair-limbed, with a pink turban and, about his throat, a jewelled necklace. How pleasant is his polished speech ! At evening by the roadside, surrounded by friends, a sweet ball of flowers in his hand, bold and amorous with reddened eyes, he laughs aloud at the passers-by.

(Rāga-mālā of Pundarika Vitthala)

GROUP: Kalyāna

TUNING OF INSTRUMENT:

CLASS *(Jāti)*:
Sampūrna (heptatonic)

Āroha Ascent   *Avaroha* Descent

SONANT *(Vādī)*: D(Ri)   **CONSONANT** *(Samvādī)*: G (Pa)

TIME OF PLAY: first quarter of the night

MODE TYPE *(Thāta)*: Khammāja   **SCALE TYPE:** Diatonic

CHARACTERISTICS: both B natural (Ni shuddha) and B♭ (Ni komal). One additional ornamental F♯ (Ma tīvra) very rarely used, and this only in the later part of the development of the rāga. Whenever a motive ends on G(Pa) the next melodic figure should start from D(Ri). B(Ni) is rarely used in ascent.

EXPRESSION: prayer and joy with tenderness. B♭ (Ni k.) means supplication.

SHRUTI-S: **expression**

tonic

confident, joyful

calm, pleasing

peace, loving

joyful, active

soft, aspiration, modest

tender, beautiful, supplication

soft, pleasure-loving

THEME (*Rūpā*):

OUTLINE

STHĀYĪ

ANTARĀ

KEDĀRĀ[1]

Her matted locks are crested with the silver moon, her breast and shoulders wreathed with snakes. Wearing the veil that Yogins use in meditation, her mind immersed in contemplation of the Lord of Sleep upholder of the Ganges, Kedārikā is the rāginī of Dīpaka, the rāga of fire. *(Sangīta-darpana 2, 65 ; Shiva-tattva-ratnākara 6, 8, 93)*

I ever think of Kedārī. A rare book in her hand, she sits, beautifully dressed, in front of the temple of Shiva, Lord of Sleep. *(Rāga-sāgara 3, 41)*

TUNING OF INSTRUMENT:

GROUP: Kalyāna

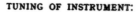

CLASS (*Jāti*): Sampūrṇa (heptatonic)

Āroha Ascent   *Avaroha* Descent:

---

[1] Also known as *Kedārikā, Keduri, Ketārā.*

SONANT (*Vādī*): F natural (Ma)   CONSONANT (*Samvādī*): C(Sa)

TIME OF PLAY: first quarter of the night

MODE TYPE (*Thāta*): Bilāval with both F natural (Ma shuddha) and F♯ (Ma tīvra)

SCALE TYPE: diatonic

CHARACTERISTICS: no D(Ri) and usually no E(Ga) in ascent.   Ornamental sharp F♯ (Ma t.)

EXPRESSION: pleasing, tender

SHRUTI-S: expression

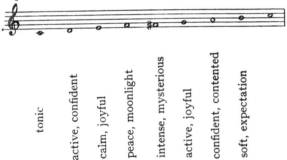

tonic — active, confident — calm, joyful — peace, moonlight — intense, mysterious — active, joyful — confident, contented — soft, expectation

THEME (*Rūpa*):

OUTLINE

STHĀYĪ

BHŪPĀLĪ

High-breasted, her radiant white body reddened with
saffron, her face a heart-entrancing moon. When all is still,
with bitter grief Bhūpālī remembers her absent Lord.

(Rāga-kalpa-druma p. 32 ; *Sangīta-
darpana* 2, 79 ; *Shiva-tattva-ratnākara*
6, 8, 121)

GROUP: Kalyāna

TUNING OF INSTRUMENT:

CLASS (*Jāti*):
Audava (pentatonic)

| *Āroha* Ascent | *Avaroha* Descent |

SONANT (*Vādī*): E₊(Ga₊)   CONSONANT (*Samvādī*): A₊(Dha₊)

SONANT (*Vādī*): $E_+(Ga_+)$ CONSONANT (*Samvādī*): $A_+(Dha_+)$

TIME OF PLAY: second quarter of the night

MODE TYPE (*Thāta*): Bilāval

SCALE TYPE: Chromatic harmonic $(6/5 \times 10/9 = 4/3)$

CHARACTERISTICS: basic Pythagorean pentatonic (as used in Tibetan and
Chinese music)

EXPRESSION:

The rāga of cosmic movement; harmony, contentment, in the dusky oppressive night, the joy of saintly detachment. (Ni (B) is physical pleasure, Ma (F) is loving); the absence of B(Ni) and F(Ma) means non attachment. $E_+(Ga_+)$, meaning confidence, self reliance, in the tender night, is the basis of the expression of Bhūpālī.

satisfaction

G (Pa) is plenitude and $E_+(Ga_+)$ contentment but their union expresses some tenderness, some devotion.

SHRUTI-S: expression

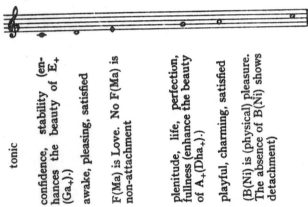

tonic

confidence, stability (enhances the beauty of E_+ $(Ga_+).$)

awake, pleasing, satisfied

F(Ma) is Love. No F(Ma) is non-attachment

plenitude, life, perfection, fullness (enhance the beauty of $A_+(Dha_+).$)

playful, charming, satisfied

B(Ni) is (physical) pleasure. The absence of B(Ni) shows detachment)

THEME (*Rūpā*):

OUTLINE

STHĀYĪ

ANTARĀ

Variation

15. KHAMMĀJA GROUP
(Night, first quarter)

Durgā
Hambīr
Khammāja

DURGĀ

GROUP: Khammāja

TUNING OF INSTRUMENT:

CLASS (*Jāti*): Audava
(Pentatonic)

Āroha Ascent   *Avaroha* Descent

SONANT (*Vādī*): D (Ri)   CONSONANT (*Samvādī*): A (Dha)

TIME OF PLAY: first quarter of the night

MODE TYPE (*Thāta*): Bilāval

SCALE TYPE: Basic chromatic. The lower tetrachord is in the Pythagorean chromatic (the hard chromatic of Greek music), while the higher tetrachord forms the soft chromatic.

CHARACTERISTICS: No E (Ga) and no B (Ni). (Bhātkhande gives a different Durgā in Khammāja Thāta.)

EXPRESSION: Early night, life, joy, energy, as in a dancing child. Pure joy which does not lead to action (no E (Ga)), nor to pleasure (no B (Ni)).

clear night, happy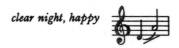

SHRUTI-S: expression

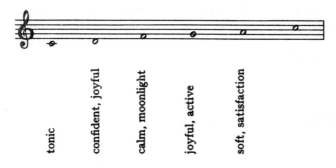

THEME *(Rūpa)*:

OUTLINE

Scale

STHĀYĪ

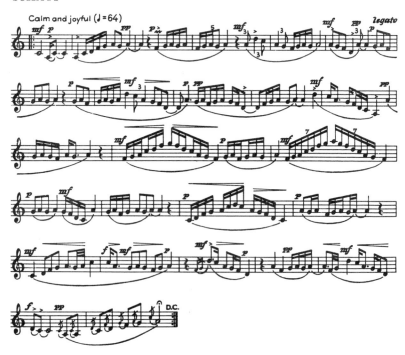

HAMBĪR

"Caressing a vīnā with his lovely hands, Hambīr rāga, a fresh Karnikā-flower at his ear, is seated at the house of rendezvous. The sages call him the image of Desire."

(*Rāga-kalpa-druma*, p. 26)

GROUP: Khammāja

TUNING OF INSTRUMENT:

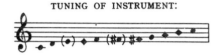

CLASS (*Jāti*): Shādava-sampūrna
(Hexatonic in ascent, heptatonic in descent)

Āroha Ascent   *Avaroha* Descent

SONANT (*Vādī*): E (Ga)　　　　CONSONANT (*Samvādī*): A (Dha)

TIME OF PLAY: first quarter of the night

MODE TYPE (*Thāta*): Kalyāna　　　SCALE TYPE: Diatonic Pythagorean

CHARACTERISTICS: Both F natural (Ma shuddha) and F♯ (MaT). The ascent should always be broken on F (Ma). Scale very similar to Kedārā.

EXPRESSION: Charming and lovely.

SHRUTI-S: expression

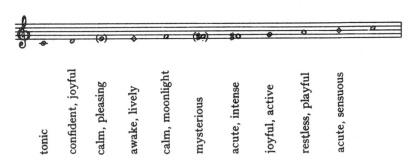

tonic   confident, joyful   calm, pleasing   awake, lively   calm, moonlight   mysterious   acute, intense   joyful, active   restless, playful   acute, sensuous

THEME (*Rūpa*):

OUTLINE

STHĀYĪ

KHAMMĀJA

A lovely girl in the flower of youth, robed in yellow, Kāmbhojikā of the beautiful hair. Searching everywhere in the forest with her maids, the thought of her lover makes her weep with tenderness.

(Shiva-tattva-ratnākara 6, 8, 99)

Bearing arrows of flowers and adorned with the blue lotus, moon-faced Kambhojā, her breasts like lily buds.

(Chatvārimshach'hata-rāga-nirūpanam p. 18)

In a sensuous mood, ever ready to sing, Kāmbhojī holds wooden clappers near her left temple. Her dancing feet seem to write, restless, on the ground. I ever think of her.

(Rāga-sāgara 3, 31)

GROUP: Khammāja

TUNING OF INSTRUMENT:

CLASS (*Jāti*):
Sampūrna (heptatonic)

Āroha Ascent   Avaroha Descent

SONANT (*Vādī*): E(Ga)   CONSONANT (*Samvādī*): B natural (Ni)

TIME OF PLAY: first quarter of the night

MODE TYPE (*Thāta*): Khammāja

SCALE TYPE: Pythagorean diatonic with both B natural (Ni shuddha) and B♭ (Ni komal)

CHARACTERISTICS: both B and B♭ (Ni and Ni k.)

EXPRESSION: early night, tender remembrance of joy, contentment with hope and desire

SHRUTI-S: expression

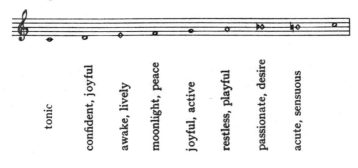

tonic — confident, joyful — awake, lively — moonlight, peace — joyful, active — restless, playful — passionate, desire — acute, sensuous

OUTLINE

STHĀYĪ

ANTARĀ

CHAPTER VI
RĀGA-S OF THE DEEP OF NIGHT

16. KĀNADĀ GROUP
(Second quarter of the night)

Suhā
Sindhurā
Sahānā
Kāfī
Sinddha Kāfī
Kānadā
Bageshrī
Jayajavantī
Bahār

SUHĀ

GROUP: Kānadā

TUNING OF INSTRUMENT:

CLASS (*Jāti*): Audava-shādava
(Pentatonic—hexatonic)

Āroha Ascent   *Avaroha* Descent

SONANT (*Vādi*): C (Sa)   CONSONANT (*Samvādi*): F (Ma)

TIME OF PLAY: second quarter of the night

MODE TYPE (*Thāta*): Kāfī

SCALE TYPE: Basic chromatic, except for the lower descending tetrachord
which is diatonic.

CHARACTERISTICS: No A (no Dha) ; no E (Ga) in ascent.

EXPRESSION: Gay, lovely, light.

SHRUTI-S: expression

tonic   confident, joyful   tender, loving   moonlight, peace   joyful, active   desire, anxiety

THEME (*Rūpa*):

OUTLINE

Scale

STHĀYĪ

Gaily (♩ = 104)

SINDHURĀ (SAINDHAVĪ)

"United in love with Shiva, robed in red and in her hand
the flower of friends, brandishing a trident in the fearful anger
of the hero mood, Saindhavī, the rāginī of Bhairava."

(Shiva-tattva-ratnākara 6, 8, 65)

GROUP: Kānadā

TUNING OF INSTRUMENT:

CLASS (*Jāti*): Audava-sampūrna
(Pentatonic in ascent, heptatonic
in descent)

Āroha Ascent   *Avaroha* Descent

SONANT (*Vādī*): C (Sa)   CONSONANT (*Samvādī*): G (Pa)

TIME OF PLAY: second quarter of the night

MODE TYPE (*Thāta*): Kāfī with an ornamental B natural (shuddha Ni).

SCALE TYPE: Chromatic ascent (with an ornamental B natural) ; mixed
diatonic descent.

CHARACTERISTICS: Both B (Ni) and B♭ (NiK) ; the B natural (Ni shuddha)
being used rarely and only as an ornament from C (Sa).

EXPRESSION: Loving and pleasing.

SHRUTI-S: expression

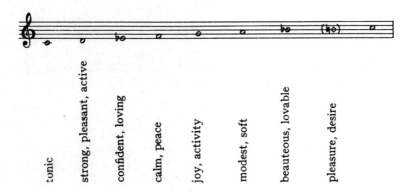

tonic

strong, pleasant, active

confident, loving

calm, peace

joy, activity

modest, soft

beauteous, lovable

pleasure, desire

THEME (*Rūpa*):

OUTLINE

Scale

STHĀYĪ

ANTARĀ

SAHĀNĀ

GROUP: Kānadā

TUNING OF INSTRUMENT:

CLASS (*Jāti*): Audava-sampūrna
(Pentatonic—heptatonic)

Āroha Ascent   *Avaroha* Descent

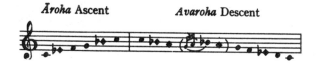

SONANT (*Vādī*): G (Pa)   CONSONANT (*Samvādī*): C (Sa)

TIME OF PLAY: third quarter, after midnight

MODE TYPE (*Thāta*): Kāfī   SCALE TYPE: Diatonic

CHARACTERISTICS: No Ri (D) and no Dha (A) in ascent (āroha). Two distinct
B♭ (NiK), the one in ascending being slightly higher. E♭ (GaK) is always
trembling.

B♭ (NiK) is used only with an ornamental A+ (Dha+) in ascent as in:

This actually is a change of rāga, since
A (Dha) should not be used in ascending, hence the corresponding change in
the expression of the B♭ (NiK).

EXPRESSION: Charming and graceful.

SHRUTI-S: expression

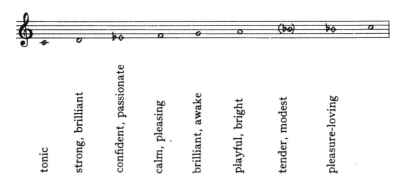

tonic — strong, brilliant — confident, passionate — calm, pleasing — brilliant, awake — playful, bright — tender, modest — pleasure-loving

THEME (*Rūpa*):

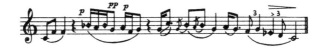

OUTLINE

Scale

STHĀYĪ

Graceful (♩=36)

ANTARĀ

KĀFĪ

Of shining whiteness, Kāpikā who inspires lust tenderly sits
on the lap of her play-mate in the royal palace, fond of parrots
she is dressed in blue and decked with jewels. She is the image
of sensuousness.
In the Lotus of my heart I cherish her, lovelier than Lakshmī
the goddess of Fortune.

(*Rāga-sāgara* 3, 33)

GROUP: Kanadā

TUNING OF INSTRUMENT:

CLASS (*Jāti*): Sampūrṇa
(heptatonic)

Āroha Ascent   *Avaroha* Descent

SONANT (*Vādī*): G(Pa)   CONSONANT (*Samvādī*): C(Sa)

TIME OF PLAY: second quarter of the night

MODE TYPE (*Thāta*) Kāfī   SCALE TYPE: Diatonic

CHARACTERISTICS: the mediaeval unaltered scale

EXPRESSION: light, happy and contented, very gentle and harmonious, no
depth

SHRUTI-S: expression

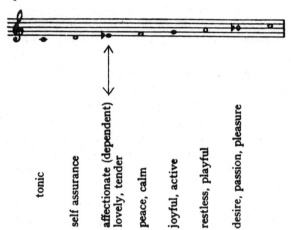

tonic

self assurance

affectionate (dependent)
lovely, tender

peace, calm

joyful, active

restless, playful

desire, passion, pleasure

THEME (*Rūpā*):

OUTLINE

STHĀYĪ

ANTARĀ

SINDDHA KĀFĪ

GROUP: Kānadā

TUNING OF INSTRUMENT:

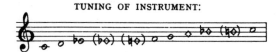

CLASS (*Jati*): Sampūrṇa
(Heptatonic)

Āroha Ascent   *Avaroha* Descent

SONANT (*Vādī*): G (Pa)   CONSONANT (*Samvādī*): C (Sa)

TIME OF PLAY: second quarter of the night

MODE TYPE (*Thāta*): Kāfī   SCALE TYPE: Diatonic (of 9 notes)

CHARACTERISTICS: This is really a mixture of two rāga-s, with an E natural (Ga shuddha) changing into a high E♭ (GaK).

EXPRESSION: Lovely and charming.
In Sinddha-Kāfī, Kāfī-Khammāja and Mishra (mixed)-Kāfī, E+ (Ga+) and B+ (Ni+) give a commanding, passionate and also light-hearted expression.

SHRUTI-S: expression

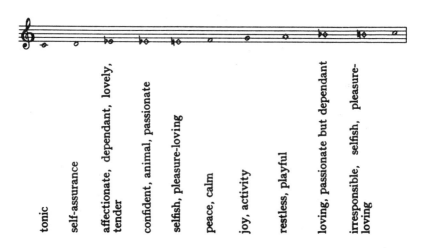

tonic

self-assurance

affectionate, dependant, lovely, tender

confident, animal, passionate

selfish, pleasure-loving

peace, calm

joy, activity

restless, playful

loving, passionate but dependant

irresponsible, selfish, pleasure-loving

THEME (*Rūpa*):

OUTLINE

Scale

STHĀYĪ

Softly (♩=46)

ANTARĀ

KĀNADĀ[1]

With uplifted sword and, in the other hand, the tusk of an elephant, the divine form of Kānadā is lauded by the hosts of heaven.

(Sangīta-darpana 2, 66 ; Shiva-tattva-ratnākara 6, 8, 95)

I see Kānadā a sensuous woman, who plays the stronger part in Love's gentle fights. Her limbs are dark, her ornaments charming and strange. Her open tresses fall to her waist. She remains playfully near a banian tree, her hand caressing the muzzle of a deer.

(Rāga-sāgara 3, 34)

GROUP: Kānadā

TUNING OF INSTRUMENT:

CLASS (*Jāti*): Audava-sampūrna
(pentatonic-heptatonic)

Āroha Ascent　　　　　Avaroha Descent

SONANT (*Vādī*): D(Ri)　　　　　CONSONANT (*Samvādī*): G(Pa)

TIME OF PLAY: second quarter of the night

MODE TYPE (*Thāta*): Yāvanapūrī

SCALE TYPE: Diatonic (with chromatic ascent)

[1] Also called Darbārī

CHARACTERISTICS: very particular style of play [on the Vīnā never use the E(Ga) or A(Dha) keys but pull the string from D(Ri) and G(Pa)]

EXPRESSION:
deep emotion and satisfaction, with some happiness and passion.
E♭ (Ga k.) and A♭ (Dha k.) mean satisfaction, contentment, but the particular shake expresses passion.

E♭(Ga k.) and A♭(Dha k.) are high and light, not heavy as in Yavanāpurī.

D(Ri) renders the expression definite, accurate, clear and precise.

SHRUTI-S: expression

tonic

strong, clear, definite

sensuous, satisfied, happy but with passion (shake)

peace, calm

joy, activity

loving, enterprising, with passion (shake)

pure, noble, beautiful

(desire, anxiety)

THEME (*Rūpā*):

OUTLINE

Scale

STHĀYĪ

ANTARĀ

BAGESHRĪ

Her voice seductive when she is near her lover, Vāgīshvarī is lovely, desirable. With eyes large like the lotus and a flawless pale body, she plays upon the lute her songs of love.

(*Rāga-kalpa-druma* p. 19)

GROUP: Kānadā

CLASS (*Jāti*): Shadava-sampūrna (hexatonic in ascent, heptatonic in descent)

TUNING OF INSTRUMENT:

Āroha Ascent   Avaroha Descent

SONANT (*Vādī*): F(Ma)   CONSONANT (*Samvādī*): C(Sa)

TIME OF PLAY: second quarter of the night

MODE TYPE (*Thāta*): Kāfī

SCALE TYPE: Diatonic (with chromatic and enharmonic ascent)

CHARACTERISTICS: in ascent no G(Pa) and almost no D(Ri)

EXPRESSION: calm and profound night, deep and moving

SHRUTI-S: **expression**

tonic

confident, powerful

tender, loving

peace, calm

(rare) joyful, active

restless, playful

desire, anxiety

THEME (*Rūpă*):

OUTLINE

Scale

STHĀYĪ

JAYAJAVANTĪ

Buxom and comely, with eyes like a gazelle's, her golden skin fragrant with divine flowers, Jayajavantī is the consort of Megha-rāga, god of rains. Drunken, playing upon a lute, she carols like a Kokila.

(Rāga-kalpa-druma p. 33)

Dark of limb, dressed in yellow with a necklace of precious gems, his forehead is elaborately marked with saffron. His body graceful in its triple curve, noble amorous, companion of the God of love whose arrows are of flowers, Jijāvanta plays charmingly a heart-enchanting flute.

GROUP: Kānadā

TUNING OF INSTRUMENT:

CLASS (*Jāti*): Sampūrna (heptatonic)

Āroha Ascent   *Avaroha* Descent

SONANT (*Vādī*): D(Ri)   CONSONANT (*Samvādī*): G(Pa)

TIME OF PLAY: second quarter of the night

MODE TYPE (*Thāta*): Kāfī   SCALE TYPE: Pythagorean diatonic

CHARACTERISTICS: both E natural (Ga shuddha) and E♭ (Ga komal). An ornamental B natural (Ni shuddha) is sometimes used.

EXPRESSION: vigour and tenderness

B natural (Ni shuddha)
is used only in

interrogation,
pleading

helplessness
surrender

SHRUTI-S: expression

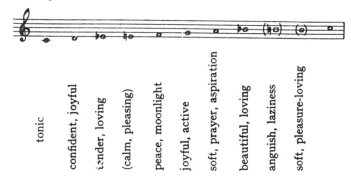

tonic

confident, joyful

tender, loving

(calm, pleasing)

peace, moonlight

joyful, active

soft, prayer, aspiration

beautiful, loving

anguish, laziness

soft, pleasure-loving

THEME (*Rūpă*):

OUTLINE

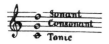 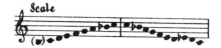

STHĀYĪ

ANTARĀ

BAHĀR

GROUP: Kānadā

CLASS (*Jāti*):
Sampūrna-shadava
(heptatonic in ascent, hexatonic in descent)

TUNING OF INSTRUMENT:

Āroha Ascent   *Avaroha* Descent

SONANT (*Vādī*): C(Sa)   **CONSONANT** (*Samvādī*): F(Ma)

TIME OF PLAY: second quarter of the night

MODE TYPE (*Thāta*): Kāfī   **SCALE TYPE:** Diatonic (peculiar)

CHARACTERISTICS: no Dha (A) in descent, two peculiar B flats (Ni komal). If the B- - is not on the instrument it should be replaced by the higher B♭₊ (Ni k.₊), never by B natural (Ni shuddha).

EXPRESSION: lovely and charming love songs

SHRUTI-S: expression

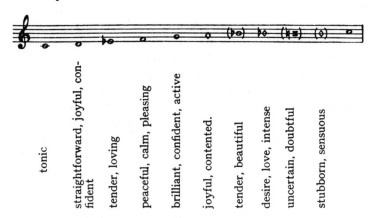

tonic

straightforward, joyful, con-fident

tender, loving

peaceful, calm, pleasing

brilliant, confident, active

joyful, contented.

tender, beautiful

desire, love, intense

uncertain, doubtful

stubborn, sensuous

THEME (*Rūpă*):

OUTLINE

STHĀYĪ

ANTARĀ

CHAPTER VII
RĀGA-S OF MIDNIGHT AND LATE NIGHT

17. MĀLAKOSHA

His mace running with blood, garlanded with the skulls of heroes, Mālakosha, surrounded by braves, and bravest of the brave!

(Rāga-kalpa-druma p. 18 ; *Sangīta-darpaṇa* 2, 52 ;
Shiva-tattva-ratnākara 6, 8, 67)*

GROUP: Malakosha

CLASS (*Jāti*): Audava (Pentatonic)

TUNING OF INSTRUMENT:

Āroha Ascent   *Avaroha* Descent

SONANT (*Vādī*): F(Ma)   CONSONANT (*Samvādī*): C(Sa)

TIME OF PLAY: midnight (but can be played at midday)

MODE TYPE (*Thāta*): Bhairavī

SCALE TYPE: Basic chromatic (of 5 notes)

CHARACTERISTICS: all the flat notes of the chromatic-harmonic

EXPRESSION: prayer, deep, peaceful and sublime. Humble, abandon in the peace of the night.

love    surrender

SHRUTI-S: expression

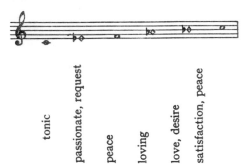

THEME (*Rūpă*):

OUTLINE

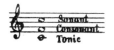

STHĀYĪ

Very slow and expressive (♩ = 72)

ANTARĀ

18. BIHĀGA

TUNING OF INSTRUMENT:

, GROUP: Bihāga

CLASS (*Jāti*):
Audava-sampūrna
(pentatonic-heptatonic)

Āroha Ascent   *Avaroha* Descent

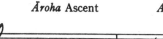 

SONANT (*Vādī*): E(Ga)   CONSONANT (*Samvādī*): B(Ni)

TIME OF PLAY: Midnight (when everyone is asleep)

MODE TYPE (*Thāta*): Kalyāna

SCALE TYPE: mixed (the ascent is enharmonic, the descent diatonic)

CHARACTERISTICS: Both F (Ma) and F♯ (Ma ṭ), no D and A (Ri and Dha) in
ascent

EXPRESSION: melancholy in the calm of night, thirst for enjoyment. (Gauda
Sāranga which has a similar scale is more restful, lovely, and satisfied.)

contentment   *sadness*   *crying*

The combination of F natural (Ma shuddha) and F♯ (Ma tīvra) always
adds to the intensity of the expression whether it is sadness or joy. Here
it shows more intense anguish and desire.

SHRUTI-S: expression

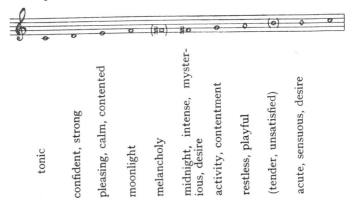

tonic

confident, strong

pleasing, calm, contented

moonlight

melancholy

midnight, intense, mysterious, desire

activity, contentment

restless, playful

(tender, unsatisfied)

acute, sensuous, desire

THEME (*Rūpă*):

OUTLINE

STHĀYĪ

Soothing and quiet (♩=60)

ANTARĀ

19. PARĀJ GROUP
(After midnight)
Parāj
Sohinī

PARĀJ

GROUP: Parāj

TUNING OF INSTRUMENT:

CLASS (*Jāti*): Shādava-sampūrna
(Hexatonic-heptatonic)

Āroha Ascent   *Avaroha* Descent

SONANT (*Vādī*): C(Sa)   CONSONANT (*Samvādī*): G(Pa)

TIME OF PLAY: after midnight

MODE TYPE (*Thāta*): Shrī   SCALE TYPE: Chromatic

CHARACTERISTICS: no D (Ri) in ascent [Bhātkhande gives no Pa(G) in ascent, and begins from the higher Sa(C)]

EXPRESSION: satisfaction, contentment, appeal

SHRUTI-S: expression

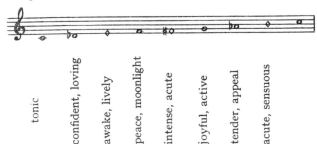

THEME (*Rūpă*):

OUTLINE

STHĀYĪ

ANTARĀ

SOHINĪ

"Tall, virgin, charming, her eyes like lotuses, ears clustered with celestial flowers, Sohanī's is a lovely form. She holds a lute, and her songs are amorous."

(Rāga-kalpa-druma, p. 19)

GROUP: Parāj

TUNING OF INSTRUMENT:

CLASS *(Jāti):* Audava-shādava (Pentatonic in ascent, heptatonic in descent)

Āroha Ascent   *Avaroha* Descent

SONANT *(Vādī):* A (Dha)   CONSONANT *(Samvādī):* E (Ga)

TIME OF PLAY: end of the night (after Parāj, before Kalingadā and Lalitā)

MODE TYPE *(Thāta):* Pūravī (without G (Pa))

SCALE TYPE: Chromatic (special)

CHARACTERISTICS: No G (no Pa), but both F (Ma) and F♯ (MaT). F natural
(Ma shuddha) is used only as an ornament from E (Ga).
Some musicians omit altogether the F natural (Ma shuddha). This F (Ma)
is, however, essential to bring out the expression of late night, or early
dawn.
This F natural (Ma shuddha) is necessary in Sohinī although not in the
similar scale of Vasanta because, in Vasanta, one starts from E (Ga) to
return to E (Ga) without stopping on the A (Dha), while in Sohinī one
stops on A (Dha) in the ascent and, therefore, after F♯ (Ma tīvra), a soft
(natural) F (Ma) is necessary for the balance of the expression.

EXPRESSION: E (Ga) accentuated in the rāga-s of late night expresses the
effort to remain awake. It represents the musician's self which remains
conscious in the middle of the outward dream.

SHRUTI-S: expression

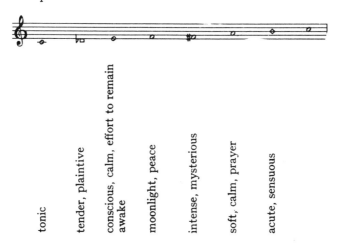

THEME (*Rūpa*):

OUTLINE

STHĀYĪ

20. SHANKARĀ
(At the end of the night)

GROUP: Independent

TUNING OF INSTRUMENT:

CLASS (*Jāti*): Shādava
(Hexatonic)

Āroha Ascent   *Avaroha* Descent

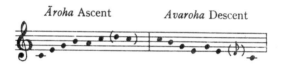

SONANT (*Vādī*): E (Ga)   CONSONANT (*Samvādī*): B (Ni)

TIME OF PLAY: third quarter of the night

MODE TYPE (*Thāta*): Bilāval

SCALE TYPE: Diatonic (defective) ; chromatic and enharmonic in descent.

CHARACTERISTICS: No F (no Ma).

EXPRESSION: Long before dawn, manliness, full satisfaction. carelessness
towards everything.
The dance of Shiva.

SHRUTI-S: expression

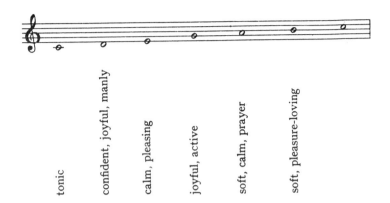

tonic | confident, joyful, manly | calm, pleasing | joyful, active | soft, calm, prayer | soft, pleasure-loving

THEME (*Rūpa*):

OUTLINE

Scale

STHĀYĪ

With humour (♩=60)

ANTARĀ

21. KALINGADĀ
before dawn

ɜROUP: Kalingadā

CLASS (*Jāti*): Shadava-Sampūrna
(Hexatonic-heptatonic)

TUNING OF INSTRUMENT:

Āroha Ascent   *Avaroha* Descent

SONANT (*Vādī*): Ab(Dha k.)   CONSONANT (*Samvādī*): E(Ga)

TIME OF PLAY: early morning, before dawn (before Lalita)

MODE TYPE (*Thāta*): Bhairava   SCALE TYPE: Chromatic

CHARACTERISTICS: $E_+(Ga_+)$ is very much accentuated. (Like all the late
night rāgas (Vasanta, Sohinī, Parāj) Kalingadā begins from the higher
C (Sa)).
E(Ga) is never flat (komal) in late night rāga-s.
(Kalingadā, the rāga of morning twilight, is considered a son of Dīpaka,
the rāga of evening twilight.)

EXPRESSION: E_+ (Ga_+) has a clear, satisfied, expression which seems, however, a disturbance, almost painful, to those who have sung all night and
feel sleepy. E_+ $(Ga_{+\blacklozenge})$ has, therefore, two meanings, sometimes it
shows the musician in good mood and ready to play on, and sometimes
troubled and remaining painfully awake.

SHRUTI-S: **expression**

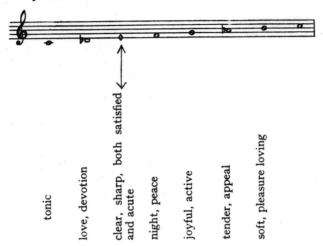

tonic

love, devotion

clear, sharp, both satisfied and acute

night, peace

joyful, active

tender, appeal

soft, pleasure loving

THEME (*Rūpă*):

OUTLINE

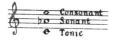 

STHĀYĪ

ANTARĀ

CHAPTER VIII
SEASONAL RĀGA-S

22. SPRING RĀGA-S[1]

Hindola
Vasanta
Panchama

[1] The rāga-s of spring have characteristics similar to the rāga-s of sunrise.

HINDOLA

Dwarf, with the sheen of a dove, on a swing pleasantly placed for play Hindola is gently rocked, the sages say, by women with ample hips.

(Rāga-kalpa-druma p. 20 ; *Sangīta-darpana* 2, 58 ; *Chatvārimshach'hata-rāgā-nirūpanam* p. 20 ; *Shiva-tattva-ratnākara* 6, 8, 79)

Her pale golden body with great hips is fragrant like the flowers of heaven. Well favoured, long-eyed, she holds a lute.

(Rāga-kalpa-druma p. 20)

My heart dreams of Hindolā, whose breasts are firm, dressed in colourful garments.

With the flowers of the Lotus she worships the Lord Krishnǎ who sits on a swing tied to the hanging roots of a banian tree. She listens to the notes of the flute, her heart full of love, her fair limbs covered with jewels.

(Rāga-sāgara 3, 61)

TUNING OF INSTRUMENT:

GROUP: Spring rāga-s

CLASS (*Jāti*): Audava (pentatonic)

Āroha Ascent   *Avaroha* Descent

SONANT (*Vādī*): A+ (Dha+)   CONSONANT (*Samvādī*): E+(Ga+)

TIME OF PLAY: in Spring time (otherwise, morning 2nd half (9 to 12))

MODE TYPE (*Thāta*): Kalyāna

SCALE TYPE: mixed chromatic and enharmonic

CHARACTERISTICS: no D(Ri) and no G(Pa).
More expressive if B (Ni) is also omitted.

EXPRESSION: spring, bursting life, like a war dance. (Hindola means 'swing'.)
No softness. Passionate, but not loving, Hindola is violent. All spring
rāga-s have this same creative impulse yet Panchama is milder and
Vasanta very soft and delicate.

Virile,
rough,
challenging

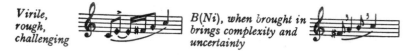

B(Ni), when brought in
brings complexity and
uncertainty

SHRUTI-S: expression

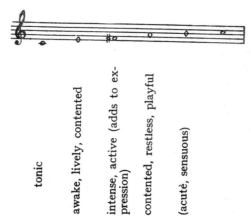

tonic

awake, lively, contented

intense, active (adds to expression)

contented, restless, playful

(acuté, sensuous)

THEME (*Rūpá*):

OUTLINE

STHĀYĪ

ANTARĀ

VASANTA

With ear-rings of mango flower and a high diadem spread wide like the fan of a peacock, her indigo body dark like the black bee, lovely, voluptuous, fortunate, is Vasantī the darling of Spring. *(Rāga-kalpa-druma* p. 20 ; *Sangīta-darpana* 2, 71 ; *Shiva-tattva-ratnākara* 6, 8, 105)

Parrots, Cuckoos and Shāri birds flutter about Vasanta, Lord of Spring, who dances in the garden of Love surrounded by lovely women. His image never leaves my heart.

(Rāga-sāgara 3, 17)

TUNING OF INSTRUMENT:

GROUP: Spring rāga-s

CLASS (*Jāti*): Audava-Shadava (Pentatonic in ascent, hexatonic in descent)

Āroha Ascent   *Avaroha* Descent

SONANT (*Vādī*): C(Sa)   CONSONANT (*Samvādī*): F♯ (Ma t.)

TIME OF PLAY: Spring time

MODE TYPE (*Thāta*): Pūravī   SCALE TYPE: Chromatic

CHARACTERISTICS: no fifth (no Pa)

EXPRESSION: the feminine aspect of spring. F(Ma) and D♭- (Ri k.) are very womanly and delicate.

D♭-(Ri k.-) is very tender (and very prominent) in this rāga. B₊ (Ni₊) is clear and sincere (B (Ni) would be hazy insincere) the use of both F natural (Ma shuddha) and F♯ (Ma tīvra) always accentuates the expression. The relation between D♭-(Ri k.-) and F natural (Ma) brings great delicacy. All melodic figures begin from E (Ga) and end on D♭-(Re k.-).

SHRUTI-S: expression

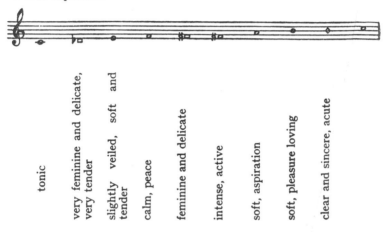

tonic

very feminine and delicate, very tender

slightly veiled, soft and tender

calm, peace

feminine and delicate

intense, active

soft, aspiration

soft, pleasure loving

clear and sincere, acute

THEME (*Rūpă*):

OUTLINE

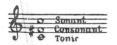

STHĀYĪ

With delicacy and phantasy

ANTARĀ

PANCHAMA

"Golden, with blood-red scarf, his ruddy eyes wide open
and heavenly blossoms at his ears, this amorous youth,
victorious, dear to all, the very form of Love, talks charmingly
᾿ᵛᵉ the Kokila-bird at dawn."

(Sangīta-darpana 2, ⁹8)

GROUP: Spring rāga-s

TUNING OF INSTRUMENT:

CLASS (*Jātī*): Audava-shādava
(Pentatonic in ascent, hexatonic in descent)

Āroha Ascent   *Avaroha* Descent

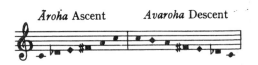

SONANT (*Vādī*): F♯ (MaT)   CONSONANT (*Samvādī*): C (Sa)

TIME OF PLAY: night

MODE TYPE (*Thāta*): Māravā   SCALE TYPE: Chromatic

CHARACTERISTICS: No fifth note (no Pa), same scale as Vibhāsa. D (Ri) is
light (not accentuated).

EXPRESSION: The sonant F♯ (MaT) seems bashful while the consonant is the
elegant and manly young god of spring. C (Sa) is strong and energetic.
E+ (Ga+) in Panchama is energetic, active, joyful (E (Ga) in Vasanta is
slightly veiled, soft and tender).

challenge

SHRUTI-S: expression

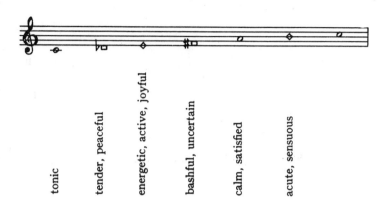

tonic

tender, peaceful

energetic, active, joyful

bashful, uncertain

calm, satisfied

acute, sensuous

THEME (*Rūpa*):

OUTLINE

Scale

STHĀYĪ

ANTARĀ

23. RĀGA-S OF THE RAINY SEASON[1]

Mīyān Mallār
Desha Mallār
Gauda Mallār
Surat Mallār
Shuddha Mallār
Megha Mallār[1]

[1] The scales of Mallār (mid-year) always resemble those of Sāranga (midday).

MĪYĀN MALLĀR

GROUP: Mallār
(rainy season)

TUNING OF INSTRUMENTS:

CLASS (*Jāti*): Audava-sampūrna
(Pentatonic in ascent and
heptatonic in descent)

Āroha Ascent   *Avaroha* Descent

SONANT (*Vādī*): C (Sa)

CONSONANT (*Samvādī*): F (Ma)

TIME OF PLAY: rainy season

MODE TYPE (*Thāta*): Kāfī

SCALE TYPE: Pythagorean diatonic (first plagal mode), with chromatic ascent.

CHARACTERISTICS: No E (Ga) is ascent. Mīyān Mallār is a combination of Mallār and Jayajavantī, a Mallār played in Darbārī style.

EXPRESSION: (Shuddha Mallār and Megha Mallār combined) Monsoon rains, passionate and happy although more melancholy than Dhānī which has a similar scale.

D (Ri) *comforts*

SHRUTI-S: expression

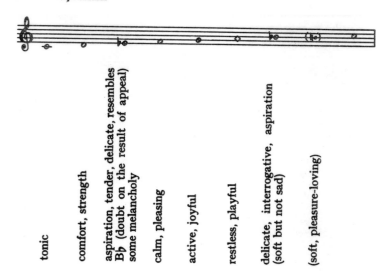

tonic

comfort, strength

aspiration, tender, delicate, resembles
B♮ (doubt on the result of appeal)
some melancholy

calm, pleasing

active, joyful

restless, playful

delicate, interrogative, aspiration
(soft but not sad)

(soft, pleasure-loving)

THEME (*Rūpa*):

OUTLINE

STHĀYĪ

ANTARĀ

DESHA MALLĀR

GROUP: (Mallār
(rainy season)

TUNING OF INSTRUMENT:

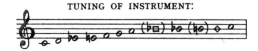

CLASS (*Jāti*): Audava-sampūrna
(Pentatonic in ascent and
heptatonic in descent)

Āroha Ascent   *Avaroha* Descent

SONANT (*Vādī*): D (Ri)

CONSONANT (*Samvādī*): G (Pa)

TIME OF PLAY: rainy season

MODE TYPE (*Thāta*): Kāfī with additional E and B natural (Ga and Ni shuddha).

SCALE TYPE: Complete diatonic of 9 notes (with chromatic-enharmonic ascent).

CHARACTERISTICS: It is the first mūrch'hanā (plagal mode) of the full diatonic scale of 9 notes (with Kākalī Ni and Antara Ga).

EXPRESSION: Monsoon, rains, passion, love, desire; the question of the love's acceptance depends upon the presence of E (Ga).

SHRUTI-S: expression

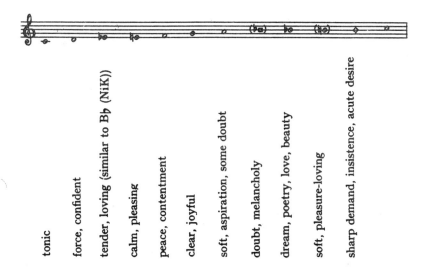

tonic

force, confident

tender, loving (similar to B♭ (NiK))

calm, pleasing

peace, contentment

clear, joyful

soft, aspiration, some doubt

doubt, melancholy

dream, poetry, love, beauty

soft, pleasure-loving

sharp demand, insistence, acute desire

THEME (*Rūpa*):

OUTLINE

STHĀYĪ

ANTARĀ

GAUDA MALLĀR

TUNING OF INSTRUMENT:

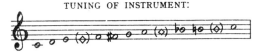

CLASS (*Jāti*): Sampūrna
(Heptatonic)

Āroha Ascent   *Avaroha* Descent

SONANT (*Vādi*): F (Ma) and also E (Ga)

TIME OF PLAY: rainy season

CONSONANT (*Samvādi*): C (Sa)
and also A (Dha)

MODE TYPE (*Thāta*): mixed Yaman and Khammāja (this is but the plagal
mode of F (Ma mūrch'hanā) in the diatonic of 9 notes (with Kākali Ni
and Antara Ga).

SCALE TYPE: Diatonic

CHARACTERISTICS: Uses both F (Ma) and F♯ (MaT), and both B natural
(Ni shuddha) and B flat (NiK) and, according to motives, two distinct
vādi-s and two samvādi-s, these being sometimes F and C (Ma and Sa)
and sometimes E and A (Ga and Dha).

F♯ (MaT) is very rare ; so is B♭ (NiK). This rāga is often played without
B♭ (NiK). The F♯ (MaT) is just an ornament from G (Pa); it is, however,
indispensable for the rāga while B♭ (NiK) can be dispensed with.

EXPRESSION: Rains, beauty and charm, the end of the monsoon with altern-
ance of rain (Mallār) and sunshine (Gauda-Sāranga).
Combination of diatonic harmonic based on the scale of C (Sa mūrch'hanā)
and of diatonic Pythagorean based on the Ma mūrch'hanā (scale of F):
Gauda Mallār receives, by the subtle contrast of these two scales (residing in
the difference of one comma occurring on E, A and B (Ga, Dha and Ni)), a
peculiar versatility and charm.

SHRUTI-S: expression

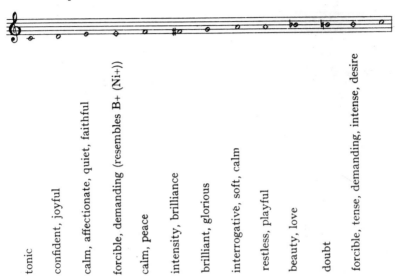

- tonic
- confident, joyful
- calm, affectionate, quiet, faithful
- forcible, demanding (resembles B+ (Ni+))
- calm, peace
- intensity, brilliance
- brilliant, glorious
- interrogative, soft, calm
- restless, playful
- beauty, love
- doubt
- forcible, tense, demanding, intense, desire

THEMÉ (*Rūpa*):

OUTLINE

STHĀYĪ

ANTARĀ

SURAT MALLĀR

GROUP: Mallār (Rāga-s of the rainy season)

TUNING OF INSTRUMENT:

CLASS (*Jāti*): Shādava-sampūrna (Hexatonic in ascent and pentatonic in descent)

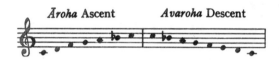

Āroha Ascent   *Avaroha* Descent

SONANT (*Vādī*): A (Dha)   **CONSONANT** (*Samvādī*): D (Ri)

TIME OF PLAY: rainy season

MODE TYPE (*Thāta*): Khammāja   **SCALE TYPE:** Diatonic

CHARACTERISTICS: Resembles Desha Mallār, but has only B flat (NiK) and no B natural (Ni shuddha). E (Ga) should be very light, never should one stop on it.

EXPRESSION: Rains
F (Ma) always means satisfaction, peace

heavy emotion, search for enjoyment, call to the playmates.

SHRUTI-S: expression ·

tonic

powerful, satisfied, contented, self-confident

calm, pleasing

peace. satisfaction

joy, activity (enchances A (Dha))

very joyful

beautiful, loving, tender

THEME (*Rūpa*):

OUTLINE

Scale

STHĀYĪ

With peaceful contentment (♩=48)

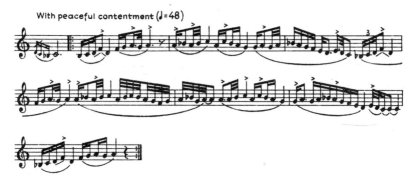

ANTARĀ

SHUDDHA MALLĀR

Pale and weak, her voice like the song of the kokila-bird, some cadence reminds her of her lord. Clasping her lute, Mallārikā cries out in misery—heart-anguished with the pain of youth.

(Sangīta-darpana 2, 77; Shiva-tattva-ratnākara 6, 8, 117)

I meditate upon Malahārī, who constantly worships Shiva, the Lord of Sleep. Pure, She rests surrounded with the lotuses of the cool season below the divine tree of ages. Her pure, pale body has the glow of the winter clouds.

(Rāga-sāgara 3, 7)

GROUP: Mallār (Rainy season)

TUNING OF INSTRUMENT:

CLASS (*Jati*): Audava
(pentatonic)

Āroha Ascent   *Avaroha* Descent

SONANT (*Vadī*): Sa (C)   CONSONANT (*Samvādī*): Ma (F)

TIME OF PLAY: Rainy season

MODE TYPE (*Thāta*): Bilāval   SCALE TYPE: Chromatic

CHARACTERISTICS: no Ga (E) no Ni (B)

EXPRESSION: rains, monsoon.   Manly.   It is the less delicate of Mallār-s. It has no flattened notes, hence no tenderness or melancholy.   All the notes give a feeling of determination, even A(Dha) which is soft but without hesitation.

Expression of rains in all Mallār-s    Lightning

SHRUTI-S: expression

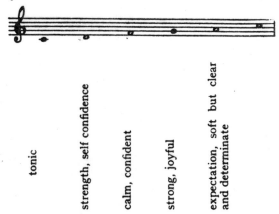

tonic

strength, self confidence

calm, confident

strong, joyful

expectation, soft but clear and determinate

THEME (*Rūpă*):

OUTLINE

STHĀYĪ

ANTARĀ

MEGHA MALLĀR

The ancients tell of Megha rāga, lustrous like a blue lotus, the divine smile of his moon-like face is sweeter than ambrosia. Clothed in yellow in the midst of heavy clouds, he shines among the heroes. The thirsty Chātaka-birds that drink only raindrops, at the sight of him cry out for water.

(Sangīta-darpana 2, 76 ;
Shiva-tattva-ratnākara 6, 8, 119)

Ever should Megha ranjinī be praised who brings flower garlands for the worship of Indra god of rains. Her body looks like lightning ; a blue veil enhances her beautiful hips.

(Rāga-sāgara 3, 3)

GROUP: (Rāga-s of the rainy season)

TUNING OF INSTRUMENT:

CLASS (*Jāti*): Audava-shādava (Pentatonic-hexatonic)

Āroha Ascent   *Avaroha* Descent

SONANT (*Vādī*): Sa (C)   CONSONANT (*Samvādī*): Ma (F)

TIME OF PLAY: at night, or at all times during the rainy season

MODE TYPE (*Thāta*): Khammāja   SCALE TYPE: Chromatic

CHARACTERISTICS: no A(Dha); E(Ga) only used as ornament of F(Ma). Portamento (Mīda) between Ri and Pa (D and G).

EXPRESSION: monsoon, rains, commanding, deep, happy

Rains
(*pleasing,*
calming)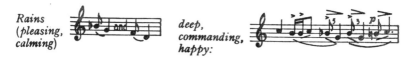

deep,
commanding,
happy:

expectation

satisfaction

sharp, like
the throwing
of an arrow

SHRUTI-S: expression

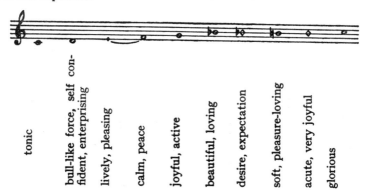

tonic

bull-like force, self confident, enterprising

lively, pleasing

calm, peace

joyful, active

beautiful, loving

desire, expectation

soft, pleasure-loving

acute, very joyful

glorious

THEME (*Rūpā*):

OUTLINE

 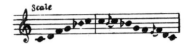

STHĀYĪ

ANTARĀ

BIBLIOGRAPHY

I. SANSKRIT WORKS, PUBLISHED

Mānduki Shikshā (Atharva Veda).
Benares Sanskrit Series, 1893.
Nāradīya Shikshā (of Nārada) (Sāma Veda) (w'th the Shikshā Vivarana, commentary of Shrī Bhatta Shubhākara).
Benares Sanskrit Series, 1893. Mysore, 1946.
Gītālamkara (of Bharata) edited with French translation and notes by Alain Daniélou and N. R. Bhatt.
Pondicherry 1959.
Nātya Shāstra (of Bharata) (chapters 28, 29 and 38 deal with Music).
text only: Benares 1929.
With text and commentary of Abhinava Gupta: Baroda 1926-1964, in four parts.
Asiatic Society edition with English translation by Manamohan Ghosh, Calcutta 1961.
Rudra-damarūdbhava-sūtra-vivarana (of Nandikeshvara?).
"New Indian Antiquary", June 1943.
Bharatārnava (of Nandikeshvara) with English and Tamil translations.
Tanjore, 1957.
Brihaddeshī (of Matanga).
Trivandrum Sanskrit Series, 1928.
Vishnu-dharmottara Purāna (Part III, chs. 18-19).
Bombay, 1912.
Vāyu Purāna (chs. 24 and 25).
Poona, 1905.
Mārkandeya Purāna (ch. 23).
Mathura, 1941.

SECOND PERIOD

Dattilam (of Dattila-āchārya) (mentioned in Nātya Shāstra).
Trivandrum Sanskrit Series, 1930.
Sangīta-makarandah (of Nārada).
Baroda, 1920.
Chatvārimshach'hata-rāga-nirūpanam (of Nārada).
Bombay, 1914.
Amara Kosha (of Amara Simha), second or third century A.D.
(With commentaries: Amarakoshodghātana of Kshīrasvāmin and Tīkāsarvasva of Sarvānanda.)
Kudimiyamālai Inscription (Pudukottai).
Seventh century.

376

Bharata Bhāshya (of Nānya Bhūpāla, c. A.D. 1097) with Hindi commentary
by Pundarika Desaī, Vol. 1 (chs. 1 to 5).
Delhi, 1961.
Mānasollāsa or Abhilāshitārtha-chintāmani (an encyclopedia with chapter on
music of Someshvara Deva, 1131).
Baroda
Rāga-tarangiṇī (of Lochana Kavi, 1160 or 1700).
Bombay, Darbhanga. ·
Sangīta-samaya-sāra (of Parshva Deva, twelfth century).
Trivandrum Sanskrit Series, 1925.
Sangīta Chūdāmani (of Jagadekamalla, 1138-1150).
Baroda ,1958.
Bhāva-prakāsha (of Shāradātanaya, twelfth century) (ch. 7).
Baroda, 1930.
Sangīta-ratnākara.
(of Shārngadeva, thirteenth century.)
Ānandāshrama, Poona, 1897; and Adyar Library, 1943.
(Commentary of Kallinātha, fifteenth century).
(Commentary of Simhabhūpāla, fourteenth century) Adyar ed. only.
Sangītopanishad-saroddhara (of Sudhākalasha, 1350).
Baroda.
Brihaddharma Purāna. (ch. 44).
Calcutta ed.

Abhinava-tāla-manjarī
(of Appā Tulsi, modern).
Bombay, c. 1920.
Abhinava-rāga-manjarī
(of Vishnu Sharmā (Pt. Bhātkhande) modern).
Bombay, 1921.
Anūpa-sangīta-ankusha
(of Bhāva Bhatta, seventeenth century).
Bombay, c. 1916.
Anūpa-sangīta-ratnākara
(of Bhāva Bhatta, seventeenth century).
Bombay, c. 1916.
Anūpa-sangīta-vilāsa
(of Bhāva Bhatta, seventeenth century).
Bombay, 1921.
Ashtottara-shata-tāla-lakshanam.
Bombay, early twentieth century.
Bāhattara-melakartā
(of Venkata Makhin, c. 1620).
Adyar, 1938.
Chaturdandī-prakāshikā
(of Venkata Makhin, c. 1620).
Madras, 1934.
Hridaya-kautuka
(of Hridaya Nārāyana, c. 1667).
Bombay, c. 1920.

Hridaya-prakāsha
(of Hridaya Nārāyana, c. 1667).
Bombay, c. 1920.
Nartana-nirnaya
(of Pundarīka Vitthala, sixteenth century).
Bombay, early twentieth century.
Nrityādhyaya
(of Ashokamalla, c. 15th century).
Baroda, 1963.
Rāga-chandrikā
(of Appā Tulsi, modern).
Bombay, 1911.
Rāga-kalpa-druma
(of Krishnānanda Vyāsa).
In Bengali and Hindi scripts, Calcutta, 1842.
Rāga-kalpa-drumānkura
(of Appā Tulsi, modern).
Bombay, 1914.
Rāga-lakshanam
(of Venkata Makhin, c. 1620).
Madras, early twentieth century.
Rāga-mālā
(of Pundarīka Vitthala, sixteenth century).
Bombay, c. 1916 (Mss. Poona).
Rāga-manjarī
(of Pundarīka Vitthala, sixteenth century).
Bombay, c. 1916.
Rāga-tattva-vibodha
(of Shri Nivāsa, late seventeenth century).
Bombay, c. 1916 and Graekwad's Oriental Series, 1956.
Rāga-vibodha
(of Somanatha, 1610).
Lahore, 1910; Madras 1945.
Rasa-kaumudī
(of Shri Kantha, eighteenth or nineteenth century). Gaekwad's Oriental
Series, 1963.
Sāhitya-sangīta-nirūpanam
(same work as Sangīta-mālā, Mss. dated 1778).
Delhi, 1817.
Samgraha-chūdāmani
(of Govinda).
Adyar, 1938.
Sangīta-āditya.
Baroda, early twentieth century.
Sangīta-darpana
(of Dāmodara Mishra, 1625).
Calcutta, 1880.
Sang. Darp. (abbreviation).
Sangīta Dāmodara
(of Subhankara, c. 15th century).
Calcutta, 1960.

Sangīta-gangā-dharana
(of Nangarāja).
Belgaum, 1936.
Sangīta-kritayah
(of Rāma Varmā Mahārāja).
Trivandrum, 1932.
Sangīta-pārijāta
(of Ahobala, thirteenth or seventeenth century).
Calcutta, 1884.
Sangīta rāja
(of Kumbhakarna, 15th century.) Vol. 1ᐧ
Benares University, 1963.
Sangīta-sampradāya-pradarshinī
(a compilation from Venkata Makhin).
Ettayapuram, early twentieth century.
Sangīta-sārāmritam
(of King Tulajendra Bhonsale of Tanjore, (1729–35)).
Madras Music Acad., 1942.
Sangīta (sāra) sangraha
(of Ghanashyāma Naraharidāsa)
edited with notes by Swami Prajnānanā-nanda, Calcutta.
Sangīta-sāra-sangraha
(of Sourindro Mohan Tagore).
Calcutta, 1875.
Sangīta-sudhā
(of King Raghunātha of Tanjore, 1614).
Madras Music Acad., 1940.
Sangīta-sudhākara
(of Appā Tulsi, modern).
Bombay, 1917.
Shadrāga-chandrodaya
(of Pundarīka Vitthala, sixteenth century).
Bombay, early twentieth century (Mss. Poona).
Shiva-tattva-ratnākara
(an encyclopedia of Bāsava Rājā, 1798-1815).
Madras, 1927. Sh. tat. Ratn. (abbreviation).
Shrimallakshya-sangītam
(a compilation from older texts).
By Vishnu Sharmā (Pt. Bhātkhande).
Bombay, 1910.
Svaramela-kalānidhi
(of Rāmāmātya, 1550).
Annamalai University, 1932.
Svar. Kal. (abbreviation).
Vīnā Lakshana
(of Parameshvara, 15th-18th century).
Baroda, 1959.
Vīnā Prapāthaka
(17th cent.)
Baroda, 1959.

II. SANSKRIT WORKS, UNPUBLISHED

From the following libraries:
Adyar Library
Central Library, Baroda
Maharajah of Benares
Maharajah of Bikaner
Royal Asiatic Society, Calcutta
Government Sanskrit College, Calcutta
Maharajah of Kashmir
India Office Library, London
Govt. Oriental Library, Madras
Govt. Oriental Library, Mysore
The Bodleian Library, Oxford
Palace Library, Tanjore
Palace Library, Trivandrum
Bhandarkar Oriental Institute, Poona,
etc.*

Copies of most of these works are available in the author's personal library at the International Institute for Comparative Music Studies in Berlin.

* A few known works often considered lost but which Mr. O. C. Gangoly (in *Rāgas and Rāginīs*, London, Bombay, 1948) say he has consulted are mentioned here with due reference.

Abhilashitārtha-chintāmani
(of King Someshvara, 1131), an encyclopedia with a large section on music.
(Mysore, Baroda).
Abhinava-bharata-sāra
(Mysore).
Abhinava-bhārati
(of Abhinava Gupta)
(Madras, Trivandrum).
Same work as Nātya Veda-vivritti.
Ādi-bharata
(Mysore, Tanjore).
Telugu script. Incomplete.
Ānanda-(san)jīvana or Ānanda-sanjīvanī Sangīta
(of Madanapala, 1528).
(Bikaner, Calcutta).
Angahāra-lakshana
(Trivandrum).
Arjunādimata-sāra
(of Shuddha Sattva Venkatāchārya).
(Madras). Incomplete.
Arjuna-bharata
(of Arjuna).
(Tanjore). Incomplete.
Aumapatam-gīta-shāstram
(later than ninth century).
(Madras). Incomplete.

Bālarāma-bharata
    (of Bālarāma Kulashekhara Varmā, 1798–1810).
    (Madras, Trivandrum).
Bharata-arnava
    (of Nandikeshvara)
    (Madras, Tanjore).
    Same work as Nandi-bharata.
Bharata-arnava-sangraha
    (Grantha script)
    (Tanjore).
Bharata-artha-chandrikā
    (of Nandikeshvara) with Telugu comm.
    (Madras).
Bharata-bhāshya or sangīta-sarasvatī-hridayālamkāra
    (of Nānya Deva, twelfth century).
    (Poona).
Bharata-gāna-shāstra
    (Calcutta).
Bharata-lakshanam
    (Tanjore).
    A late compilation.
Bharata-nāma-dipaka Nada-shāstram
    (Nepal).
Bharata-sarvārtha-grantha
    (of Mudumbai Narasimhachariar).
    (Madras).
Bharata-sāra
    (Mysore).
Bharata Shāstra
    (anon.) (India Office).
Bharata Shāstra
    (of Raghunātha)
    (Tanjore).
Bharata Shāstra
    (of Tulajādhipa).
    (Tanjore). A late compilation.
Bharata Shāstra-grantha
    (of Lakshmīdhara, sixteenth century).
    (Poona).
Dattila-Kohalīyam
    (Tanjore).
Dakshinī Rāga-mālā
    (Poona). See Rāga-mālā.
Gamaka-manjarī
    (Bikaner).
Gāna Shāstra
    (Calcutta).
Gāndharva-vidyā or Veda
    (Calcutta).
Gīta-prakāsha
    (sixteenth century).
    (Madras). Oriya script.
Gīta-sangraha
    (Calcutta).

Gīta-sāra
    (Calcutta).
Hanumanta-rāga-vibhāshā
    (Bikaner).
Jātih
    (Tanjore).
Kalpatarutīkā
    (of Ganesha Deva) (Bikaner).
    Same work as Subodhinī.
Kohala-rahasya
    (Madras). Incomplete.
Kohalīya Abhinaya-shāstra
    (Madras).
    With Telugu comm.
Māna-manoranjana
    (of Māyā Shankara)
    (Baroda).
Mānasollāsa or Abhilāshitārtha-chintāmani
    (of Someshvara Deva, 1131).
    (Baroda).
Matanga-bharata
    (of Lakshmanarya) (Tanjore).
    An incomplete work on Matanga Bharata.
Melādhikāra-lakshanam
    (Tanjore).
    Not earlier than eighteenth century.
Mela-rāga-svara-sangraha
    (Oppert's catalogue of South India).
Mukhādi-chālī
    (Bikaner).
Muralī-prakāsha
    (of Bhāva Bhatta, c. 1700)
    (Bikaner).
Nandi-bharata
    (of Nandikeshvara)
    (Mysore).
    Same work as Bharata-arnava.
Nāda-dipaka
    (Benares).
Nashtoddishta-prabodhaka Dhraupada-tīkā
    (of Bhāva Bhatta, c. 1700) (Bikaner).
Nātya-sarvasva-dīpikā
    (of Rāmānanda yogin).
    (Poona).
Nātya-chūdāmani
    (of Somanarya, c. 1650).
    (Madras).
Nātya-lochana
    (ninth century).
    (O.C. Gangoly's bibliography).
Nātya Veda
    (Trivandrum).

Nātya Veda-āgama
(of Tulaja rājā, c. 1729–35).
Telugu script
(Tanjore). Incomplete.
Nātya Veda-vivritti
(Trivandrum, Madras, Poona, Benares).
Abhinava Gupta, tenth century comm. on Nātya Shāstra.
Same work as Abhinava-bhārati.
Nritta-ratnāvalī
(of Jayasena, c. 1235).
(Calcutta, Tanjore).
Nrittāla Purāna
(Madras).
Nritya-adhyāya
(of Ashoka Malla)
(Bikaner).
Nritya-nirnaya
(attributed to Pundarīka Vitthala, c. 1590)
(Tanjore).
Oddisha Mahāmantrodaya
(Madras).
Same work as Tāla-vidhāna.
Panchama-sāra Samhitā
(of Nārada) (Calcutta).
(Mss. dated 1440).
Rāga-bodha-viveka
(of Somanātha).
(Adyar).
Rāga-chūdāmani
(Calcutta).
Rāga-dhyāna
(Bikaner).
Rāgādivichārah
(Tanjore).
Rāga-kāvya-ratna
(Bikaner).
Rāga-mālā
(of Jīvarāja Dīkshita).
(Poona, Calcutta).
Rāga-mālā
(of Kshemakarna).
(Oxford, Bikaner).
Rāga-mālā
(of Meshakarna).
(Calcutta).
(Mss. dated 1509).
Rāga-mālā
(Dakshinī).
(Poona).
Rāga-lakshmāni
(India Office).
Rāga-pradīpa
(Madras).

Rāga-prastāra
(Tanjore).
Rāga-rāginī svarūpānī
(Poona).
Rāga-ratna
(of Mānikya)
(Calcutta).
Rāga-ratnākara
(of Gandharva Rāja)
(Tanjore).
Rāgārnava
(Anonymous, earlier than 1300).
(O.C. Gangoly's bibliography).
Rāgārnava-nirūpanam
(Madras).
Rāga-sāgaram
(a dialogue between Nārada and Dattila).
Telugu script (Madras).
Rāga-sārāvalī
(Benares).
Rāga-tattva-vichāra
(of Shrīrāma Malla)
(Bikaner).
Rāga-varna nirūpanam.
Telugu script
(Madras).
Rāga-vibodha-viveka
(Bikaner).
Rāga-vishaya
(Madras).
Rāgotpatti
(Oppert's catalogue of South India).
Rāghava-prabandha
(Tanjore).
Rāma-kautuhala
(of Rāma Krishna Bhatta)
(Bikaner).
Same work as Sangīta-sāroddhāra.
Ratnākara Vyākhyā
(Mysore).
Ratna-mālā
(of Jāthara Bhūpati)
(Bikaner).
Ratna-mālā
(of Kshemakarna)
(Bikaner).
Same work as Rāga-mālā
Rasārnava-sudhākara
(Trivandrum).
Sangāna-sāgara
(of Shubhākara, 1308).
(Calcutta).
Sangīta-adhyāya
(Madras).

Sangīta-amrita
    (of Kamala Lochana, fifteenth century ?)
    (Aufrecht's cat.)
Sangīta-anūpa-rāga-sāgara
    (Bikaner).
Sangīta-bhāskara
    (of Vangamani, seventeenth century)
    (Nepal).
Sangīta-chandra
    (of Abhilasa, seventeenth century).
    (Nepal).
Sangīta-chandrikā
    (of Mādhava Bhatta, earlier than 1614).
    (Tanjore).
Sangīta-chintāmani
    (of Vema Bhūpālā, fourteenth century).
    (Trivandrum).
Sangīta-chintāmani
    (of Kamala Lochana, fifteenth century).
    (Calcutta, Tanjore).
Sangīta-chūdāmani
    (of Kavi Chakravarti)
    (Baroda).
Sangīta-chūdāmani
    (of Haripāla Mahīpati).
    (Mysore).
Sangīta-chūdāmani
    (Trivandrum).
Sangīta-darpana
    (of Haribhatta).
    (Bikaner, Madras, Tanjore).
Sangīta-kalānidhi
    (of Haribhatta, seventeenth century).
    (N.W. Province cat.)
Sangīta-kalpa-druma
    (Calcutta).
Sangīta-kalpa-latā
    (Calcutta).
Sangīta-kalpa-taru
    (Bikaner).
Sangīta-kāmadah
    (Adyar).
    Oriya script.
Sangīta-kaumudī
    (of King Sanasena).
    (Madras).
Sangīta-kautuka
    (Calcutta).
Sangīta-lakshana
    (Mysore).
Sangīta-lakshana-dīpikā
    (of Gauranārya).
    (Mysore).

Sangīta-makaranda
   (of Veda, seventeenth century)
   (Bikaner, Poona, Tanjore).
Sangīta-mālā
   (Mss.dated 1778).
   Same work as Sāhitya-sangīta-nirūpanam, publ. Delhi, 1817.
Sangīta-mīmānsā
   Same work as Sangīta-rāja.
Sangīta-muktāvalī
   (of Devendra, c. 1420).
   (Bikaner, Tajore).
Sangīta-nārāyana
   (of Nārāyana Deva).
   (Kashmir, Oxford).
Sangīta-nārāyana
   (of Purushottama Mishra).
   (Calcutta).
Sangīta-nārāyana
   (of King Nārāyana, eighteenth century).
   (Madras).
Sangīta-nritya
   (of Shārngadeva Suri).
   (Oudh cat.).
Sangīta-nrityākāra
   (of Bharatāchārya).
   (Oudh cat.).
Sangīta-padyāvalī
   (Mysore).
Sangīta-pushpānjali
   (of Veda, seventeenth century).
   (Bikaner, Tanjore).
Sangīta-rāga-kalpadruma
   (of Krishnānanda Vedavyāsa).
   (Poona).
Sangīta-rāghava
   (of Chinabommabhūpāla).
   Telugu script.
   (Tanjore).
Sangīta-raghunānanda
   (of Vishvarātha Simha).
   (Adyar, Benares).
Sangīta-rāja
   (of Kumbharkarna, 1433–1468).
   (Cent. Prov. and Poona).
Sangīta-rāja-ratnakosha
   (Bikaner).
Sangīta rāma-kautuka
   (Bikaner).
Sangīta-rasa-kaumudī
   (Baroda, Calcutta).
Sangīta-ratnākara
   (of Varunaka).
   (Bikaner).

Sangīta-ratnākara
(of Vitthala).
(Poona).
Sangīta-ratnākara-vyākhyā-setuh
(of Gangārāma).
(see: Hindi).
Sangīta-ratna-mālā
(of Mammata, 1050–1150).
(O.C. Gangoly's bibliography).
Sangīta-ratnāvalī
(Baroda, Calcutta).
Sangīta-sāgara
(of Pratāpa Simha, 1779–1804).
(Jaipur ?)
Sangīta-saṅgraha
(Calcutta).
Sangīta-sangraha-chintāmani
(of Appala-Āchārya, nineteenth century).
(Adyar).
Sangīta-sārā
(of Harināyaka, c. 1500).
(O.C. Gangoly's bibliography).
Sangīta-sārā
(late eighteenth century).
(Bikaner).
Sangīta-sārakalikā
(of Shuddha Svarnakara Mosha Deva).
(Bikaner).
Sangīta-sārāmrita
(of Tulajārāja, eighteenth century).
(Tanjore).
Sangīta-sarani
(of poet Nārāyana, eighteenth century)
(Madras).
Sangīta-sāra-sangraha
(of Sourindra Mohan Sharmā, Rājā Tagore, 1875).
(Madras).
Sangīta-sāra-sangraha
(Anonymous).
(Conjeevaram).
Sangīta-sāra-sangraha
(of Jagajjyotirmalla, seventeenth century).
(Nepal).
Sangīta-sarasvatī-hridayālamkāra
(of Nānya Deva, twelfth century).
Same work as Bharata-bhāshya.
Sangīta-sārāvalī
(Benares).
Sangīta-sāroddhāra
(of Hari Bhatta, seventeenth century).
(Bikaner).
Sangīta-sāroddhāra
(of Kikarājā, seventeenth century).
(Poona).

Sangīta-sāroddhāra
(Bikaner).
Same work as Rāma-kautuhala.
Sangīta-shārīra
(Bikaner).
Sangīta Shāstra
(Tanjore).
Sangīta Shāstra-sankshepa
(of Govinda, eighteenth century).
(Adyar).
Sangīta-siddhānta
(of Rāmānanda Tīrtha).
(Aufrecht's cat.)
Sangīta-shiromani
(Bikaner, Calcutta).
Sangīta-sudhā
(of Bhīma Narendra).
(Oudh).
Sangīta-sudhākara
(of Haripāla Deva, 1309–1312).
(Adyar, Madras, Tanjore).
Sangīta-sūryodaya
(of Lakshmī Nārāyana, sixteenth century).
(Madras).
Sangīta Sūtra
(Bikaner).
Sangīta-upadesha
(Bikaner).
Sangīta-upanishad
(of Sudhākalasa, 1323).
(Bikaner).
Sangīta-upanishatsāra
(Sudhākalasa, 1349).
(Bikaner).
Sangīta-vartamāna
(Bikaner).
Sangīta-vidyābhidhāna
(Calcutta).
Sangīta-vinoda
(of Bhāva Bhatta, c. 1700).
(Bikaner).
Sangīta-vishaya,
Telugu script.
(Madras).
Sangīta-vrittaratnākarah
(attributed to Pundarika Vitthala, c. 1590).
(Tanjore).
Sankīrna-rāga
(Bikaner, Poona).
Sankīrna-rāga-lakshana
(Calcutta).
Sapta-svara-lakshanam
(Trivandrum).

Shārngadhara-paddhati
    (of Shārngadhara, c. 1300–1350).
    (Bikaner).
Shringāra-hāra
    (Bikaner).
Shruti-bhāskara
    (of Bhīma Deva).
    (Bikaner).
Someshvara-mata
    (Calcutta).
Subodhinī
    (of Ganesha Deva, seventeenth century).
    (Bikaner).
Sulādi
    (Tanjore).
Svarādhyāya-bhāshā
    (Bikaner).
Svara-prastāra
    (Mysore).
Svara-rāga-sudhārasa
    (Madras).
Svarārnava
    (of Somanārya).
    (Tanjore).
Svara-samuch'aya
    (Oppert's cat.).
    Incomplete.
Svara-tālādi-lakshanam
    (Trivandrum).
Tāla-adhyāya
    Telugu script
    (Madras).
Tāla-dasha-prāna-dīpikā
    (Tanjore).
Tāla-dasha-prāna-lakshanam
    Telugu script.
    (Madraš).
Tāla-dīpikā
    (of Gopendra Tippa Bhūpāla, fifteenth century).
    (Madras, Tanjore).
Tāla-lakshanam
    (Anonymous).
    (Madras).
Tāla-lakshanam
    (of Kohala).
    Telugu script,
    (India Office) (Madras).
Tāla-lakshanam
    (of Nandikeshvara).
    (Ānandāshram, Tanjore).
Tāla-prakaranam
    (Madras).
Tāla-prastāra
    (Tanjore).

Tāla-vidhāna
  (Madras).
  Same work as Oddisha Mahāmantrodaya.
Tāla-vishaya
  Telugu script
  (Madras).
Tāna-nighantu
  (Tanjore).
  Incomplete.
Varna-laghu-vyākhyāna
  (of Rāma).
  (Madras).
Vitthalīyah
  (of Vitthala).
  (Tanjore).
  Incomplete.

III. PERSIAN AND URDU MANUSCRIPTS

Ukde-gushā
  (Benares)
  Persian.
Nagmāt-e-Asaphi
  (of Muhammad Rezza, 1813)
  (Benares) Persian.
Rāga-mālā
  (of Saiyid "Abd-al Wali" Uzlat)
  1759 (Hindusthani).

IV. HINDI MANUSCRIPTS

Māna-kautūhala
  (of Rājā Māna-simha Tomār, 1496–1518)
  (Baroda).
Rāga-mālā
  (attributed to Tānsen, 1549).
Rāga-vichāra
  (of Shrīrāma Malla)
  (Bikaner).
Sangīta-darpana
  a Hindi version of Dāmodara's work by Harivallabha
  (Bikaner, British Museum, Mss. dated 1673).
Setu
  a Hindi comm. on Sangīta-ratnākara by Gangārām.
  (Benares, Tanjore).
Buddhiprakāsha-darpana
  (of Diwān Lachhirām, 1823).
Rāga-ratnākara
  (of Deo Kavi, 1673).
Rāga-kutūhala
  (of Kavi Krishna, 1781).
Sangīta-sāra
  (compiled by Mahārāja Sawai Pratāpa Simha Deva of Jaipur, 1779–1804).

V. HINDI AND MARATHI WORKS, PUBLISHED

Abhinava Gīta-manjarī
(Hindi)
By K. N. Ratanjankar (Bombay, 1945).
Bhāratīyā Sangīta
(Marāthī)
by G. K. Mulay (Bombay, 1941).
Bhāratīya Shruti-svara-rāga Shāstra
(Hindi)
by Pandit Firoze Framjee (Poona, 1935).
Gītamālikā
(Hindi)
(Bombay).
Hindusthānī Sangīta-paddhati
(Marāthī and Hindi)
by Pandit Vishnu Nārāyana Bhātkhande, 7 vol. (Bombay, 1937).
Kāvya-prabhākara
(Hindi)
by Bhānu Kavi (Jagannāth Prasad) (1909).
Nāda Vinoda
(Hindi)
by Gossain Chunnilālji (1896).
Pāda Ratnāvalī
(Hindi)
by Chhatra Nripati (Benares, 1854).
Pārijāta-praveshikā
(Marāthī)
(Bombay).
Pranava Bharati
by Pandit Omkarnath Thākur (1960).
Rāga-chandrikā Sāra
(Hindi)
by Appā Tulsi (Bombay).
Rāga Kalpadruma
(Hindi and Bengali versions)
by Krishnānanda Vyāsa-deva (Calcutta, 1842).
Rāga-Lakshana Gīta-mālikā
(Hindi)
by Pandit Firoze Framjee (Poona).
Rāga Pravesha
(Hindi)
by Pandit Vishnu Digambar (Bombay, 1921).
Rāga Sumana-mālā
(Hindi)
by Bālābhau Umadekar (Gwalior).
Rāga-vibodha praveshikā
(Marāthī)
(Bombay).
Sangīta Darpana
A Marāthī version of the work of Dāmodar Mishra
(Bombay, 1910).
Sangīta Kalā Prakāsha
(Hindi).
by Rāmakrishnabua Vaze (Poona, 1941).

Sangīta Kaumudī
(Hindi)
by Vikramāditya Sinha (Lucknow, 1945).
Sangītānjali
by Pandit Omkarnāth Thākur (1960).
Sangīta Praveshikā
(Hindi and English)
by Shivendra Nāth Basu.
Benares Hindu University.
Sangīta Samuch'aya
(Hindi)
by Shivendra Nāth Basu (Benares, 1942).
Sangīta Shikshā
(Hindi)
by K. N. Ratanjankar. 3 vol. (Lucknow, 1938).
Sugama Rāga-mālā
(Hindi)
(Bombay).
Tāna Sangraha
(Hindi)
by K. N. Ratanjankar 2 vol. (Bombay, 1946).

VI. BENGALI WORKS, PUBLISHED

Amiya Nāth Sanyal
Prāchīn Bhārater Sangīta Chintā
(Calcutta, 1946).
Brajendra Kishore Roy Choudhury
A series of articles in the Sangīta Vijnāna Praveshikā
(1929–1934).
Hindusthānī Sangīte Tānsener Sthān
(Gauripur, Mayanmansingh, 1939).
O.C. Gangoly
Rāg Rāginīr nāma rahasya
(a series of articles in Sangīta Vijnāna Praveshikā, 1941).
Rādhā Mohan Sen
Sangīta Taranga
(1819).
Swāmi Prajnānānanda
Rāga o Rūpa
(2 vols, Calcutta).
Sangīta o Samskriti
(2 vols, Calcutta).
Dhrupada mālā
(with notations, Calcutta).

VII. URDU AND PERSIAN WORKS, PUBLISHED

Mārfat ul Naghmāt (in Urdu)
by Nawab Ali Khān
(Lucknow, c. 1910) (reprinted Hathras, 1952)
Tuhfat ul Hind (in Persian)
by Mirza Jan (chapter on music).
Shir ul Ajam (in (Persian)
by Shibli (chapter on music).
Iilaskah Musiqi (in Persian)
by Sādat Ali Khān (The Music and Life of Tānsen).

VIII. TELUGU WORKS, PUBLISHED

Bāsava Purāna
(of Pālkuriki Somanātha Kavi, thirteenth-fourteenth century)
(Andhra grantha mālā, Madras, 1926).
Contains a chapter on music.
Shrī-Mallikārjuna Panditārādhyacharitra
(of Pālkuriki Somanātha Kavi, thirteenth-fourteenth century)
(Andhra grantha mālā, Madras, 1939).
Contains a chapter on music.
Sangīta-sāra Sangrahamu
(Anon., c. 1800)
(Music Academy, Madras, 1940).

IX. GUJARATI WORKS, PUBLISHED

Music During the Reign of the Sultans of Gujarat
by Muhammad Umar Kokil
(Quarterly journal of Forbes Gujarati Sabha, Bombay, 1938).

X. ENGLISH AND FRENCH WORKS

Atya Begum Fyzee Rahamin
The Music of India
(London, 1926).
Bandopādhyāya (S.)
The Music of India
(Bombay, 1945).
The Origin of Rāga
(Delhi, 1946).
Batra (R. L.)
Science and Art of Indian Music
(Lahore, 1945).
Bhātkhande (Pt. V. N.)
A Short Historical Survey of the Music of Upper India
(Bombay, 1917; reprinted 1934).
A Comparative Study of some of the Leading Music Systems of the
fifteenth, sixteenth, seventeenth and eighteenth centuries.
(Lucknow 1930–1931 in Sangeeta; Bombay, 1940).
Chatterji (Bani)
Applied Music
(Calcutta, 1948).
Clements (E.)
Introduction to the Study of Indian Music
(London, 1913).
Rāgas of Tanjore
(Lectures on Indian Music)
(Poona).
Daniélou (Alain)
Introduction to the Study of Musical Scales
(India Society, London, 1943).
(Taken over by David Marlowe Ltd., London, 1946).
Traité de Musicologie Comparée
(Hermann, Paris, 1959).

Le Gītālamkāra,
the original work of Bharata, Sanskrit text, French translation,
(Institut Français d'Indologie, 1959).
Textes des Purānas sur la Musique
Sanskrit text with French translation,
(Institut Français d'Indologie, 1959).
Les Traditions Musicales—Inde du Nord
Buchet/Chastel, Paris, 1965)
Musikgeschichte in Bildern—Indien
(Leipzig, 1967).
Deval (K. V.)
Theory of Indian Music as expounded by Somanathꞔ
(Poona, 1916).
The Rāgas of Hindustan, 3 vol.
(Poona, 1918-23).
Report of the First All India Music Conference
(Baroda, 1916).
Report of the Second All India Music Conference
(Delhi, 1919)
Report of the Fourth All India Music Conference
(Lucknow, 1925).
Dharampur (Maharānā Vijayadevji of)
Sangīta Bhāva, 1st vol.
(Bombay, 1933),
2nd vol. (Bombay, 1939).
Firoze Framjee (Pandit)
Theory and Practice of Indian Music
(Poona, 1938).
Fox Strangways (A. H.)
The Music of Hindosthan
(Oxford, 1914).
Grosset (Joanny)
Inde, Histoire de la musique depuis l'origine jusqu'à nos jours
Encyclopédie de la musique (Paris, 1924)
Contribution à l'Étude de la Musique Hindoue
(Paris, 1888).
Bhārātīya Nātya-çāstram
(Paris, 1888).
Jones (William) and Willard (N. Augustus)
Music of India
(Calcutta, 1793)
(Second edition Calcutta, 1962).
Kunhan Rājā (C.)
The Sangīta-ratnākara of Shārngadeva
(English translation 1st part)
(Madras, 1945).
Krishna Rao (H. P.)
The first steps in Hindu Music in English notation
(Bangalore)
The Psychology of Music
(Bangalore, 1923).
Mahāvaidyanātha Shiva
Mela-rāga-malikā
(Madras, 1937).

Mukerji (D. P.)
    Indian Music
    (Bombay, 1945).
Pingle (B. A.)
    Indian Music
    (Byculla, 1898, 2nd edition Calcutta, 1962).
Popley (H. A.)
    The Music of India
    (Calcutta-London, 1921).
Prajnānānanda (Swāmī)
    Historical development of Indian Music
    (Calcutta, 1960).
Raghavan (V.)
    Some Names in early Sangīta Literature
    (Journal of the Music Academy, Vol. III, no. 1, 2, 3, and 4, Madras,
    1932).
    Later Sangīta Literature
    (id., Vol. IV, 1933).
Ramachandran (N. S.)
    The Rāgas of Karnatic Music
    (University of Madras, 1938).
Ramaswamy Aiyar (M. S.)
    The Svaramela-kalānidhi of Rāmāmatya
    (With introduction and translation, Annamalai University, 1932).
    The Rāga Vibodha of Somanātha
    (With introduction and translation, Madras, 1933).
Ranade (G. H.)
    Hindusthani Music,
    an outline of its physics and aesthetics
    (Sangli, 1938).
Rosenthal (Ethel)
    The story of Indian music and its instruments
    (London, 1928).
Roy (Hemendra Lal)
    Problems of Hindusthani Music
    (Calcutta, 1937).
Sambamoorty (P.)
    South Indian Music, 3rd edition
    (Madras, 1941).
Simon (R.)
    The musical compositions of Somanātha
    critically edited with a table of notations
    (Leipzig, 1904).
Subramanya Ayyar (C.)
    The grammar of South Indian Music
    (Bombay, 1939).
Svarup (Bishan)
    Theory of Indian Music
    (Swarup Bros., Maithan, Agra, 1933).

Tagore (Rājā Sourindra Mohun)
  Hindu Music from Various Authors
  (Calcutta, 1882).
  Six Principal Rāgas of the Hindus
  (Calcutta, 1877).
  The Eight Principal Rāgas of the Hindus with tableaux and dramatic
  pieces illustrating their character
  (Calcutta, 1880).
Wilson (Anne C.)
  A short account of the Hindu system of music
  (London, 1904).

ARTICLES AND ESSAYS

Coomaraswamy (A. K.)
  Hindi Rāgamālā texts
  (Journal of the American Oriental Society, 1933).
  Dīpaka Rāga
  (Year book of Oriental Art and Culture, London, 1925).
Dennis Stoll
  The Philosophy and Modes of Hindu Music
  (Asiatic Review, 1941).
Dharampur (Maharana Saheb of)
  Music in India
  (Indian Arts and Letters, 1938).
Dharma (Miss P. C.)
  Musical Culture in the Rāmāyana
  (Indian Culture Vol. IV, 1938).
Gangoly (O. C.)
  Non-Aryan Contribution to Aryan music
  (Annals of the Bhandarkar Research Institute, Poona).
  Date of the Sangīta Rāga Kalpadrumah (id. 1934)
  Dhruva: A type of old Indian Stage-songs
  (The Journal of the Music Academy, Madras, Vol 14, 1943).
  The Meaning of Music
  (The Hindoosthan, Calcutta, 1946).
Kanhere (S. G.)
  Some remarks on Indian Music
  (Bulletin of the School of Oriental Studies, Vol. IV., London).
Kannoo Mal (Lāla)
  Notes on Rāginis
  (Rupam, 1922).
Lakshmana Shankara Bhatta
  The mode of Singing Sāma Gāna
  (Poona Orientalist, 1939).
Manji (P. V.)
  Rāg mālā
  (a series of articles in Suvarna-Mālā, Bombay, 1923–1926).
Mehta (N. C.)
  Rāgas and Rāginis in a Landian Mss.
  (The Bodleian Quarterly Record, Vol. VI, Oxford, 1932).
Menon (V. K. R.) and V. K. Raghavan
  "Govinda" the greatest musical theorist of South India

Mukherjee (Jogendra Nath)
A lecture on Rāgas and Rāginis
(Indian Society of Oriental Art, Calcutta, 1921).
Narasimhachary (V. V.)
The Early Writers on Music
(Journal of the Music Academy, Madras, 1930).
Ramakrishna Kavi (M.)
King Nānyadeva on Music
(The Quarterly Journal of Andhra Historical Research Society, October, 1926).
Literature on Music
(ibid. July, 1928).
Literary gleanings: Sangītāchāryas Nānya deva, Jagadekamalla, Someshvara, Sāranga deva, Pārashva deva, Devana Bhatta, Aliya Rāmarāya
(ibid. October, 1928–April, 1929).
Rice (Stanley)
Hindi Music
(The New Criterion, June, 1926).
Rukminiyama (K. D.)
Music (Journal of Indian History, 1941).
Sambamurti (P.)
A History of Sacred Music in India
(K. V. Rangaswami Aiyangar Commemoration Volume, Madras, 1940).
Stern (Philippe)
La musique Indoue
(La revue musicale, Paris, May 1923).
The Music of India and the Theory of the Rāga
(Indian Arts and Letters, London, 1933).
Tarun Ghoshal
Hindi Contribution to Music
(Calcutta Review, 1940).
Venkatarama Iyer (T. L.)
The Musical Element in Kālidāsa
(Journal of Oriental Research, Madras, 1930).

DISCOGRAPHY

GERMANY

Unesco Collection: A musical Anthology of the Orient. Edited under the direction of Alain Daniélou. Commentary in French, English, German. Bärenreiter Musicaphon, Kassel.

India I (Vedic chant): BM 30 L 2006. 30 cm. 33
  Recordings and notes by Alain Daniélou.
India III (Dhrupad): BM 30 L2018.
  Rāga Āsāvarī
  Rāga Bhairavī

ENGLAND

Music of India: Rāgas and Tālas HMV ALP 1665. 30 cm. 33 (Instrumental)
  4 items: Rupaka tāla (tablā solo), Rāga Madhukosha, Rāga Odiyā, Dhun (piece in lighter style). Played by Ravi Shankar (sitār), Alla Rakha (tablā) and a tānpūrā. Rec. issued 1959. Notes.
Music of India ALP 1893. 30 cm. 33 (also issued in stereo, on ASD 463) (Instrumental)
  3 items: Rāga Hamsadhvani, Dhun Kāfī, Rāga Rāmakalī. Played by Ravi Shankar (sitār) K. Dutt (tablā), N. Mullick (tānpūrā). Issued 1962. Notes.
Music of India HMV ALPC 7. 30 cm. 33. (Also issued in USA on Angel 3548) (Instrumental)
  3 Rāgas: Joga, Ahir-Bhairava, Simhendra-Madhyaman. Played by Ravi Shankar (sitār), Chatur Lal (tablā), Prodyot Sen (tānpūrā). 3 photographs, notes by Ravi Shankar and Prodyot Sen.
India's Master Musician Vogue VA 160156 30 cm. 33. (Instrumental)
  5 items performed by Ravi Shankar (sitār), Chatur Lal (tablā), and Nodu C. Mullick (tānpūrā): Kāfī (Hori), Dhun, Mishra Pilū in Thumrī style, Rāga Dhanāshrī, Rāga Chārukeshī.
Morning and Evening Rāgas HMV ALPC 2, 30 cm. 33. (Instrumental)
  2 items: Rāga Pilū, Rāga Sind Bhairavī. Played by Ali Akbar Khan (sarod), Chatur Lal (tablā), accomp. by Shirish Gor (tānpūrā). Spoken introduction by Yehudi Menuhin. Issued 1956. Introductory note by Yehudi Menuhin. (Also issued in France on HMV FALP 472
Musique de l'Inde, 30 cm. 33, and in USA on Angel 35283
Morning and Evening Rāgas, 30 cm. 33.)

FRANCE

Anthologie de la Musique Classique de l'Inde. Ducretet-Thomson, Paris 320 C 096-7-8. Three records 30 cm. 33.
  32 items, vocal and instrumental. Recordings and notes by Alain Daniélou (17 pages), introduction by Serge Moreux (14 pages), photographs by Raymond Burnier. Issued 1955. (In England: DTL 93111-2-3. Re-issued Pathe-Marconi, Paris, 1962.)

USA
The sounds of India Columbia WL 119, 30 cm. 33. (Instrumental).
4 Rāgas played by Ravi Shankar (sitār), Chatur Lal (tablā), Nodu
Mullick (tānpūrā). Spoken introduction by Ravi Shankar. Issued
1958. Notes (with musical transcriptions) by Alan Hovhaness.
Indian Music World Pacific WP 1248, 30 cm. 33. (Instrumental).
Performers: Ravi Shankar (sitār), Chatur Lal (tablā), Nodu Mullick
(tānpūrā). Issued 1958.
The Rāgas of India Folkways FI 8368, 30 cm. 33. (Vocal)
Sung by Dr. B. R. Deodhar accomp. by tablā and tānpūrā. Issued 1962.
Nⴲtes by Dr. B. R. Deodhar. 4 items: Rāga Yaman, Rāga Mīyān
Mallār, Rāga Desha, Rāga Jayajavantī.
Religious Music of India, Ethnic Folkways FE4431. Recorded with notes
by Alain Daniélou.
Indian Folk Music. Columbia World Library of Folk and Primitive
Music, Vol. XIII, SL215. Recorded and Edited with notes by Alain
Daniélou.

INDIA
I. INSTRUMENTAL MUSIC
Abdul Halim Jafar Khan (sitār)
    Columbia 33 ESX 4253, 33 cm. 33
    Rāga Māravā
    Rāga Pāhadī

Ali Akbar Khan (sarod)
1. HMV EALP 1255, 33 cm. 33
    Rāga Todī
    Rāga Lajvanti
2. HMV EALP 1290
    Rāga Mīyān kī Todī
    Rāga Zilha Kāfī
3. HMV 1281
    Rāga Pāhadī-Jhinjotī
    Mishra Shrīranjanī
4. HMV 7 EPE 1243
    Rāga Alhaiyā Bilāval
    Rāga Desha
5. HMV EALP 1268
    Rāga Chandranandan
    Rāga Bhairavī
6. HMV EALP 1274
    Rāga Rāmdāsī Mallār
7. HMV EALP 1286
    Rāga Prabhātkali
8. Odeon PMAE 502
    Rāga Yaman Kalyāna
See also Ravi Shankar, 7 and 8.

Allā Rakhā (tablā)
    HMV 7 EPE 1252
    Rūpaka Tāla and Tīntāla

Amir Hussain Khan (tablā) and Madhavrao Alkutkar (pakhāvaj)
    HMV 7 EPE 1216, 17 cm, 45.
    Ekatāla, Chautāla, Tritāla, Āditāla

Bismallah Khan (shahnaī)
1. The Magic Shahnai of Bismillah Khan
    HMV EALP 1262, 30 cm. 33. Notes. Issued 1961. Accomp. by a
    second shahnaī.
    Rāga Pūriyā Dhanāshrī
2. HMV EALP 1254, 30 cm. 33.
    Rāga Todī
    Rāga Mishra (Thumrī)
3. HMV 7 EPE 1214, 17 cm. 45.
    Rāga Bilāval
    Rāga Chandrakosha
4. HMV 7 EPE 1203, 17 cm. 45.
    Rāga Vasanta
    Rāga Sur Mallār
5. HMV 7 EPE 1255, 17 cm. 45.
    Rāga Desha (Dhun)
    Horī
6. HMV EALP 1253
    Rāga Mālakosha
    Rāga Desha
7. HMV EALP 1271
    Rāga Bāgeshrī
    Rāga Sohini
8. HMV EALP 1285
    Rāga Bhairavī
    Rāga Multānī
9. HMV EALP 1270
    Rāga Lalitā
    Rāga Madhyamādi Sāranga
10. HMV 7 EPE 1248
    Rāga Mālakosha
11. Odeon PMAE 503
    Rāga Kedārā

Choudhury, Devabrata (sitār)
    HMV 7 EPE 1853
    Rāga Desha

Ganguly, Shyām (sarod)
    HMV 7 EPE 1011
    Rāga Ahir Bhairava
    Rāga Desha

Moitra, Radhikā Mohan (sarod)
    HMV ECLP 2301
    Introduction to the Music of India
    Rāga Bhairavī

Pannalal Ghosh (flute)
1. HMV EALP 1252, 30 cm. 33.
   Rāga Yaman
   Rāga Shrī
2. HMV 7 EPE 1240, 17 cm. 45.
   Rāga Shuddha Bhairavī
   Rāga Sāranga
3. HMV 7 EPE 1226, 17 cm. 45.
   Rāga Māravā
4. HMV EBLB 1752, 30 cm. 33.
   Rāga Chandramauli
   Rāga Vasanta
Parvatikar, Dattatreya (vīnā)
   HMV ECLP 2301
   Rāga Bhairava
   Rāga Pilū Paharī

Ramnarain (sarod)
   HMV 7 EPE 1251
   Rāga Bhairavī
   Rāga Joga

Ravi Shankar (sitār)
1. HMV EALP 1261, 30 cm. 33. Issued 1961
   Rāga Deshi
   Rāga Suddha Sāranga
   Rāga Yaman
2. HMV EALP 1276, 30 cm. 33.
   Rāga Madhuvanti
   Mishra Mand
3. HMV ALP 1895
   Rāga Hansadhvani
   Rāga Rāmakalī
4. HMV EALP 1273
   Rāga Hema Bihāga
   Mishra Mand
5. HMV EALP 1283
   Rāga Puriyā Dhanāshrī
   Rāga Kāfī
6. Odeon PMAE 502
   Rāga Jhinjotī
7. Music of India, HMV EALP 1251, 30 cm. 33.
   Rāga Palas Kāfī
   Rāga Vilāsakhānī Todī
   Played by Ravi Shankar (sitār) and Ali Akbar Khan (sarod)
8. HMV 7 EPE 57, 17 cm. 45.
   Rāga Todī
   Rāga Khammāja
   Played by Ravi Shankar (sitār), Ali Akbar Khan (sarod), and K. L.
   Dutt (tablā)

Roy, Kalyani (sitār)
    HMV 7 EPE 1015
    Brindābani Sāranga
    Simhendra Madhyaman

Sharan Rani (sarod)
    HMV ECLP 2283, 33 cm. 33. Issued 1963. Accomp. Chatur Lal
    (tablā)
    Rāga Darbārī-Kānadā
    Rāga Nat-Bhairava

Vilayat Khan (sitār)
  1. The Genius of Vilayat Khan, HMV EALP 1266, 30 cm. 33.
    Rāga Ahir Bhairava
    Rāga Khammāja
  2. HMV ALP 1946
    Rāga Mīyān kī Mallār
    Rāga Mīyān kī Todī
    Rāga Pilū
  3. HMV ALP 1988
    Rāga Suhā-Sughrai
    Rāga Pilū (Thumrī)

Other records of instrumental Music:
    HMV 7 EPE 1003–1004, 1201, 1204, 1209, 1211–1212, 1219–1220,
    1223, 1228, 1231, 1237–1238, 1602, 1605, 1608

II VOCAL MUSIC
Abdul Karim Khan
    Columbia 33 ECX 3251, 33 cm. 33.
    Thumrī and Khyāl: Bilāval, Tilang, Vasanta, Shuddha Pilū, Sarpada,
    Gārā, Mālakosha, Bhairavī.

Amir Khan
    HMV EALP 1253, 30 cm. 33.
    Rāga Māravā
    Rāga Darbārī-Kānadā

Bade Ghulam Ali Khan
  1. HMV EALP 1258, 30 cm. 33.
    Rāga Gunakalī
    Rāga Mālakosha
  2. HMV EALP 1256, 30 cm. 33. Issued 1961.
    Rāga Darbārī-Kānadā
    Rāga Kāshi-Dhani
  3. HMV 7 EPE 1252
    Rāga Gurjarī Todī
    Rāga Kāmoda
  4. HMV EALP 1751
    Thumrī
    Janglā Bhairavī
  5. HMV 7 EPE 1256
    Paharī
    Thumrī

6. HMV EALP 1265
   Rāga Darbārī Kānadā

Bhimsen Joshi
1. HMV ECLP 2264, 30 cm. 33.
   Rāga Lalitā
   Rāga Shuddha Kalyāna
2. HMV ECLP 2253, 30 cm. 33.
   Rāga Mīyān Mallār
   Rāga Purva Kalyāna
3. HMV 7 EPE 1246
   Rāga Mīyān ki Todī
   Rāga Yogiyā
4. HMV EALP 1280
   Rāga Mīyān ki Todī
   Rāga Dhanāshrī

Rahimuddin Khan Dagar
1. *Dhrupad* HMV 7 EPE 1206, 17 cm. 45.
   Rāga Todī
   Rāga Mallār
2. *Dhamar* HMV 7 EPE 1218, 17 cm. 45.
   Rāga Bihāga
   Rāga Kedāra

Gangu Bai Hangal
   HMV 7 EPE 1239, 17 cm. 45.
   Rāga Devagirī
   Rāga Jayajavantī

Hira Bai Barodekar
   HMV 7 EPE 1205, 17 cm. 45.
   Rāga Bhairavī
   Rāga Shyāma Kalyāna

Kesar Bai Kerkar
1. HMV 7 EPE 1., 17 cm. 45.
   Rāga Todī (Thumrī)
   Rāga Jayajavantī (Horī)
2. HMV 7 ERE 1., 17 cm. 45.
   Rāga Jayajavantī (Khyāl)
   Rāga Khammāja (Horī)
   Rāga Todī (Khyāl)
   Rāga Bhairavī (Thumrī)

Kumar, Gandharva
   HMV ECLP 2301
   Rāga Sanjarī
   Rāga Bāgeshrī

Nazakat Ali and Salamat Ali
1. HMV EALP 1264, 30 cm., 33. Issued 1961.
   Rāga Madhuvantī
   Rāga Purvī

HMV EALP 1282
 Rāga Abhodi Kānadā
 Rāga Gaurī

Niaz Ahmed Khan and Fayyaz Ahmed Khan
 HMV ECLP 2282
 Rāga Yaman
 Rāga Bairagi Bhairava

Nirmala Devi
 HMV 7 EPE 1250
 Thumrī

Pandit Omkarnath Thakur
 1. Columbia 33 EC 3751, 25 cm. 33. With Notes. Issued 1961.
    Rāga Devagirī Bilāval
    Rāga Bhairavī
 2. Columbia 33 EX 3252
    Rāga Deshī Todī
    Rāga Mālakosha

Pandit Omkarnath Thakur, Siddeshwari Devi, Hira Bai Barodekar
 Columbia SEDE 3302, 3304, 3306, 3308.
 4 records, 17 cm. 45.

Rajguru, Basvaraj
 HMV 7 EPE 1251
 Rāga Chandani-Kedāra
 Rāga Sahanā-Kānadā

Rasūlan Bai
 Columbia SEDE 3301, 17 cm. 45.
 Purvī

Roshan Ara Begum
 1. HMV 1530, 30 cm. 33. With Notes. Issued 1962.
    Rāga Shuddha Kalyāna
    Rāga Shankarā
 2. HMV CLP 1514
    Rāga Vasanta
    Rāga Kedāra
 3. HMV CLP 1530
    Rāga Shuddha Kalyāna
    Rāga Shankarā

Other records of vocal music
 HMV 1001–1002, 1202, 1207, 1210, 1213, 1215, 1217, 1222, 1224–1225.
 1229–1230, 1232, 1234, 1236, 1242, 1245.